Finite Element Method: Concepts and Applications

Finite Element Method: Concepts and Applications

Edited by Connie McGuire

CLANRYE
INTERNATIONAL
www.clanryeinternational.com

Clanrye International,
750 Third Avenue, 9ᵗʰ Floor,
New York, NY 10017, USA

ISBN: 978-1-63240-852-5

Cataloging-in-Publication Data

Finite element method : concepts and applications / edited by Connie McGuire.
    p. cm.
Includes bibliographical references and index.
ISBN 978-1-63240-852-5
1. Finite element method. 2. Isogeometric analysis.
3. Numerical analysis. I. McGuire, Connie.
QC20.7.F56 F56 2019
518.25--dc23

For information on all Clanrye International publications
visit our website at www.clanryeinternational.com

Contents

Preface

Finite element method refers to the numerical method, which is used to solve problems in mathematical physics and engineering. The areas where finite element method is mostly applied are fluid flow, structural analysis, mass transport, heat transfer and electromagnetic potential problems. This method divides the problem into simpler and smaller parts called finite elements, in order to solve it. Algebraic equations are formulated for each element, which are then assembled into a larger set of equations that models the whole problem. Variational methods are then applied to find an approximate solution by minimizing the associated error function. The different finite element methods are applied element method (AEM), extended finite element method (XFEM), meshfree methods, Loubignac iteration, finite element limit analysis, spectral element method, etc. This book outlines the concepts and applications of finite element method in detail. It strives to provide a fair idea about this discipline and to help develop a better understanding of the latest advances within this area of mathematics. Those in search of information to further their knowledge will be greatly assisted by this book.

This book is a comprehensive compilation of works of different researchers from varied parts of the world. It includes valuable experiences of the researchers with the sole objective of providing the readers (learners) with a proper knowledge of the concerned field. This book will be beneficial in evoking inspiration and enhancing the knowledge of the interested readers.

In the end, I would like to extend my heartiest thanks to the authors who worked with great determination on their chapters. I also appreciate the publisher's support in the course of the book. I would also like to deeply acknowledge my family who stood by me as a source of inspiration during the project.

Editor

Evaluation of Adaptive Bone Remodeling after Total Hip Arthroplasty Using Finite Element Analysis

Yutaka Inaba, Hiroyuki Ike, Masatoshi Oba and

Tomoyuki Saito

Additional information is available at the end of the chapter

Abstract

We compared equivalent stress and strain energy density (SED) to bone mineral density (BMD) in the femur after total hip arthroplasty (THA) using subject-specific finite element analysis (FEA). Equivalent stress and BMD were maintained in the distal femur after THA, whereas both decreased in the proximal femur. A significant correlation was observed between the rates of changes in BMD and equivalent stress before and after THA. Therefore, FEA can predict adaptive bone remodeling after mechanical loading changes. Additionally, we evaluated the effects of two different types of stem geometries (Zweymüller-type stem and fit-and-fill-type stem) on load distribution and BMD using the same method. Equivalent stress and BMD in the medial side of the proximal femur were significantly lower with the Zweymüller-type stem than with the fit-and-fill-type stem. Therefore, FEA can assess the effects of stem geometry on bone remodeling after THA. Moreover, we evaluated the effects of bone geometry on load distribution and BMD after THA. Equivalent stress in the medial side of the proximal femur was significantly lower in the stovepipe model implanted with large tapered wedge-type stems than in the champagne flute and intermediate models, and there was a significant loss of BMD in the stovepipe model. Therefore, a large tapered wedge-type stem and stovepipe femur may be associated with significant proximal BMD loss.

Keywords: finite element analysis, dual-energy X-ray absorptiometry, bone remodeling, hip, arthroplasty

1. Introduction

Periprosthetic bone loss, i.e., a decrease in bone mineral density (BMD) around an implant, is a major concern following total hip arthroplasty (THA) [1, 2]. Severe periprosthetic bone loss may contribute to aseptic loosening of the prosthesis or the risk of periprosthetic fracture [3] and presents serious problems if revision surgery becomes necessary [4]. Several studies have reported that BMD decreases following THA, particularly in the proximal femur [5, 6]. Most changes in BMD occur during the first postoperative year, and subsequently, BMD is maintained [7–9]. This phenomenon is considered to be an adaptive remodeling response of the bone structure to alter its stress environment owing to the presence of an implant. Therefore, mechanical stress may be associated with the patterns of BMD changes. In particular, in cementless THA, an optimal fit of the stem into the metaphyseal region of the femur has been reported to lead to a reduction in periprosthetic bone loss [10].

Wolff [11] proposed that trabecular bone in the proximal femur adapts to external mechanical loads. This structural change is caused by bone remodeling, which couples bone resorption by osteoclasts and bone formation by osteoblasts [12]. It is generally accepted that bone tissue can detect and respond to its mechanical environment, but the exact mechanical signal that drives remodeling remains controversial [13]. Various biomechanical parameters have been investigated to determine the remodeling stimulus. Huiskes et al. [14] examined whether strain energy density (SED) controls bone remodeling. Carter et al. [15] examined stress, and Stulpner et al. [16] examined equivalent strain as signals for remodeling. Adachi et al. [17] proposed that the driving force of remodeling is the local nonuniformity of the scalar function of stress. The existence of various theories indicates that the mechanism of bone remodeling is not well understood.

Subject-specific finite element (FE) models based on geometry and mechanical properties derived from computed tomography (CT) scans have been described in several studies [18–20]. Furthermore, relationships between results of subject-specific finite element analysis (FEA) and bone density have been investigated previously. Cody et al. [21] performed subject-specific FEA and bone density measurements for predicting the fracture load of the femur. Tawara et al. [22] evaluated vertebral strength using subject-specific FEA and BMD. We previously examined the usefulness of subject-specific FEA, which was validated by BMD changes, after THA. We found that equivalent stress through subject-specific FEA correlated with BMD changes before and after THA [23]. The distribution of mechanical loads within the femur after THA might be influenced by the stem geometry and the femur structure. Our previous results suggest that subject-specific FEA could be used to evaluate the effects of stem and femoral geometry on adaptive bone remodeling after THA [24].

This chapter initially provides general information on subject-specific FEA and then presents a brief overview of our work regarding adaptive bone remodeling after THA.

2. Finite element analysis

2.1. Finite element analysis and bone mineral density

It is difficult to assess the stress and strain distributions throughout the entire bone using simplified mathematical models or implanted prostheses or through experiments with cadaveric tissue. An alternative approach to analyze bone mechanics is the FE method, which can accommodate large intersubject variations in bone geometry and material properties [25]. When the ability to perform three-dimensional FE contact analysis is available, subject-specific geometry should be analyzed. This provides the opportunity to examine normal populations of individuals and populations with specific injuries or other pathologies. Ultimately, patient-specific modeling might be used in surgical planning and large-scale studies of treatment efficacy [26]. As mentioned above, we investigated the relationships between the FEA results and BMD. Several previous studies have described the application of FEA for investigating bone-remodeling patterns around implants. However, most of these were not subject-specific models. Weinans et al. [27] reported that subject-specific FE models might be useful for explaining variations in bone adaptation responsiveness among different subjects.

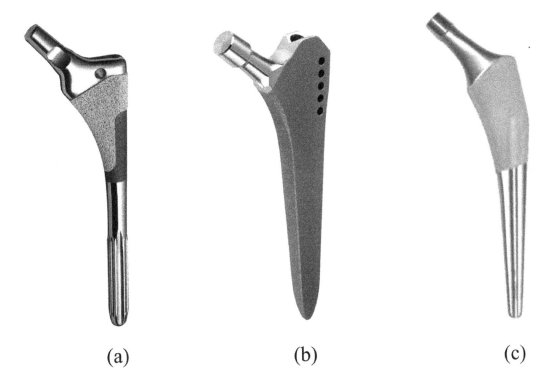

(a)   (b)   (c)

Figure 1. Diagrams of (a) collarless VerSys Fiber Metal MidCoat, (b) SL-PLUS, and (c) Accolade TMZF stems. (a) Collarless VerSys Fiber Metal MidCoat (Zimmer Inc., Warsaw, IN) is a fit-and-fill-type stem composed of titanium alloy with fiber-metal porous coating at the proximal region. (b) SL-PLUS (Smith & Nephew Inc., Memphis, TN) is a Zwey-müller-type stem composed of titanium alloy with a dual taper, rectangular, and trochanteric wing design. (c) Accolade TMZF stem (Stryker Orthopaedics, Mahwah, NJ) is a cementless tapered wedge-type stem composed of beta titanium alloy with a proximal hydroxyapatite-coated porous surface and a distal smooth-finished surface.

We investigated 24 patients (16 women and 8 men) who underwent primary cementless THA using the same fit-and-fill type of prosthesis (collarless VerSys Fiber Metal MidCoat, Zimmer Inc., Warsaw, IN) (**Figure 1**). Collarless VerSys Fiber Metal MidCoat is a stem composed of titanium alloy with a fiber-metal porous coating at the proximal region. Patients were excluded from the study if they were receiving systemic estrogen, vitamin D, or bisphosphonate for osteoporosis. The mean patient age at surgery was 63 years (range, 44–82 years). After surgery, all patients were allowed to use a wheelchair, with full weight bearing, on postoperative day 1, and gait exercise was performed as soon as possible [23]. BMD was assessed with dual-energy X-ray absorptiometry (DEXA) using the Hologic Discovery system (Hologic Inc., Waltham, MA). Baseline DEXA measurements were performed 1 week after surgery as reference, and subsequent measurements were performed at 3, 6, and 12 months postoperatively. Patients were placed in the supine position, and the affected leg was maintained in 20 ° internal rotation to minimize measurement errors. DEXA measurements were performed using the "array prosthetic" mode, which excludes metal from analysis of the regions of interest (ROIs). ROIs were defined according to Gruen's system [28]. The pixel size was 1.1 × 0.56 mm.

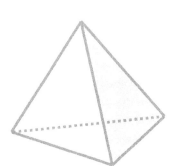

Tetrahedral element

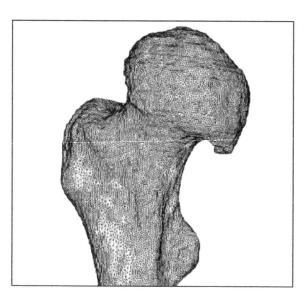

Mesh model

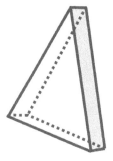

Shell element

Figure 2. Finite element mesh of the femur. Three-dimensional FE models are constructed using 1- to 4-mm tetrahedral elements for the trabecular and inner cortical bone. The outer surface of the cortical bone is represented with three nodal-point shell elements having a thickness of 0.3 mm.

CT scans of the femurs of all patients were performed pre- and postoperatively (1 week after surgery). The scanner settings were approximately 140 kV and 300 mA, with a slice thickness of 2 mm, pixel resolution of 512 × 512, and voxel size of 0.70 × 0.70 × 2 mm. Three-dimensional FE models of the femur and stem were constructed according to pre- and postoperative CT data using the Mechanical Finder ver. 6.0 software (Research Center of Computational Mechanics Inc., Tokyo, Japan). This software creates FE models after considering individual bone shape and density distribution [29]. We used a global threshold algorithm for determining the bone area with a threshold of 200 mg/cm³ and with manual correction if necessary. We applied a closing algorithm in addition to the global threshold algorithm for determining the bone area when the density was extremely low [29]. In addition, the global threshold algorithm was applied to determine the stem area with a threshold of 2,000 Hounsfield units. We used 1 to 4 mm tetrahedral elements to construct three-dimensional FE models for the trabecular and inner cortical bone. The outer surface of the cortical bone was represented with three nodal-point shell elements having a thickness of 0.3 mm (**Figure 2**). The FE models of the femur consisted of approximately 600,000 elements in addition to 200,000 elements for the stem. Bone density was determined according to CT density values, using a calibration equation (**Table 1**). Additionally, the elastic modulus of the bone was determined according to bone density values, using the equations proposed by Keyak et al. [18, 30] and Keller [31] (**Table 1**). Poisson's ratio of the bone was assumed to be 0.40. The stem was an isotropic titanium alloy, and it had an elastic modulus of 109.0 GPa and a Poisson's ratio of 0.28. The models assumed a completely bonded interface between the stem and bone. The models were restrained at the distal end of the femoral shaft, and loads were applied to the femoral head and greater trochanter. We applied a load of 2400 N to the surface of the femoral head at an angle of 15° to the femoral axis and applied a load of 1200 N to the greater trochanter at an angle of 20° [32, 33]. Linear FEA was performed. Equivalent stress and SED were analyzed in ROIs 1–7 and were compared with the DEXA data.

Bone density	Elastic modulus (MPa)
$\rho = 0$	0.001
$0 < \rho \le 0.27$	$33,900\rho^{2.20}$
$0.27 < \rho < 0.6$	$5307\rho + 469$
$0.6 \le \rho$	$10,200\rho^{2.01}$

$$\rho \left(g/cm^3\right) = (H.U. + 1.4246) \times 0.001 \Big/ 1.508 \ (H.U. > -1)$$
$$= 0.0 \ (H.U. \le -1)$$

H.U. represents CT density values in Hounsfield Units. The elastic modulus of the bone is determined according to computed tomography density values, using the equations proposed by Keyak et al. [18, 30] and Keller [31].

Table 1. Equations used for calculating the elastic modulus of the bone.

Changes in the BMD of the femur during the first postoperative year are shown in **Figure 3**. BMD was maintained in ROIs 3, 4, 5, and 6, whereas it significantly decreased in ROIs 1, 2, and 7 by 19, 11, and 27%, respectively, 12 months after THA. The changes in BMD noted in this study were similar to those reported in other studies [34, 35].

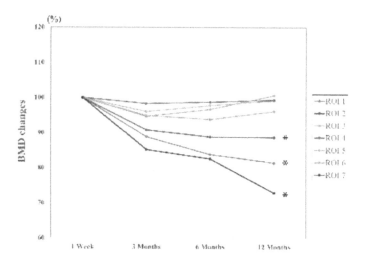

Figure 3. The median percentage change in bone mineral density (BMD) after surgery with the fit-and-fill-type stem. The periprosthetic BMDs at 3, 6, and 12 months after total hip arthroplasty (THA) are expressed as percentage changes from the baseline BMD measured at 1 week after surgery. BMD is maintained 12 months after THA in regions of interest (ROIs) 3, 4, 5, and 6, whereas it has significantly decreased by 19, 11, and 27% in ROIs 1, 2, and 7, respectively, 12 months after THA (*$p< 0.05$).

The pre- and postoperative equivalent stress and SED are shown in **Figure 4**. The equivalent stress and SED were maintained in ROIs 3, 4, and 5, whereas both decreased in ROIs 1, 2, 6, and 7 after THA (**Figure 5**). The lowest values of equivalent stress, SED, and relative BMD were observed in ROI 7 ($p < 0.05$). There was a relatively strong correlation between equivalent stress and BMD changes ($R = 0.426, p < 0.01$), whereas there was a weak correlation between SED and BMD changes ($R = 0.183, p = 0.053$) (**Figure 6**).

	preoperative	postoperative
Equivalent stress		50 MPa ... 0 MPa
Strain energy density		0.05 MPa ... 0 MPa

Figure 4. Distributions of equivalent stress and strain energy density (SED) in the femur. Equivalent stress and SED are maintained in the distal femur after total hip arthroplasty, whereas both decreased in the proximal femur.

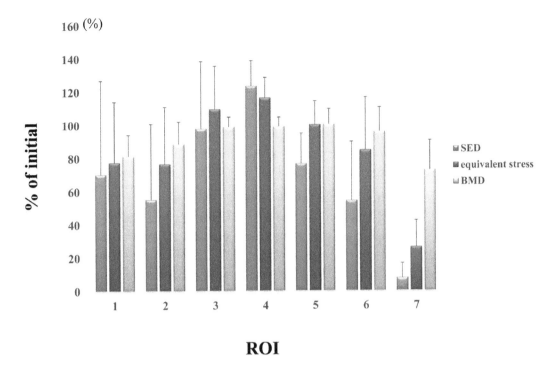

Figure 5. Strain energy density (SED), equivalent stress, and bone mineral density (BMD) 12 months after total hip arthroplasty. In ROI 7, equivalent stress, SED, and relative BMD show the lowest values of all regions examined.

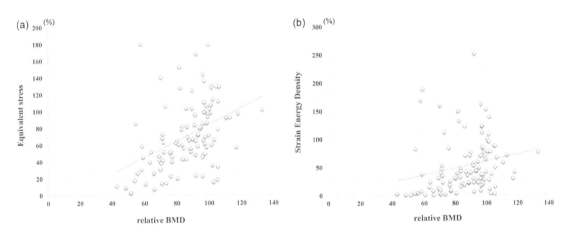

Figure 6. Scatter plots of the relationships (a) between bone mineral density (BMD) and equivalent stress and (b) between BMD and strain energy density (SED). The periprosthetic BMD at 12 months after total hip arthroplasty (THA) is expressed as the percentage change from the baseline BMD measured at 1 week after surgery. Postoperative equivalent stress and SED are expressed as percentage changes from the preoperative values. (a) Equivalent stress has a relatively strong correlation with the changes in BMD ($R = 0.426$, $p < 0.01$). (b) SED has a weak correlation with the changes in BMD ($R = 0.183$, $p = 0.053$).

Periprosthetic BMD loss may be related to changes in the mechanical loading environment. The purpose of this study was to investigate the relationships between periprosthetic BMD loss and changes in the mechanical loading environment after cementless THA according to subject-specific FEA. This subject-specific FEA exhibited a significant correlation between BMD changes and equivalent stress. After THA, the stress load is transferred to the distal femur through the stem rather than to the periprosthetic bone owing to the high elastic modulus of the stem [36, 37]. Therefore, equivalent stress in the proximal femur may decrease after stem implantation. These results are consistent with those of previous studies [20, 33]. We investigated the effect of a porous-coated titanium-alloy fit-and-fill-type stem on bone remodeling after THA. Although this implant is designed to achieve proximal fixation, equivalent stress and BMD decreased postoperatively at the proximal femur. These results indicate that load transmission to the proximal femur may not be sufficient for maintaining BMD.

The present study demonstrated that equivalent stress correlates with BMD changes in the femur 12 months after THA. In this study, CT scans were performed from all patients pre- and postoperatively, and subject-specific FE models were constructed to investigate bone heterogeneity by using the equations proposed by Keyak et al. [18, 30] and Keller [31]. Our results suggest that the rate of changes in equivalent stress could be an important factor for BMD changes.

The strain-adaptive bone-remodeling theory has been used to simulate BMD changes after THA; Huiskes et al. [14] reported that the SED distribution indicates the regions where resorption and apposition are expected. However, other studies have reported that bone remodeling can be better predicted with stress parameters than with strain parameters. Simulation results and clinical data have shown that there is a positive correlation between average equivalent stress and BMD [38, 39]. Therefore, controversy still exists with regard to whether equivalent stress or SED is an appropriate parameter for evaluating bone remodeling. Our results suggest that a decrease in equivalent stress caused a decrease in BMD in the proximal femur after THA.

2.2. Effects of stem geometry

A number of factors, such as geometry, roughness and coating of the stem, technique of preparation, and bone quality, influence initial stability or primary fixation. Femoral stems with various geometries are currently in use. The implant shape has been shown to determine cortical contact and initial stability [40]. Our recent study showed that differences in stem design could affect the postoperative BMD loss of the proximal femur [41]. We studied the effects of stem geometry on BMD changes and equivalent stress in the femur after THA.

We investigated 20 patients who underwent primary cementless THA for osteoarthritis or osteonecrosis of the hip. Of these patients, 10 underwent THA with a Zweymüller-type stem (SL-PLUS; Smith & Nephew Inc.), and the other 10 underwent THA with a fit-and-fill-type stem (collarless VerSys Fiber Metal MidCoat; Zimmer Inc.) (**Figure 1**). The mean age of the patients at the time of THA was 63 years (range, 54–72 years) in the Zweymüller-type stem group and 64 years (range, 57–69 years) in the fit-and-fill-type stem group. There was no significant difference in age between the two groups. In the Zweymüller-type stem group, all patients were diagnosed with osteoarthritis, while in the fit-and-fill-type stem group, eight patients were diagnosed with osteoarthritis, and two were diagnosed with osteonecrosis. We compared equivalent stress and BMD between the two groups.

In the preoperative models, no significant differences in equivalent stress were observed between the two groups. In the postoperative models, maximum equivalent stress was observed in ROI 4, and minimum equivalent stress was observed in ROI 1 in both groups. In ROI 4, equivalent stress was significantly higher in the Zweymüller-type stem group than in the fit-and-fill-type stem group ($p < 0.05$). On the other hand, in ROI 7, equivalent stress was significantly higher in the fit-and-fill-type stem group than in the Zweymüller-type stem group ($p < 0.05$) (**Figure 7**).

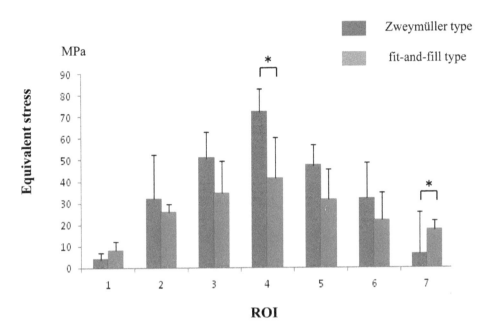

Figure 7. Comparison of equivalent stress between the fit-and-fill-type stem and Zweymüller-type stem groups. The equivalent stress in ROI 4 is higher, and the stress in ROI 7 is lower in the Zweymüller-type stem group than in the fit-and-fill-type stem group *$p < 0.05$.

Changes in the BMD of the femur during the first postoperative year are shown in **Figure 8**. In both the Zweymüller-type stem and fit-and-fill-type stem groups, BMD decreased in ROIs 2, 6, and 7, whereas BMD was maintained in ROIs 3, 4, and 5. In ROIs 6 and 7, BMD was significantly lower in the Zweymüller-type stem group than in the fit-and-fill-type stem group ($p < 0.05$). In ROI 1, the fit-and-fill-type stem group showed a continuous decrease in BMD for 12 months after surgery, while the Zweymüller-type stem group showed a decrease in BMD up to 6 months after surgery and then showed an increase 12 months after surgery. In ROI 4, BMD was significantly lower in the fit-and-fill-type stem group than in the Zweymüller-type stem group at 3 months after surgery ($p < 0.05$); however, there were no differences in BMD between the two groups at 6 months or 12 months after surgery [24].

Stress at the proximal femur was lower, and stress at the distal femur was higher in the Zweymüller-type stem group than in the fit-and-fill-type stem group. BMD at the proximal femur was significantly lower in the Zweymüller-type stem group than in the fit-and-fill-type stem group ($p < 0.05$). The FEA results and postoperative BMD changes in the femur suggest that implantation of the Zweymüller-type stem leads to insufficient load transmission to the proximal femur and may be associated with proximal BMD loss. These findings indicate that subject-specific FEA can assess the effects of stem geometry on adaptive bone remodeling after THA.

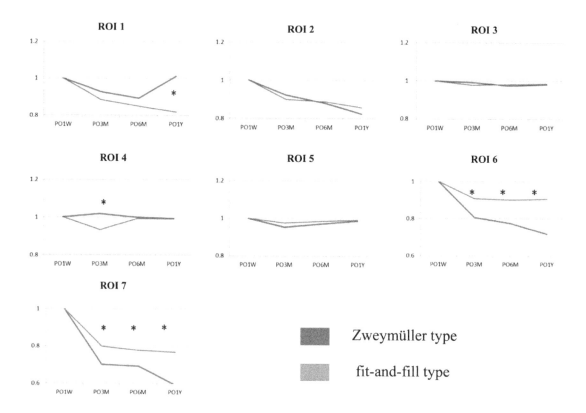

Figure 8. Median percentage change in bone mineral density (BMD) after surgery in the fit-and-fill-type stem and Zweymüller-type stem groups. The periprosthetic BMDs at 3, 6, and 12 months after surgery are expressed as percentage changes from the baseline BMD measured at 1 week after surgery (*$p< 0.05$).

2.3. Effects of bone geometry

Noble et al. [42] demonstrated the femoral anatomy variations in the mediolateral and anteroposterior dimensions and the need for multiple stem designs to achieve a close fit. Close adaptation of the prosthesis to the bone geometry is required to achieve optimal primary stability and secondary biologic fixation [43]. We studied the effects of bone geometry on BMD changes and equivalent stress in the femur after THA.

We investigated 20 patients who underwent THA using the Accolade TMZF stem (Stryker Orthopaedics) after reviewing the preoperative anterior-posterior hip radiographs of 90 consecutive patients who had undergone THA using the Accolade TMZF stem (**Figure 1**). The width of the proximal femoral canal on the operated side was measured from preoperative anterior-posterior hip radiographs, and Noble's canal flare index (CFI) was calculated for each patient [42]. Based on Noble's classification, the femurs were divided into the following three groups of femoral canal shapes: champagne flute (CFI ≥ 4.7), intermediate (CFI 3–4.7), and stovepipe (CFI < 3). Among the 20 study femurs, 7 had a champagne flute canal shape, 5 had a stovepipe shape, and 8 had an intermediate canal shape. The 8 femurs with an intermediate canal shape were randomly selected from among the remaining 78 hips with an intermediate canal shape to balance the groups for analysis.

The mean percentage changes in equivalent stress in each ROI between the pre- and postoperative femur models were calculated from the FEA results, and they are plotted in **Figure 9**. Between-group differences in the pattern of postoperative changes in equivalent stress were identified, and specific differences were observed in ROIs 6 ($p = 0.01$) and 7 ($p = 0.02$). Post hoc analysis indicated that the decrease in equivalent stress in ROI 6 was significantly greater in the stovepipe group (−63.8%) than in the champagne flute group (−38.8%) and intermediate group (−47.2%) ($p = 0.01$). Additionally, the decrease in equivalent stress in ROI 7 was significantly greater in the stovepipe group (−70.9%) than in the champagne flute group (−53.7%) and intermediate group (−51.4%) ($p = 0.03$).

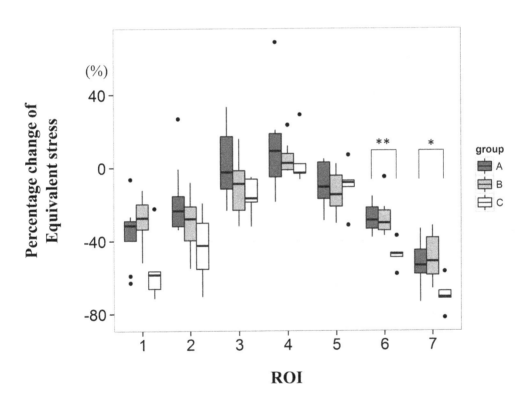

Figure 9. Comparison of the relative percentage changes in equivalent stress between the pre- and postoperative femur models for the three femoral canal shape groups. Postoperative relative percentage changes in equivalent stress in each region of interest compared to that of the preoperative models. Dots in the box plot show the outliers (*$p = 0.02$, **$p = 0.01$).

BMD changes in the femurs during the first postoperative year are shown in **Figure 10**. Significant between-group differences in BMD were evident in ROIs 6 ($p = 0.01$) and 7 ($p = 0.04$). In ROI 6, a marked decrease in BMD was identified only in the stovepipe group during the first postoperative year; the ROI 6 BMD showed a significantly higher decrease in the stovepipe group (−14.3%) than in the champagne flute group (−1.4%) and intermediate group (+3.6%) (p = 0.01). A postoperative decrease in ROI 7 BMD was evident in all the groups during the first postoperative year (champagne flute group, −23.1%; intermediate group, −22.7%; and stovepipe group, −36.5%). Additionally, the ROI 7 BMD showed a significantly higher decrease in the stovepipe group than in the other two groups (p = 0.045). BMDs in ROIs 1 and 2 were relatively lower in the stovepipe group than in the champagne flute and stovepipe groups during the first postoperative year; however, the differences were not significant.

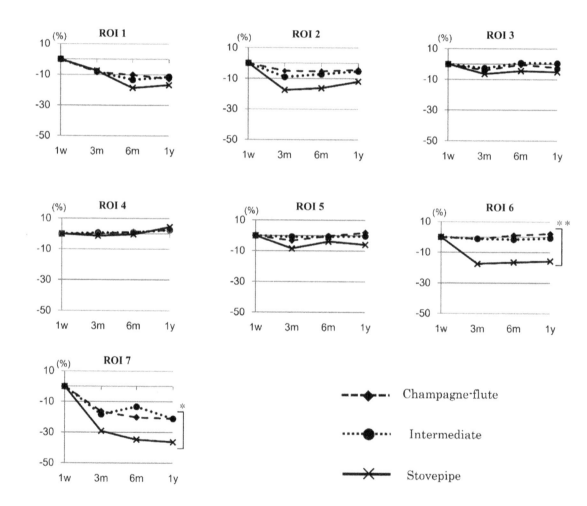

Figure 10. Comparison of bone mineral density (BMD) in the three femoral canal shape groups. The periprosthetic BMDs at 3, 6, and 12 months after surgery are expressed as percentage changes from the baseline BMD measured at 1 week after surgery (*p = 0.04, **p = 0.01).

The percentage changes in equivalent stress in each ROI were positively correlated with the postoperative BMD changes (**Figure 11**). A significant correlation was observed between equivalent stress and BMD changes ($p < 0.01$), and the adjusted R^2 value showed that the percentage changes in equivalent stress (adjusted R^2 = 0.79) could predict the postoperative BMD changes in our simulation model.

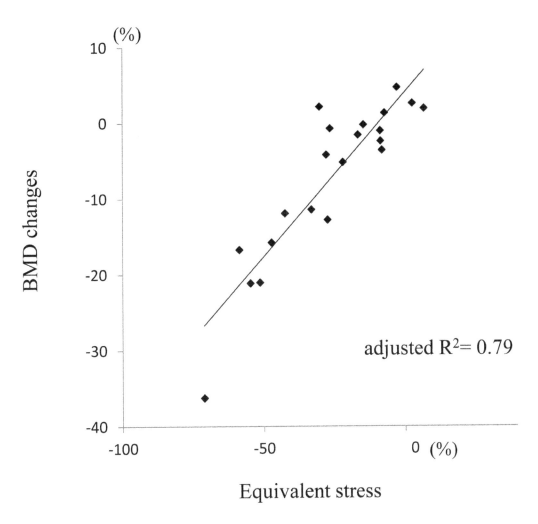

Figure 11. Scatter plot illustrating the relationship between the percentage changes in equivalent stress and postoperative bone mineral density (BMD). The 21 points plotted in this scatter plot display the average relative percentage changes in equivalent stress (finite element analysis results) and BMD for the three femoral canal shape groups. A significant correlation is observed between equivalent stress and BMD changes (adjusted R^2 = 0.79, $p < 0.01$).

The FEA results and postoperative BMD changes of the femur suggest that the combination of a large, tapered wedge-type stem and stovepipe femur may be associated with proximal BMD loss. Our simulation-based outcomes predicted a stronger stress-shielding effect in the stovepipe femur group than in the other groups. These results indicate that subject-specific FEA can assess the effects of bone geometry on adaptive bone remodeling after THA.

The present studies have limitations. First, the interface condition between the stem and the femur in the FEA model was assumed to be fully bonded. Consideration of the surface properties of the implant and degree of stem fixation would be useful for constructing realistic models. Second, the maximum length of the tetrahedral elements (4 mm) was relatively large, and therefore the elements might straddle the boundary between the cortical and cancellous area in the FE models. Therefore, the elastic modulus of the elements straddling the boundary would contain some errors.

3. Summary

We focused on equivalent stress as a mechanical parameter associated with adaptive bone remodeling and found that equivalent stress changes were positively correlated with postoperative BMD changes in the femur. BMD and equivalent stress were maintained in the distal femur and decreased in the proximal femur after THA. Thus, the proposed subject-specific FEA is useful for evaluating adaptive bone remodeling after THA and could predict BMD changes after THA. Furthermore, subject-specific FEA can be used to evaluate the effects of stem geometry and bone geometry on bone remodeling and can help in the understanding of the altered mechanical environment after THA.

Abbreviations

BMD, bone mineral density

CFI, canal flare index

CT, computed tomography

DEXA, dual-energy X-ray absorptiometry

FEA, finite element analysis

ROIs, regions of interest

SED, strain energy density

THA, total hip arthroplasty

Author details

Yutaka Inaba*, Hiroyuki Ike, Masatoshi Oba and Tomoyuki Saito

*Address all correspondence to: yute0131@med.yokohama-cu.ac.jp

Department of Orthopaedic Surgery, Yokohama City University, Yokohama, Japan

References

[1] Malchau H, Herberts P, Ahnfelt L. Prognosis of total hip replacement in Sweden. Follow-up of 92,675 operations performed 1978-1990. Acta Orthop Scand. 1993; 64:497–506.

[2] Dorr LD, Lewonowski K, Lucero M, Harris M, Wan Z. Failure mechanisms of anatomic porous replacement I cementless total hip replacement. Clin Orthop Relat Res. 1997; 334:157–167.

[3] Bougherara H, Bureau M, Campbell M, Vadean A, Yahia L. Design of a biomimetic polymer-composite hip prosthesis. J Biomed Mater Res. 2007; 82:27–40.

[4] Kerner J, Huiskes R, van Lenthe GH, Weinans H, van Rietbergen B, Engh CA, Amis AA. Correlation between pre-operative periprosthetic bone density and post-operative bone loss in THA can be explained by strain-adaptive remodelling. J Biomech. 1999; 32:695–703.

[5] Kroger H, Miettinen H, Arnala I, Koski E, Rushton N, Suomalainen O. Evaluation of periprosthetic bone using dual-energy X-ray absorptiometry: precision of the method and effect of operation on bone mineral density. J Bone Miner Res. 1996; 11:1526–1530.

[6] Kim YH, Yoon SH, Kim JS. Changes in the bone mineral density in the acetabulum and proximal femur after cementless total hip replacement: alumina-on-alumina versus alumina-on-polyethylene articulation. J Bone Joint Surg Br. 2007; 89:174–179.

[7] Nishii T, Sugano N, Masuhara K, Shibuya T, Ochi T, Tamura S. Longitudinal evaluation of time related bone remodeling after cementless total hip arthroplasty. Clin Orthop Relat Res. 1997; 339:121–131.

[8] Kroger H, Venesmaa P, Jurvelin J, Miettinen H, Suomalainen O, Alhava E. Bone density at the proximal femur after total hip arthroplasty. Clin Orthop Relat Res. 1998; 352:66–74.

[9] Rosenthall L, Bobyn JD, Brooks CE. Temporal changes of periprosthetic bone density in patients with a modular noncemented femoral prosthesis. J Arthroplasty. 1999; 14:71–76.

[10] Ostbyhaug PO, Klaksvik J, Romundstad P, Aamodt A. An in vitro study of the strain distribution in human femora with anatomical and customised femoral stems. J Bone Joint Surg Br. 2009; 91:676–682.

[11] Wolff J. Das Gesetz der Transformation der Knochen. Berlin, Germany: Verlag von August Hirschwald; 1892.

[12] Jaworski ZF. Coupling of bone formation to bone resorption: a broader view. Calcif Tissue Int. 1984; 36:531–535.

[13] Zadpoor AA. Open forward and inverse problems in theoretical modeling of bone tissue adaptation. J Mech Behav Biomed Mater. 2013; 27:249–261.

[14] Huiskes R, Weinans H, Grootenboer HJ, Dalstra M, Fudala B, Slooff TJ. Adaptive bone-remodeling theory applied to prosthetic-design analysis. J Biomech. 1987; 20:1135–1150.

[15] Carter DR, Van Der Meulen MC, Beaupre GS. Mechanical factors in bone growth and development. Bone. 1996; 18:5S–10S.

[16] Stulpner MA, Reddy BD, Starke GR, Spirakis A. A three-dimensional finite analysis of adaptive remodelling in the proximal femur. J Biomech. 1997; 30:1063–1066.

[17] Adachi T, Tomita Y, Sakaue H, Tanaka M. Simulation of trabecular surface remodeling based on local stress uniformity. Jpn Soc Mech Eng. 1997; 40:782–792.

[18] Keyak JH, Rossi SA, Jones KA, Skinner HB. Prediction of femoral fracture load using automated finite element modeling. J Biomech. 1998; 31:125–133.

[19] Taddei F, Schileo E, Helgason B, Cristofolini L, Viceconti M. The material mapping strategy influences the accuracy of CT-based finite element models of bones: an evaluation against experimental measurements. Med Eng Phys. 2007; 29:973–979.

[20] Pettersen SH, Wik TS, Skallerud B. Subject specific finite element analysis of stress shielding around a cementless femoral stem. Clin Biomech (Bristol, Avon). 2009; 24:196–202.

[21] Cody DD, Gross GJ, Hou FJ, Spencer HJ, Goldstein SA, Fyhrie DP. Femoral strength is better predicted by finite element models than QCT and DXA. J Biomech. 1999; 32:1013–1020.

[22] Tawara D, Sakamoto J, Murakami H, Kawahara N, Oda J, Tomita K. Mechanical evaluation by patient-specific finite element analyses demonstrates therapeutic effects for osteoporotic vertebrae. J Mech Behav Biomed Mater. 2010; 3:31–40.

[23] Ike H, Inaba Y, Kobayashi N, Hirata Y, Yukizawa Y, Aoki C, Choe H, Saito T. Comparison between mechanical stress and bone mineral density in the femur after total hip arthroplasty by using subject-specific finite element analyses. Comput Methods Biomech Biomed Engin. 2015; 18:1056–1065.

[24] Hirata Y, Inaba Y, Kobayashi N, Ike H, Fujimaki H, Saito T. Comparison of mechanical stress and change in bone mineral density between two types of femoral implant using finite element analysis. J Arthroplasty. 2013; 28:1731–1735.

[25] Anderson AE, Peters CL, Tuttle BD, Weiss JA. Subject-specific finite element model of the pelvis: development, validation and sensitivity studies. J Biomech Eng. 2005; 127:364–373.

[26] Ateshian GA, Henak CR, Weiss JA. Toward patient-specific articular contact mechanics. J Biomech. 2015; 48:779–786.

[27] Weinans H, Sumner DR, Igloria R, Natarajan RN. Sensitivity of periprosthetic stress-shielding to load and the bone density-modulus relationship in subject-specific finite element models. J Biomech. 2000; 33:809–817.

[28] Gruen TA, McNeice GM, Amstutz HC. "Modes of failure" of cemented stem-type femoral components: a radiographic analysis of loosening. Clin Orthop Relat Res. 1979; 141:17–27.

[29] Bessho M, Ohnishi I, Matsuyama J, Matsumoto T, Imai K, Nakamura K. Prediction of strength and strain of the proximal femur by a CT-based finite element method. J Biomech. 2007; 40:1745–1753.

[30] Keyak JH, Lee IY, Skinner HB. Correlations between orthogonal mechanical properties and density of trabecular bone: use of different densitometric measures. J Biomed Mater Res. 1994; 28:1329–1336.

[31] Keller TS. Predicting the compressive mechanical behavior of bone. J Biomech. 1994; 27:1159–1168.

[32] Bergmann G, Deuretzbacher G, Heller M, Graichen F, Rohlmann A, Strauss J, Duda GN. Hip contact forces and gait patterns from routine activities. J Biomech. 2001; 34:859–871.

[33] Herrera A, Panisello JJ, Ibarz E, Cegonino J, Puertolas JA, Gracia L. Comparison between DEXA and finite element studies in the long-term bone remodeling of an anatomical femoral stem. J Biomech Eng. 2009; 131:041013.

[34] Aldinger PR, Sabo D, Pritsch M, Thomsen M, Mau H, Ewerbeck V, Breusch SJ. Pattern of periprosthetic bone remodeling around stable uncemented tapered hip stems: a prospective 84-month follow-up study and a median 156-month cross-sectional study with DXA. Calcif Tissue Int. 2003; 73:115–121.

[35] Boden H, Adolphson P. No adverse effects of early weight bearing after uncemented total hip arthroplasty: a randomized study of 20 patients. Acta Orthop Scand. 2004; 75:21–29.

[36] Maistrelli GL, Fornasier V, Binnington A, McKenzie K, Sessa V, Harrington I. Effect of stem modulus in a total hip arthroplasty model. J Bone Joint Surg Br. 1991; 73:43–46.

[37] Decking R, Puhl W, Simon U, Claes LE. Changes in strain distribution of loaded proximal femora caused by different types of cementless femoral stems. Clin Biomech (Bristol, Avon). 2006; 21:495–501.

[38] Herrera A, Panisello JJ, Ibarz E, Cegonino J, Puertolas JA, Gracia L. Long-term study of bone remodelling after femoral stem: a comparison between dexa and finite element simulation. J Biomech. 2007; 40:3615–3625.

[39] Kwon JY, Naito H, Matsumoto T, Tanaka M. Estimation of change of bone structures after total hip replacement using bone remodeling simulation. Clin Biomech (Bristol, Avon). 2013; 28:514–518.

[40] Khanuja HS, Vakil JJ, Goddard MS, Mont MA. Cementless femoral fixation in total hip arthroplasty. J Bone Joint Surg Am. 2011; 93:500–509.

[41] Inaba Y, Kobayashi N, Oba M, Ike H, Kubota S, Saito T. Difference in postoperative periprosthetic bone mineral density changes between 3 major designs of uncemented stems: a 3-year follow-up study. J Arthroplasty. DOI: 10.1016/j.arth.2016.02.009.

[42] Noble PC, Alexander JW, Lindahl LJ, Yew DT, Granberry WM, Tullos HS. The anatomic basis of femoral component design. Clin Orthop Relat Res. 1988; 235:148–165.

[43] Massin P, Geais L, Astoin E, Simondi M, Lavaste F. The anatomic basis for the concept of lateralized femoral stems: a frontal plane radiographic study of the proximal femur. J Arthroplasty. 2000; 15:93–101.

2

The Role of Finite Element Analysis in Studying Potential Failure of Mandibular Reconstruction Methods

Raymond C.W. Wong, John S.P. Loh and I. Islam

Additional information is available at the end of the chapter

Abstract

Defects of the mandible occur after trauma or resection after infection or tumours. There have been many methods espoused, but many methods can fail especially if the biomechanics of the mandible is not considered fully. As the only moveable, load-bearing bone of the skull, the mandible is subject to loads and stresses unique to it due to its shape, location and function. This chapter reviews the basic knowledge of the mandible necessary to perform finite element analysis, the challenges and then reviews several studies that have been done. The authors' personal research is detailed to illustrate how finite element analysis can be used to look at potential failure of a new method for mandibular reconstruction and implant evaluation.

Keywords: mandible reconstruction, finite element analysis, potential failure

1. Introduction

The lower jaw or mandible is the only load bearing, moveable bone of the skull. Defects in the lower jaw or mandible can happen as a result of trauma, infection or after a resection for pathology, which can be benign or malignant. The field of medicine or surgery has never been able to satisfactorily reconstruct a mandible after the original tissue has been gone. An unrepaired defect in the mandible, depending on the location of the defect would lead to (1) constriction of the remaining tissue around the defect leading to a malocclusion due to the pull of the muscles, (2) collapse of the arches leading to inability to eat and function and (3) difficulty swallowing or even breathing especially when lying flat due to loss of attachment of the tongue, sometimes leading to aspiration or asphyxiation.

2. Methods for mandibular reconstruction

There have been many methods advocated for reconstruction of the mandible, most of which have never fully considered the biomechanical forces acting on the mandible both in the short and long term. These methods have been "tried", most times with catastrophic results. Among the methods for mandibular reconstruction advocated are:

1) Soft tissue flap

2) Autogenous bone blocks

3) Mandibular reconstruction/bridging plate

4) Cancellous bone in titanium mesh

5) Vascularized free flap

6) Newer methods like the endoprosthesis or alloplastic replacement

7) Tissue engineered bone scaffold

The current gold standard is still the vascularized free flap, which needs a long operation time and harvest of tissue from another part of the body [1, 2].

This brings the question of "what is the ideal method of mandibular reconstruction?" to the fore.

2.1. Ideal method

The ideal method of mandibular reconstruction would:

1) Reconstruct the missing soft tissue and bone

2) Allow replacement of teeth

3) Not need a long surgery

4) Easy to learn without needing extensive training and skills that are hard to learn

5) Not need to take tissue from another part of the body

6) Cost effective

7) Not need prolonged hospitalization and recovery

8) Allow the patient to eat and function early or immediately

9) Be able to withstand the forces of biting and chewing permanently or for a long time

No such ideal method exists.

2.2. Challenges to mandibular reconstruction

The challenges to replacing a section of the mandible lie in its form and function as well as its unique location in the body. Any hardware (plates and screws) used to fix the mandible would undergo unique stresses not seen in other parts of the body. There is a non-axial load in that the long axis of the teeth is about perpendicular to the long axis of the mandible. The overlying tissue in the mouth is thin; any break in the soft tissue could lead to exposure of the hardware to the bacteria and saliva in the mouth, leading to the formation of biofilms. Ingestion of hot and cold food and liquids can cause expansion and contraction of the hardware, which is dissimilar to that of the underlying bone.

3. Mandibular biomechanics

The biomechanics of the mandible has not been very well studied. Mandibular biomechanics can be studied with finite element analysis, strain gauges or photoelastic models. Finite element analysis allows study of the forces throughout an entire structure but is limited to static forces. An understanding of the anatomy and biomechanics of the intact mandible is necessary prior to looking at how to conduct a finite element analysis of the mandible.

3.1. Anatomy of the mandible

The mandible is a U-shaped bone, connected at the temporomandibular joints at both ends to the skull. It consists of a corpus (body), the symphysis, which connects both right and left at the midline, the alveolar bone, which supports the teeth, the ramus with the condylar as well as the coronoid processes (**Figure 1**).

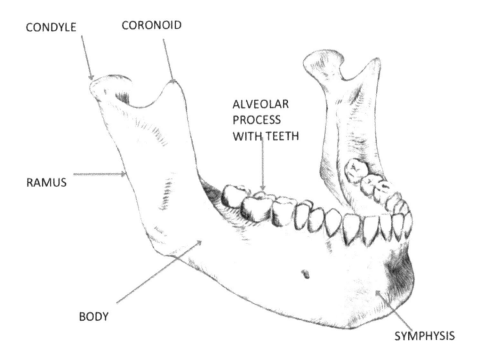

Figure 1. Schema showing the gross anatomy of the mandible.

The teeth are connected to the alveolar bone by periodontal ligaments, which act as a gomphosis (allowing minute movement). These ligaments are inserted into the bone on one end and into the cementum of the teeth.

The muscular attachments can be divided into three groups:

1) Muscles of mastication—medial pterygoid, lateral pterygoid, masseter and temporalis; only the lateral pterygoid muscle assist in opening the mandible, the rest closes the mandible.

2) Suprahyoid muscles that assist in some opening of the mouth and swallowing—mylohyoid, hyoglossus, genioglossus, digastric muscles.

3) Muscles of facial expression that insert into the mandible—buccinators, depressor anguli oris, mentalis.

The outer surface of the mandible consists of dense cortical bone, the thickness of which varies. In certain areas, there is only cortical bone throughout. The alveolar processes and in the middle of the mandibular body and part of the ramus consist of cancellous bone (bone marrow). There is a nerve coursing through the mandible in a canal, which usually does not play a role in terms of biomechanics.

The attachment of the mandible to the skull consists of the attachments of the muscles of mastication and the temporomandibular joint. The temporomandibular joint consists of two joint spaces, the superior and inferior joint spaces, surrounded by a capsule consisting of elastic collagen fibres and divided by the articular cartilage, which is a fibrocartilage. The movement of the joint consists of two distinct movements, which are Phase I (rotation) about a hinge for the first 20 mm followed by Phase 2 (translation), which is affected mainly by the action of the lateral pterygoid muscle pulling the entire condyle to the front and out of the glenoid fossa onto the part of the zygomatic process of the temporal bone. The forward movement of the condyle is limited somewhat by a protrusion called the articular eminence.

3.2. Biomechanics of the intact mandible

The mandible functions as a Class III lever. During function, there is a zone of tension on the alveolar part of the mandible and a zone of compression on the lower border. Studies by Meyer [3, 4] showed bone deformation in the mandibular condyle region, with tensile stress along the anterior ramus as well as along the sigmoid notch area and compressive stress along the posterior ramus border. This suggested that there is a tendency of the mandible to straighten during function. This somewhat simplistic model holds true when there is bilateral and equal function and bite forces (**Figure 2**).

Upon contraction of the muscles of mastication, the mandible is bent in a sagittal plane; this is produced by the vertical component of the muscle forces, the joint reaction forces and the reaction forces from chewing motions. During asymmetrical loading (biting on one side), the largest shear forces happen between the bite force and the muscle force on the working side (the biting side) and between the muscle force and joint force on the balancing side (non-biting side). This produces then a converse load distribution with a zone of tension on the lower border and a zone of compression on the alveolar portion in the working side and vice versa on the balancing side. This means that during incisal biting (biting on the front teeth), there is an equal amount of sagittal bending on both sides but a different deformation on the working and balancing sides during molar biting [5–7].

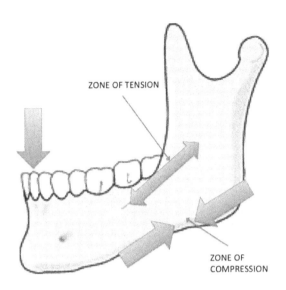

Figure 2. Zones of tension and compression in the mandible.

There is also a tendency for narrowing of the mandibular arch from parasagittal and transverse deformation upon clenching and incisal biting. This is caused by bilateral torsion of both mandibular bodies and bending at the symphyseal region leading to compression at the superior margin of the symphysis and tension at the inferior margin.

Hylander showed that the mandibular symphysis undergoes three distinct patterns of stress and deformation, that is, corporal rotation (relative outward rotation of both halves of the mandible), medial convergence (change in mandibular width during function) and dorso-ventral shear (movement of both mandibular halves relative to one another in the vertical plane) [8] (**Figure 3**).

There is also some difference in the deformation between the outer (buccal) surface of the mandible and the inner (lingual) surface. Lateral transverse bending occurs and the bending moment increases from back to front during the late power stroke of biting/clenching. The maximum magnitude of the bending occurs near the symphysis. This bending produces compressive stresses at the buccal cortex and tensile stress at the lingual cortex. The deformation has been calculated to be as large as 0.6 mm in a simulated molar bite of 526N using finite element analysis [6]. The mandible deformed in a helical pattern upwards and towards the working side, with regions of high tensile stress (15–25 MPa) from the coronoid process and ramus towards the lingual side of the symphysis. The highest value of compressive stress (15–25 MPa) was at the bite point and bilateral sigmoid notches, at the working side angle and in an area from the posterior surface of the balancing side ramus running to the lower border of the body till the symphysis. This then runs up to the buccal side from the inferior until the bite point. Overall, the shear stresses were larger on the working side with the exception of the balancing side condyle (peak shear stress of 25 MPa). In a nutshell, this means that the mandible changes in dimensions during function as a result of its shape and muscle pull with the greatest change in dimension and deformation in the midline.

What does all this information mean and what is the practical application? It means that application of any hardware to the mandible must take into account these forces and change in dimension. This has led to the creation of Champy's ideal lines of internal fixation for fixation of a mandibular fracture [9] (**Figure 4**). Placement of bone plates and screws in the area between the zones of tension and zones of compression will tend neutralize the forces and stabilize the bony fragments enough for healing. This however uses the principle of cross bracing and load sharing, that is, using inter-fragmentary bone friction to help stabilize the bony segments.

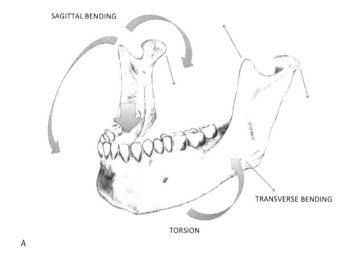

A

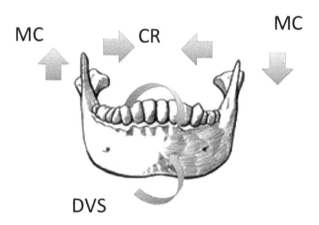

B

Figure 3. (A) Tendency for mandible to straighten as well as undergo torsion. (B) Forces acting about the midline of the mandible. CR – corporal rotation; MC – medial convergence; DVS – dorso-ventral shear.

In comminuted fractures or in a segmental mandibular defect, the principle of load sharing cannot be applied. We are then dependent on using load bearing bone plates, which means the material strength of the plate is the only thing keeping the mandibular segments together. The method of fixation of the bone plate to the bone also plays a factor.

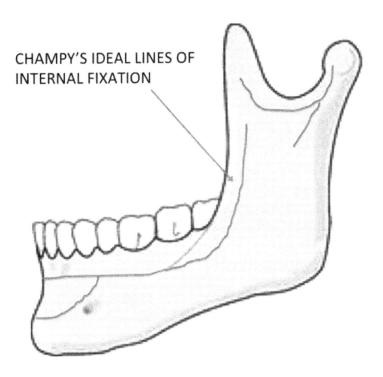

Figure 4. Champy's lines for ideal internal fixation – placement of bone plates along these lines will stabilize the bone fragments enough for healing of fractures.

4. Finite element model of the mandible

A very accurate finite element model is practically impossible to create due to the complex anatomy of the mandible. A true to accurate model that takes everything into account would need several supercomputers. Assumptions will have to be made to simplify the model and reduce the need for computing power.

Several authors have created finite element models of the mandible, each with different levels of complexity [10, 11]. Following are the steps taken to create an accurate finite element model [12].

4.1. Creation of a 3D mesh

The information about the external shaped of the mandible is needed to be able to create a mesh to input into the FEA software. Several possible methods that have been used to get the geometry of the mandible:

1) Digital creation of 3D model—not accurate representation of the anatomical detail. The question then arises: "At what level of intricacy would there be detriment to the level of accuracy?" Is it necessary to recreate all the intricacies (concavities, canals)?

2) Conversion of digitized slices or sections of a human mandible into a whole 3D structure [13].

3) Computer tomographic (CT) scans of a human mandible or mandibular equivalent and conversion of the radiographic images in Digitised Communication in Medicine (DICOM) format into a 3D structure in Standard Tessellation Language (STL). This information is then meshed with any number of software programs. This is the most popular method. Some authors have also used the cone beam CT, which is another way to get the CT images with a cone beam instead of a fan beam. This tends to produce many sharp triangles, which need to be simplified prior to mesh creation.

Once the 3D geometry has been obtained, it is subdivided into a finite, large number of geometrically simplified elements, connected together at the nodes. The mesh is a contiguous collection of these simple-shaped elements. Most FE software have automated mesh generation features, creating relatively dense meshes, which can be refined in different regions.

4.2. Input of material properties and boundary conditions

The material properties of the elements, namely the elastic modulus and Poisson's ratio must be defined. Since the mandible consists of cortical and cancellous bone together with the teeth, several assumptions need to be made to simplify the model further. It is well known that bone is anisotropic in different dimensions. For purposes of simplifying the calculations, most authors have tended to assume that bone is isotropic and that the mandible is purely cortical bone. Any teeth present, which in real life would have periodontal ligaments and allows minute movements would tend to be assumed to be ankylosed to the bone, that is, fused to the bone. The teeth are composed of enamel on the outer surface of the crown followed by dentine and the pulp (a hollow cavity which contains the nerve fibres and blood supply). The outer surface of the root is covered by cementum. All these tissues have different material properties. The values for the material properties are have already been determined by studies. Some errors abound when it comes to the values of the cancellous bone. Most studies have tended to remove a block of cancellous bone and then subject the block to mechanical testing to ascertain its material properties. There is evidence to suggest that this is not entirely accurate. Misch et al. (1999) showed that the presence of cortical bone increases the elastic modulus of cancellous bone [14]. When the cortical bone was present, the elastic modulus ranged from 24.9 to 240 MPa (mean 96.2 MPa). When cancellous bone only was tested, the elastic modulus reduced dramatically (3.5–125.6 MPa). This means that the values from the literature for cancellous bone are not accurate.

Boundary conditions are important to prevent movement of the individual units so that the model can be loaded and deformed as a rigid structure, allowing computations to be performed. It can be divided into essential boundary conditions (displacement constraints to anchor the model and the non-essential boundary conditions or loading conditions, which are the forces to be applied to the model). Decisions will need to be made also about the insertion of the muscle forces and the force of each muscle. Some muscles like the masseter have three distinct types of fibres with different vectors. Most of these values are already in the literature.

4.3. Solution

With all the information, the completed model is then solved to obtain the displacements and the resulting stress and strains. In biomechanical models, what is most often sought is information on the stresses and strains, as the force is usually known.

The external forces {F} and the mechanical properties/geometry {K} are used to solve the nodal displacements {D}. With the nodal displacements known, the displacement fields are then interpolated from the nodal values using standard interpolating polynomial functions. The strain distribution is the differentiation of the displacement field yields and the stress distribution is then determined mathematically.

4.4. Validation and interpretation

Validation can be performed by evaluating the precision and accuracy of the model. Precision, defined as how close the model's results are to the exact solution to the biomechanical model, can be ascertained by conducting a convergence test where meshes of different refinements are created and the strains/stresses at specific locations are compared. Most reported studies have tended to use precision studies as a measure of validation as it is difficult to affix strain gauges to the human subject to test for accuracy for ethical and practical purposes.

5. Finite element analysis of the various mandibular reconstruction methods

There have been very few finite element analysis conducted on reconstructed mandibles, mainly due to this being a field that is not very well understood by the people who operate in this area. In the field of orthopaedics, the biomechanics of the limbs has been well studied and there are numerous studies using finite element analysis. This section reviews the few studies that have been conducted followed by the authors' own studies. By necessity, it is impractical to go into very much detail for each study. We will concentrate on two studies in detail at the end of this section.

5.1. Marginal resection of the mandible

Marginal resection of the mandible is performed for tumours that affect the alveolar process of the mandible but does not extend to the mandibular basal bone. One of the complications that can occur is fracture of the remaining portion of the mandible, usually from the corners of the resection where areas of stress concentration occur (**Figure 5**).

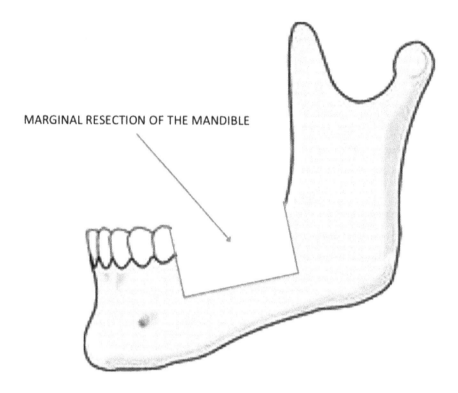

MARGINAL RESECTION OF THE MANDIBLE

Figure 5. Marginal resection of the alveolar portion of the mandible, leaving the basal bone intact.

Wittkampf et al. [13] conducted studies on prevention of mandible fracture after a marginal resection of the mandible. The authors sectioned a human mandible, photographed the slices and digitized it. Marginal resections of different radii were placed in digitally and the areas of maximum stress concentrations in the corner of the resections were compared. It was found that an enlarge radius of resection at the corners offered the best resistance to minimize fracture after resection.

5.2. Reconstruction plates for bridging mandibular defects

Reconstruction plates alone are sometime used to bridge a defect to maintain the space and contours of the jaw in patients in poor health or with advanced tumours. A patient might not be fit for a long surgery or it might not be worthwhile to subject a patient to a long surgery if the prognosis is poor. Sometimes also the reconstruction plate is placed together with bone grafts, which is then subject to other considerations in terms of biomechanics (**Figure 6**).

The most common complications in using a reconstruction plate to bridge a defect are plate fracture, sometimes after a few years, loosening of the screws and exposure of the plate (dehiscence) either in the mouth or through the skin.

For pure mandibular bridging plates alone, the size and location of the defect and whether the defect crosses the midline (symphysis region) plays a large role in terms of complications [11, 15]. Recall the earlier section where it was shown that the midline is subject to many different forces of tension, compression and torsion with changes in dimensions. The masticatory loads on the plates cause vertical discrepancies that can lead to bone resorption and screw loosening. Arden et al. [16] reported that defects larger than 5 cm of bone length are associated with a high complication rate as high as 81% when plates alone are used to repair lateral defects.

Martola et al. [17] hypothesized that residual stresses from bending a stiff plate (sometimes repeatedly) to adapt to the jaw contour can be a main reason for plate fracture. This makes sense from a material science point of view, in that repeated bending of a metal results in work hardening of the metal, sometime with creation of small micro-cracks which may affect the mean stress in fatigue loading.

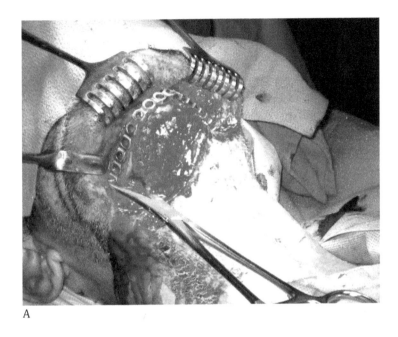

A

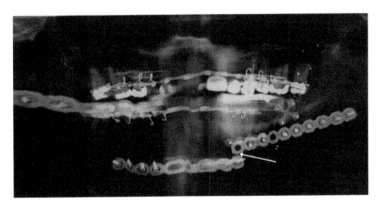

B

Figure 6. (A) Reconstruction plate bridging a defect in the anterior. (B) Fracture of the reconstruction plate, a common complication. Indicated by arrow.

Kimura et al. [18] investigated the most suitable method in dispersing stresses around the screws in plate fixation to the remnant mandible after a resection of the mandible. The authors took CT scans of dry human mandibles and created eight digital edentulous (no teeth) mandible models. Defects were created on the models in the front (midline) and lateral areas and the plates were drawn onto the defects with different screw configurations. A dental implant was drawn into the opposing (contralateral) side of the defect. The material properties (based on reported data) of all the components in the model were defined: cancellous bone, cortical bone and titanium. A maximum bite force of 300 N in a vertical load pattern was chosen and used. In the analysis, the stresses were concentrated around the implant, the screw closest to the defect on both sides (crucial screw) and the plate on the non-loaded side. Defects in the midline (central defects) placed greater maximum stress on the screws. If three screws were placed for lateral defects, there was greater stress on the crucial screws, which could have been due to bowing of the plate.

A partially dentate mandible of a cadaveric male was used to create a model with defect in the front and back. The authors (Schuller-Gotzburg et al, [19]) studied the effects and change in bone stress after caudal and buccal placement of placing a bridging plate. In this study, bridging plate alone in a conventional placement, bone grafts fixed with small miniplates to the remnant mandible and also placement of a bridging plate in a caudal and then buccal location for the reconstruction. The load was 50 N on the right mandibular second premolar. The conclusion was that there would be a better biomechanical advantage and lesser stress with the plate in a caudal position.

Knoll et al. [20] investigated replacement of angle defects with a standard 2.7 mm reconstruction plate with a linear screw configuration. An edentulous finite element mandible model was created; a defect placed in the right angle with a virtual bone plate placed and the model was loaded with 135 N of force in the front. The model showed that the stresses were far in excess of the material strength of titanium and cortical bone. This result showed that there was a high possibility of plate fracture, bone loss and screw loosening. The recommendation was to redesign the plate to allow screw placement in a triangular or square configuration to further maximize the interface between bone and plate.

5.3. Vascularized free flaps

Vascularized free flaps are flaps of soft tissue and bone, harvested from another part of the body with its own arterial blood supply and venous drainage. The flaps are then placed into the part of the body that needs it, connected to the local blood supply and then fixed to the surrounding bone and soft tissue. For defects of the mandible, the two most common flaps used are the fibula and iliac crest free flaps. This is still the gold standard after a resection.

Tie et al. [21] constructed finite element models to study which flaps, the fibula or iliac crest free flaps would be best biomechanically to replace a segment of the mandible. The authors scanned the mandible, iliac crest and fibula of a healthy 30-year old volunteer and used the images to create a finite element model of the mandible. Defects were created in the anterior and lateral mandible; the outlines of the defects outlined and extracted using the software and the volume of the fibula and iliac crest made to fit the defects. The stress distribution for the iliac crest was found to be similar to that of the intact mandible. The fibula reconstruction, however, had greater stresses (compressive and tensile) at the grafted bone with the maximum stress at the interface between native and grafted bone. The increased binding or interface between the iliac crest and native bone contributed towards better transmission of the bite forces. Their conclusion is that for smaller defects, the iliac crest would be better due to the above findings. As the fibula has greater length, it would be more suitable for larger defects.

5.4. Endoprosthesis/customized implant

An endoprosthesis is an implant, mostly titanium that is placed to replace a defect in the line of the remaining bone stumps. It is usually attached to the bone stumps with a stem, which is usually cemented or press fit. This concept has been used in orthopaedics in the long bones with great success for decades [22–25].

The concept of using an endoprosthesis for mandibular replacement was introduced by Tideman, initially as proof of concept and with several animal studies [26–28]. The decision was made to look into the mandibular endoprosthesis as a modular format rather than customized. The reasons for this were as follows:

1) Parts machined in large quantities are cheaper.

2) Customized implants require time for manufacture and are more expensive. Between the time from the scanning of the patient to the time it takes to design and manufacture as well as transport time, it may take a few weeks; this might have allowed time for the lesion if it is cancerous to grow larger in size and thus rendering the customized fit potentially inaccurate.

3) A stock endoprosthesis, which comes in different lengths and can be assembled in modules, allow variations and more flexibility during the surgery to adapt to defect length changes.

The modular endoprosthesis has been used, again with great success in the field of orthopaedics and musculoskeletal surgery.

The difference between the long limbs and the mandible has already been discussed previously. There is also the addition of the curvature of the mandible in the anterior region, which varies between individuals, making it difficult for a stock endoprosthesis.

Nevertheless, the animal experiments, which largely were conducted in the monkey model yielded interesting results. There were two designs: (1) the mandibular body replacement and (2) the condyle replacement. The condyle replacement had no problems with loosening and infection. The body replacement design had persistent problems with loosening between the module connections, causing infection and loosening. The cemented stems had no problems; however, a decision was made to investigate the biomechanical forces that acted on the entire reconstruction for the body replacement design [29].

The design of the endoprosthesis was changed as follows [30]:

1)   The stem was changed from cemented to screw retained, which was to be screwed into the marrow part of the mandible.

2)   The module connection was changed to a male and female part in a dovetail fashion, which was connected by a screw. A slight movement of 0.1 mm was designed as s tress breaker between the connection of the male and female part.

This new design was then tested for the following aims prior to any animal or human testing:

1)   Experimental evaluation of the new design to look at fatigue performance and failure patterns by mechanical testing. The entire setup was also investigated with a finite element analysis to see if the model correctly predicted the site of failure in the mechanical testing.

2)   Finite element analysis of the new design in a simulated human mandible under certain conditions. The defect was then to be made bigger and the stem length was to be changed in length to see what happens to the stress distribution to better predict the ability of the reconstruction to withstand failure (if the stress in any part is more than the material strength of the material) and also the location of failure.

The new endoprosthesis design was made to fit the dimensions of a human mandible and underwent mechanical testing in a jig, mounted on a synthetic mandible, which had similar elastic properties to cortical bone. The methods of mechanical testing depend on the question asked. It can range from simple three-point bending test, compressive and tensile strength to complex tests for load to failure or fatigue loading. The dimensions of the assembled endo-prosthesis were 18-mm stem length with 4-mm diameter and body dimensions of 15-mm length, 16-mm high and 8.5-mm thick (**Figure 7**).

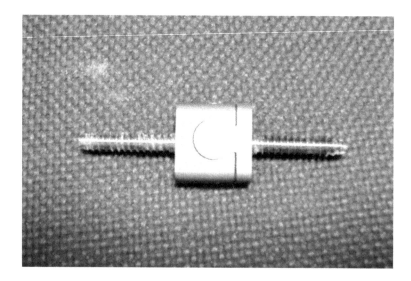

Figure 7. The endoprosthesis consisted of two screwed stems, which connected to each other in a dovetail. This was locked together by a central screw, which is inserted from the top.

Static testing revealed a tendency for the screw stem to pull out of the substrate of the synthetic mandible. Cyclic testing was then performed for up to 500,000 cycles. This revealed a tendency for the endoprosthesis to fail with fracture or bending at the superior surface of the stem but with no loosening of the module connection, which had plagued the earlier animal experiments.

The line drawings of the endoprosthesis from the manufacturer were imported into Abaqus v6.10 (Simulia, Dassault Systemes, France). The stems were modelled as smooth cylinders to simplify calculations. Rectangular cuboids were modelled as the synthetic mandibles and bores made for stem insertion. The stems of the endoprosthesis were perfectly tied to the bores of the holes as well as the central connection screw. The cuboids were assigned the elastic properties of cortical bone and meshed with linear tetrahedral elements. It was assumed that the bone was isotropic. A bolt load of 10 N was applied to simulate tightening of the central screw. A downward force of 150 N (calculated at 80% of average static load to failure of 185 N, this was the maximum force used for the fatigue testing) was loaded on to one end of the reconstruction while the other end was given fixed boundary conditions. The load was kept constant to identify peak stresses, which lead to fatigue failure (**Figure 8**).

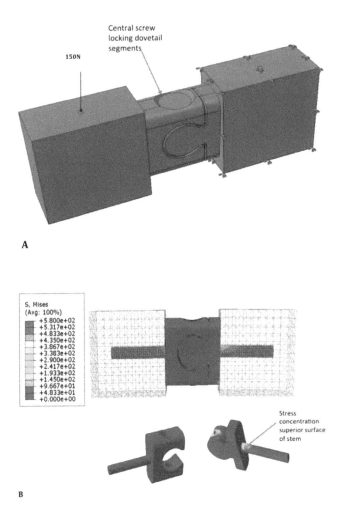

Figure 8. (A) Rendering of endoprosthesis mounted in bone blocks. (B) Von Mises stress distribution.

The finite element analysis of the setup showed areas of high stresses accumulating in the screw hole of the connection screw as well as on the superior surface of the stems. The von Mises stress recorded a maximum of 188.838 MPa, which is way below the strength of titanium alloy at 897 MPa. This corresponds well with the results of the fatigue testing with had failure of crack lines in the same areas. The conclusion of this bench top experiment was that although the forces are way below the material strength of titanium, micro-cracks as well as areas of stress concentrations from the indentation of the screw threads can lead to eventual failure over a long time of loading at a much lower load level. The connection problem of the modules seemed to have been solved.

A human-sized mandible synthetic was scanned with a cone beam CT scan to get the geometrical information of the mandible [31]. A synthetic mandible was used due to biohazard concerns. Due to the nature of the cone beam CT, using the DICOM information without alteration tended to produce a mesh with a lot of sharp, irregular and thin triangles. This was re-meshed with 3-Matics (Materialise, Belgium) into linear tetrahedrons. The mesh was dense enough to justify the use of linear elements to save on computational resources. The teeth were also removed digitally as it does not contribute structurally to the mandible.

The endoprosthesis was modelled as previously described above (termed Case I) and then the stem length was shortened (Case II) followed by Case III where the length of the body was doubled to 30 mm (**Figure 9**).

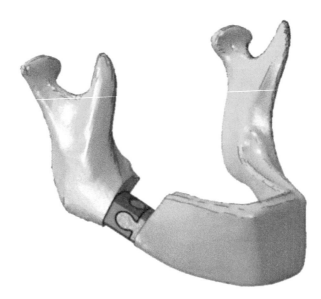

Figure 9. Endoprosthesis in mandible model.

A standardized defect as well as boreholes was created to fit the dimensions of Case I, II and III on the right side of the mandible using Abaqus. The model was assumed to be made up of only cortical bone, the bone was assumed to be isotropic and the values and vectors of the muscle pull as well as the joint reaction forces were taken from the literature. The boreholes and stems were assumed to be bonded just like the previous FEM study of the experimental setup. Case I was used as the model for the standard endoprosthesis design, Case II and III were used as models for looking at the effects of a decrease in stem length as well as an increase in defect length, respectively. A 300 N load was applied directly in the incisor region. Several studies from the literature have supported our assumptions to be relatively accurate while saving on computational resources. As a form of validation, a convergence check was conducted on a mandible with quadratic elements, which gave a finer mesh. The differences were less than 10%.

The analysis was conducted and divided into three separate parts:

1) Stress in the endoprosthesis

2) Stress in the mandible

3) Deflection of the mandible

(1) Stress in the endoprosthesis

Under the prescribed loading conditions, the intact mandible bent upwards almost equally on both sides. As this model was not totally symmetrical, there were minute differences on both sides. With a defect in place, reconstructed with an endoprosthesis, the mandible became less stiff, causing the left intact side to arch less than the right reconstructed side. This led to the mandible shifting to the left by 0.354 mm. There was a tendency for the endoprosthesis to bend outwards. There was little difference between Case I and II, which led to the conclusion that a case could be put forward for a shorter stem to reduce the amount of hardware needed. A longer/larger defect, as in Case III led to a tendency for separation at the module connection, leading to a possibility for eventual loosening of the connection screw in the long term. Although there was a tendency for separation at the module connection, the stresses in the connection screw were all below 100 MPA, below the material strength of titanium. The stress distribution for Case I and II was similar, but with slightly larger magnitudes in Case II. In Case III, however, since it was a larger defect, the endoprosthesis tended to bend more at the stem, although, again, the stresses were below the strength of titanium at 898 MPa (**Figures 10–12**).

(2) Stress in the mandible

With regard to the stresses within the mandible, areas of stress concentration were in the left condyle (due to unequal deflection of the mandible from torsional stress), lower border of the mandibular body close to the abutment with the endoprosthesis and top edge of the hole in the stumps. There tended to be a pull out tendency of the stem from the holes, as experienced in the experimental setup. This was worse in Case II and III, with the peak stress exceeding the material strength of cortical bone at 85 MPa. The condyles were restricted from moving in this model, while in real life, there would certainly be movements that could dissipate stress; thus there is some mitigation factor in vivo. Whether this would be true could only be answered in animal experimental models.

(3) Deflection of the mandible

Deflection of the mandible was measured with respect to an *x-y-z* axis in three dimensions at points of interest. Since the boundary conditions were applied to the incisors and condyles, this caused any deflection to show up in the body of the mandible. The greatest displacement for Case I was 0.638 mm, for Case II 0.8 mm and III 0.608 mm.

The conclusions drawn from the study were that the modular endoprosthesis in its current dimensions should be adequate for small defects. Altering the stem dimensions by shortening it showed a slight increase in magnitude but no significant alteration to the stress distribution. A larger defect, however, would be more difficult to reconstruct and more studies needed to be done.

This work was followed by Pinheiro and Alves [32] who performed a finite element analysis for an endoprosthesis that was not modular and comprised of a solid component, which was customized. This was a feasibility study in which the authors removed the screw stem component and designed a stem that looks to be press fit. The endoprosthesis performed well based on the finite element study. There was no tendency for separation of the module due to the entire prosthesis being a solid framework and the stress distribution as well as the displacement field were very similar to that of the intact mandible and yet did not exceed the material strength of titanium.

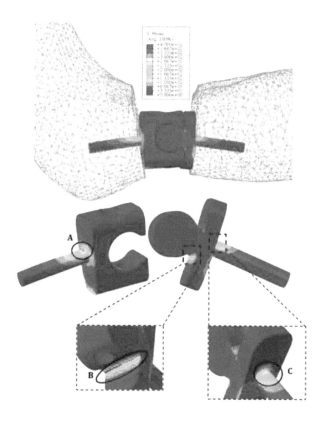

Figure 10. Case I Von Mises stress distribution.

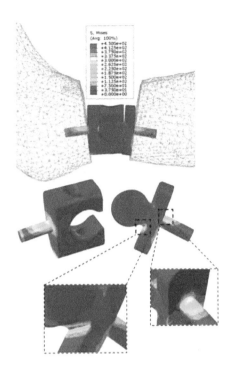

Figure 11. Case II Von Mises stress distribution. The stem length has been halved.

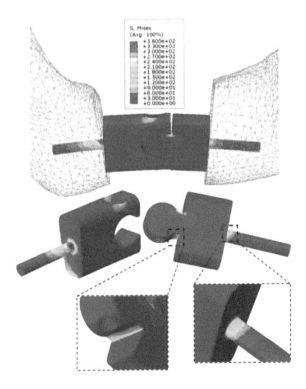

Figure 12. Case III Von Mises stress distribution. The defect length has been doubled.

6. Conclusion

Finite element analysis is a good method to analyse solid mechanics. It has been used extensively in studying the forces in the long limbs as well as the bone plates and the pattern of bone resorption and formation. In the field of head and neck surgery, there are much fewer studies. A number of studies have been recently published as surgeons notice problems with their methods of reconstruction. We have looked at some of the studies and although not exhaustive, it should serve as an illustration to how it is used to look at potential failure of mandibular reconstruction.

Author details

Raymond C.W. Wong*, John S.P. Loh and I. Islam

*Address all correspondence to: raginwcw@yahoo.com

Discipline of Oral and Maxillofacial Surgery, National University Hospital, National University of Singapore, Singapore

References

[1] Wong RC, Tideman H, Kin L, Merkx MA: Biomechanics of mandibular reconstruction: a review. Int. J. Oral Maxillofac. Surg. 2010; 39: 313–319.

[2] Goh BT, Lee S, Tideman H, Stoelinga PJ: Mandibular reconstruction in adults: a review. Int. J. Oral Maxillofac. Surg. 2008; 37: 597–605.

[3] Meyer C, Kahn JL, Boutemi P, Wilk A: Photoelastic analysis of bone deformation in the region of the mandibular condyle during mastication. J. Craniomaxillofac. Surg. 2002; 30: 160–169.

[4] Meyer C, Sehir L, Boutemi P: Experimental evaluation of three osteosynthesis devices used for stabilizing condylar fractures of the mandible. J. Craniomaxillofac. Surg. 2006; 34: 173–181.

[5] Korioth TW, Hannam AG: Deformation of the human mandible during simulated tooth clenching. J. Dent. Res. 1994; 73: 56–66.

[6] Korioth TW, Romilly DP, Hannam AG: Three dimensional finite element stress analysis of the dentate human mandible. Am. J. Phy. Anthropol. 1992; 88: 69–96.

[7] Van Eijden TMGJ: Biomechanics of the mandible. Crit. Rev. Oral Biol. Med. 2000; 11: 123–136.

[8]   Hylander WL: Stress and strain in the mandibular symphysis of primates: a test of competing hypotheses. Am. J. Phys. Anthropol. 1984; 64: 1–46.

[9]   Champy M, Lodde JP, Schmitt R: Mandibular osteosynthesis by miniature screwed plates via a buccal approach. J. Oral Maxillofac. Surg. 1978; 6: 14–21.

[10] Choi AH, Ben-Nissan B, Conway RC: Three-dimensional modelling and finite element analysis of the human mandible during clenching. Aust. Dent. J. 2005; 5: 42–48

[11] Curtis DA, Plesh O, Hannam AG, Sharma A, Curtis TA: Modeling of jaw biomechanics in the reconstructed mandibulectomy patient. J. Prosthet. Dent. 1999; 81: 167–173.

[12] Wong RC, Tideman H, Merkx MAW, Jansen J, Goh SM, Liao K: Review of biomechanical models used in studying the biomechanics of reconstructed mandibles. Int. J. Oral Maxillofac. Surg. 2011; 40: 393–400.

[13] Wittkampf ARM, Starmans FJM: Prevention of mandibular fractures by using constructional design principles. I. Computer simulation of human mandibular strength after segmental resections. Int. J. Oral Maxillofac. Surg. 1995; 24: 306–310.

[14] Misch CE, Qu ZM, Bidez MW: Mechanical properties of trabecular bone in the human mandible: implications for dental implant treatment planning and surgical placement. J. Oral Maxillofac. Surg. 1999; 57: 700–706.

[15] Markwardt J, Pfeifer G, Eckelt U, Reitemeier B: Analysis of complications after reconstruction of bone defects involving complete mandibular resection using finite element modelling. Onkologie. 2007; 30: 121–126.

[16] Arden RL, Rachel JD, Marks SC, Dang K: Volume-length impact of lateral jaw resections on complication rates. Arch. Otolaryngol. Head Neck Surg. 1999; 125: 68–72.

[17] Martola M, Lindqvist C, Hanninen H, Al-Sukhun J: Fracture of titanium plates used for mandibular reconstruction following ablative tumour surgery. J. Biomed. Mater. Res. B Appl. Biomater. 2007; 80: 345–352.

[18] Kimura A, Nagasao T, Kaneko T, Tamaki T, Miyamoto J, Nakajima T: Adequate fixation of plates for stability during mandibular reconstruction. J. Craniomaxillofac. Surg. 2006; 34: 193–200.

[19] Schuller-Gotzburg P, Pleschberger M, Rammerstorfer FG, Krenkel C: 3D-FEM and histomorphology of mandibular reconstruction with the titanium functionally dynamic bridging plate. Int. J. Oral Maxillofac. Surg. 2009; 38: 1298–1305.

[20] Knoll WD, Gaida A, Maurer P: Analysis of mechanical stress in reconstruction plates for bridging mandibular angle defects. J. Craniomaxillofac. Surg. 2006; 34: 201–209.

[21] Tie Y, Wang DM, Ji Tong, Wang CT, Zhang CP: Three-dimensional finite element analysis investigating the biomechanical effects of human mandibular reconstruction with Autogenous bone grafts. J. Craniomaxillfac. Surg. 2006; 34: 290–298.

[22] Callaghan JJ, Albright JC, Goetz DD, Olejniczak JP, Johnston RC: Charnley total hip arthroplasty with cement: minimum twenty-five year follow-up. J. Bone Joint Surg. Am. 2000; 82: 487–497.

[23] Charnley J: The reaction of bone to self-curing acrylic cement: a long-term histological study in man. J. Bone Joint Surg. Br. 1970; 52: 340–353.

[24] Henshaw R, Malawer M: Musculoskeletal Cancer Surgery: Treatment of Sarcomas and Allied Diseases: A Review of Endoprosthetic Reconstruction During Limb-sparing Surgery. Kluwer Academic Publishers 2001; 381–401.

[25] Huiskes R: Biomechanics of artificial joint fixation. Basic Orthopaedic Biomechanics. In: Van C Mowe and Wilson Hayes (Eds.). Raven Press Ltd, New York 1991; 375–437.

[26] Tideman H, Lee S: The TL endoprosthesis for mandibular reconstruction: a metallic yet biological approach (abstract). Asian J. Oral Maxillofac. Surg. 2006; 18: 5.

[27] Lee S, Goh BT, Tideman H, Stoelinga PJW: Modular endoprosthesis for mandibular reconstruction: a preliminary animal study. Int. J. Oral Maxillofac. Surg. 2008; 37: 935–942.

[28] Lee S, Goh BT, Tideman H, Stoelinga PJW, Jansen J: Modular endoprosthesis for mandibular reconstruction: a clinical, micro-computed, tomographic and histologic evaluation in 8 macaca fascicularis. Int. J. Oral Maxillofac. Surg. 2009; 38: 40–47.

[29] Wong RC, Lee S, Tideman S, Merkx MAW, Jansen J, Liao K: Effect of replacement of mandibular defects with a modular endoprosthesis on bone mineral density in a monkey model. Int. J. Oral Maxillofac. Surg. 2011; 40: 633–639.

[30] Wong RC, Tideman H, Merkx MAW, Jansen J, Goh SM: The mandibular modular endoprosthesis for body replacement. Part 1: mechanical testing of the reconstruction. J. Craniomaxillofac. Surg. 2012; 40 (8): e479–486.

[31] Wong RC, Tideman H, Merkx, MAW, Jansen J, Goh SM: The modular endoprosthesis for mandibular body replacement. Part 2: finite element analysis of the reconstruction. J. Craniomaxillofac. Surg. 2012; 40(8): e487–497.

[32] Pinheiro M, Alves JL: The feasibility of a custom-made endoprosthesis in mandibular reconstruction: implant design and finite element analysis. J. Craniomaxillofac. Surg. 2015; 43: 2116–2128

3

Improved Reduced Order Mechanical Model and Finite Element Analysis of Three-Dimensional Deformations of Epithelial Tissues

Ara S. Avetisyan, Asatur Zh. Khurshudyan and
Sergey K. Ohanyan

Additional information is available at the end of the chapter

Abstract

In this chapter, we analyse non-uniform bending of single-layer cell tissues—epithelia, surrounding organs throughout the body. Dimensionally reduced model is suggested, which is equivalent to membranes with bending stiffness: the total elastic energy of the tissue is a combination of stretching and bending energies. The energy, suggested in this chapter, is a piecewise function, the branches of which correspond to a specific deformation regime: compression, pure bending and stretch.

Under specific assumptions on a single cell, such as all cells are identical, elastic, homogeneous, have the shape of a hexagonal prism, are linked to each other by pure elastic junctions, and so on, tissues of different shapes are analysed using finite element discretization. The deformation of initially flat, cylindrical and spherical tissues is visualized to reproduce similar deformations in real epithelial tissues observed during experiments.

Keywords: morphogenesis, embryonic tissue, adherens junctions, relaxation, quasi-convex energy densities, isometric deformations, short maps, tissue mechanics, Γ-convergence, lower semi-continuity, hexagonal elements

1. Introduction

Morphogenesis, the evolutionary process of shape and structure development of organisms or their parts, is driven by certain types of cell shape changes or, in other words, deformations.

One type of such deformations is the apical constriction—visible shrinkage of the apical side of cells, leading to bending of epithelia—cell sheets, which surround organs throughout the body. First occurring at early stages of embryogenesis, the apical constriction results initially flat epithelia to be bent obtaining three-dimensional form, which, depending on physiological context and morphogenetic stage, leads to different consequences. It has been first hypothesized in [1] that in various developmental systems the apical constriction may drive the bending of epithelia. Using bulky mechanical construction, the hypothesis of Rhumbler is first practically tested in [2]. The testing mechanism consists of 13 identical bars (cell walls) that are kept apart by means of stiff tubes connecting their centres (cell kernels), and are held in a row by rubber bands connecting their ends (cell membrane). In the first stage, the rubber bands at both sides are stretched equally and the mechanism is in straight equilibrium. Shortening the rubber bands at, for instance, the upper side uniformly in each segment (cell), the mechanism is bent on the side of the greater tension, as it could be expected. Thus, Rhumbler's hypothesis could take place.

A more illustrative, computer model for verifying Rhumbler's hypothesis is suggested in [3], where bars and bands are replaced by virtual cells. Prescribing certain mechanical properties to the cell membrane and cytoplasmic components, and assuming that as a result of deformations the volume of a single cell is preserved, which is implicitly done by Rhumbler and Lewis, a model of cuboidal epithelia folding is suggested, based on the local behaviour of individual cells. The model is demonstrated on the example of ventral furrow formation in *Drosophila*. A sequence of cells in the form of a cylindrical shell, representing the cross section of ventral furrow, is deformed such that apical constriction occurs in its lower row of cells. Increasing the applied stresses, different steps of the furrow formation are illustrated. **Figure 1** expresses how much Odell's model is close to the real microscopic picture [4].

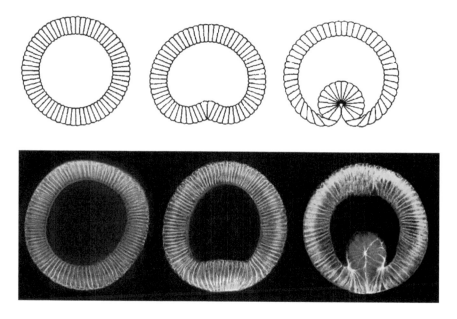

Figure 1. Ventral furrow formation in *Drosophila* according to [3] (upper) and [4] (lower).

Much is known about the causes of the apical constriction, but some issues still remain unexplored [5–8]. The most studied causes include contraction of actin filaments—fibrous network localized at the cortex of the cell, by interacting with motor protein myosin—the most known converter of chemical energy into mechanical work. Under influence of myosin, actin fibres contract leading to shrinkage of the cell in the area of their localization [9, 10]. The contraction size and principal direction of the fibres, that is, the microscopical deformation of a single cell, mainly depend on the tissue type: actin-myosin network contraction may deform columnar (occurring, for instance, in digestive tract and female reproductive system) or cuboid (resp. in kidney tubules) cells into trapezoidal-, wedge- or bottle-shaped cells. The deformation size strongly depends also on the emplacement of deforming cells: cells with different placement are constricted differently, so that macroscopically one observes localized wrinkles (see **Figure 2**).

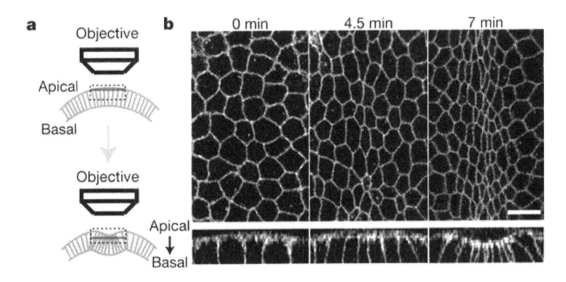

Figure 2. Apical constriction of ventral furrow at different times [10].

Because of the mechanical nature of cell shape change, in particular, apical constriction, its theoretical study first of all must rely on mechanical principles and constitutive laws. In early mechanical models, the tissue is modelled as a continuum material, so that the position and behaviour of individual cells are unimportant, that is, only macroscopic deformation of the tissue is studied. Moreover, the height of the cells (viz. the thickness of the tissue) is supposed to be negligible with respect to other measures, such that the deformation of the tissue can be described in terms of its mid-surface. In such models, the actin network is not explicitly accounted and the contraction forces are modelled as a force term acting on the outer surface of the epithelium. The actin network is explicitly accounted in [11], where thin elastic shell model based on linear Cauchy relations is derived to describe apical constriction in initially non-flat epithelia. The model is tested to simulate apical constriction in initially flat, cylindrical and spherical tissues. Ventral furrow formation in *Drosophila* is simulated (see **Figure 3**), and it becomes evident from comparison of **Figures 1** and **3** that the model, being three-dimensional, is in good correspondence with that from [3]: **Figure 1** corresponds to cross section of cylindrical shell from **Figure 3**. However, it does not involve the behaviour of individual cells and describes only macroscopic deformation. For further introduction into other mechanical models, we refer to [11–26].

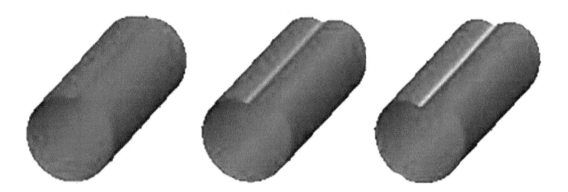

Figure 3. Ventral furrow formation in *Drosophila* according to [11].

The physical and geometrical characteristics of individual cells are taken into account by mechanical model suggested in [27] describing three-dimensional deformations of cell sheet. Both actin-myosin network contractile tensions and cell-cell adhesion stresses are involved to contribute in epithelial tissue bending. Prescribing specific mechanical characteristics to cytoplasmic components and to the kernel, the effective energy of a cell, which is assumed to be a hexagonal prism with constant volume, is expressed in terms of its basal length. As a result of simulations, it is particularly established that when adhesion stresses, distributed on lateral sides of the cell, are large enough, the effective energy has two local minima, that is, there are two equilibrium cell shapes. More particular, depending on position, cell shape may be discontinuously transited from squamous to columnar forms. **Figure 4** shows that there is a whole domain in the plane of lateral adhesion and actin-myosin tensions for which the effective energy has two local minima.

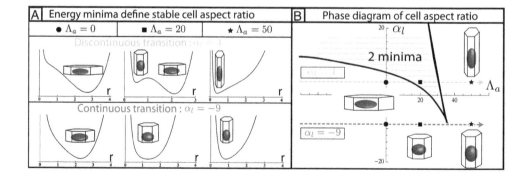

Figure 4. Epithelial cell aspect ratio as a bistable phenomenon [27]: α_l is the contractile force and Λ_a is the actin-myosin tension.

In mathematical terms, it means that the total energy of the tissue is not *lower semi-continuous*, which implies that there is no convergence of its minimizers, and, therefore, it becomes impossible to derive real deformation of the tissue [28, 29]. To be more illustrative, consider a membrane, that is, a tissue without bending stiffness, which is compressed by boundary stresses. The only way that the membrane can accommodate a compressed state is due to *wrinkling* [30]. Wrinkles may occur more and more finely, so the limiting deformation will be smooth, but evidently it will not minimize the membrane energy.

To overcome such difficulties, the membrane energy density is usually substituted by its *quasi-convex envelope* [28], which ensures the lower semi-continuity of its total energy. In calculus of variations, there are several ways to construct or even compute convex envelopes for functionals, depending on first- and second-order derivatives [28, 31–36].

Another possibility for incorporating the lack of lower semi-continuity of membrane energy functionals is accounting the bending stiffness of the membrane and adding to the energy the bending contribution [37]. So, it is established in [33, 34] that the total energy of a membrane with some bending stiffness and thickness h, that is, the functional

$$E[\mathbf{r}] = hE_m[\mathbf{r}] + h^3 E_b[\mathbf{r}] \tag{1}$$

of deformation $\mathbf{r}$ consisting of membrane (E_m) and bending (E_b) contributions is lower semi-continuous for arbitrary E_m as far as E_b is lower semi-continuous. Explicit forms for E_m and E_b as well as sufficient conditions on material constants for which E_b (and therefore E) is lower semi-continuous are derived ibid. Such materials are called *stable*.

However, the most rigorous and general approach seems to be the derivation of low-order energies from general three-dimensional non-linear elasticity by means of Γ-convergence. The concept was originally developed by De Giorgi, see [29]. It turns out that the Γ-limit of three-dimensional elastic energy functional, when the thickness of the body goes to zero, is always lower semi-continuous and since most commonly used two-dimensional energy functionals, that is, membrane energy, pure bending (Kirchhoff) energy and higher-order terms (von Kármán–like energies), are already derived as such limits (see Section 3), it becomes possible to analyze real deformations of particular tissues.

By suggested improvements, it is supposed to get rid of disadvantages of previous models and take into account the fact that the total energy of the tissue can have two local minima. Thus, we are intended

- to account the height of each individual cell, so the model is fully three-dimensional,

- to pick up strongly localized internal forces to model the phenomenon of apical constriction more precisely,

- to introduce stretching and bending contributions into the total elastic energy of the epithelial tissue, thus making the model more realistic and convenient not only for qualitative but also for quantitative analysis,

- to use the quasi-convexification of the total energy, so the real three-dimensional deformations of the epithelial tissues can be identified as minimizers of the total energy by a gradient flow technique.

The former allows making simplified toolboxes for analysing three-dimensional deformations of epithelial tissues. The rough diagram of the improved model looks like in **Figure 5**, so that the characteristics of each individual cell are important, as well as the actin belt is explicitly involved in the model.

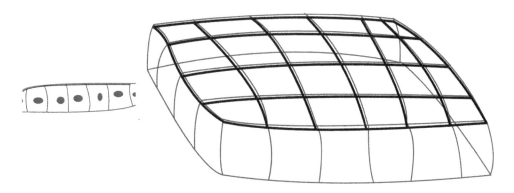

Figure 5. Diagrams of a single-cell layer: cross section (left) and 3D shape (right).

The chapter is organized as follows: In Section 2, some preliminary definitions and main notations are brought to make the chapter independent of outer sources. In Section 3, known results from Γ-convergent energies are shortly described. In Section 4, the quasi-convex envelope of membrane energy densities of general form is derived explicitly and sufficient conditions for their convexity are derived. Moreover, a specific energy is suggested for different deformation regimes that fully satisfies the needs of basic mechanical theory suggestion. Finally, in Section 5 main results of finite element analysis of tissues of particular initial shapes (flat, cylindrical, spherical) are discussed. Overall conclusion completes the body of the chapter.

2. Preliminaries

We begin with the definition of concepts used throughout the paper, which and much more on this topic can be found in [28, 29].

There are different concepts of convexity in higher dimensions, such as *quasi-, poly-, rank-one* and *separately convexity*. Here, we use all but poly-convexity, so it is of no use to enlarge the chapter by its definition.

Definition 1 (quasi-convexity). *A function* $W : \mathbb{R}^{N \times n} \to \mathbb{R} \cup \{+\infty\}$ *is said to be quasi-convex if*

$$W(\mathbf{G}) \le \frac{1}{\mu(\Omega)} \int_\Omega W(\mathbf{G} + \nabla \mathbf{r}_0(\mathbf{x})) d\mathbf{x}, \qquad (2)$$

for every bounded open set Ω, for every $\mathbf{G} \in \mathbb{R}^{N \times n}$ and for every $\mathbf{r}_0 \in W_0^{1,p}(\Omega, \mathbb{R}^N)$.

Definition 2 (rank-one convexity). *A function $W : \mathbb{R}^{N \times n} \to \mathbb{R} \cup \{+\infty\}$ is said to be rank-one convex if*

$$W(\mathbf{G} + \theta \mathbf{F}) \le (1 - \theta)W(\mathbf{G}) + \theta W(\mathbf{G} + \mathbf{F}), \qquad (3)$$

for every $\theta \in [0, 1]$, $\mathbf{G}, \mathbf{F} \in \mathbb{R}^{N \times n}$ with rank $\mathbf{F} = 1$.

Definition 3 (separately convexity). *A function $W : \mathbb{R}^N \to \mathbb{R} \cup \{+\infty\}$ is said to be separately convex if*

$$W\left(x_1, \ldots, x_{i-1}, x_i, x_{i+1}, \ldots, x_N\right) \qquad (4)$$

is convex for every $i = 1, ...,N$ and for every fixed $(x_1, \ldots, x_{i-1}, x_{i+1}, \ldots, x_N) \in \mathbb{R}^{N-1}$.

In other words, a function $W : \mathbb{R}^N \to \mathbb{R} \cup \{+\infty\}$ is separately convex if it is convex on every line parallel to a coordinate axis.

In general, convexity implies quasi-convexity, which implies rank-one convexity, and finally rank-one convexity implies separately convexity.

The quasi-convexity notion is generalized by Meyers [38] for functionals depending on higher-order derivatives. We refer to [32, 35, 36] for practical use of the definition.

Definition 4 (*k*-quasi convexity). *A function $W : \mathbb{R}^{N \times n} \to \mathbb{R} \cup \{+\infty\}$ is said to be k −quasi-convex if*

$$W(\mathbf{G}) \le \frac{1}{\mu(\Omega)} \int_\Omega W(\mathbf{G} + \nabla^k \mathbf{r}_0(\mathbf{x})) d\mathbf{x}, \qquad (5)$$

for every open-bounded set Ω, for every $\mathbf{G} \in \mathbb{R}^{N \times n \times k}$ and for every $\mathbf{r}_0 \in W_0^{k,p}(\Omega, \mathbb{R}^N)$.

In particular, 2-quasi-convex functions, which we use here, are the restriction of quasi-convex functions to symmetric matrices [39] (in the case of *k*-quasi convexity, see [40]).

We widely use the quasi-convex envelope of $W(\mathbf{G})$ or *apparent energy density*, $W_q(\mathbf{G})$, which can be defined in terms of deformations of the form $\mathbf{r}(x) = \mathbf{G}x + \mathbf{r}_0(x)$ with $\mathbf{G} \in \mathbb{R}^{N \times n}$ constant, $\boldsymbol{x} \in \mathbb{R}^n$ and $\mathbf{r}_0(x) = 0$ on the boundary $\partial\Omega$ [41, 42]:

$$W_q(\mathbf{G}) = \frac{1}{\mu(\Omega)} \inf_{\mathbf{r}_0|_{\partial\Omega}=0} \int_\Omega W(\mathbf{G} + \nabla\mathbf{r}_0)d\mathbf{x}. \tag{6}$$

It is evident that for any $\mathbf{G} \in \mathbb{R}^{N\times n}$, $0 \leq W_q \leq W$, and when $W = 0$, $W_q = 0$ as well.

Deformation is always denoted by $\mathbf{r} : \Omega \to \mathbb{R}^3$ with open-bounded $\Omega \in \mathbb{R}$. We introduce the first and second fundamental forms of a deformation $\mathbf{r}$

$$\mathbf{I} = (\nabla\mathbf{r})^T \nabla\mathbf{r}, \quad \mathbf{II} = \left\{ \frac{\partial^2\mathbf{r}}{\partial x_i \partial x_j} \cdot \mathbf{n} \right\}_{i,j=1,2}, \tag{7}$$

$$\mathbf{n} = \frac{1}{\left| \frac{\partial\mathbf{r}}{\partial x_1} \times \frac{\partial\mathbf{r}}{\partial x_2} \right|} \frac{\partial\mathbf{r}}{\partial x_1} \times \frac{\partial\mathbf{r}}{\partial x_2}$$

respectively, in which   is the unit of the outer normal to Ω. The first fundamental form quantitatively characterizes the stretch or compression of the membrane, while the second fundamental form characterizes its curvature.

Definition 5. *Energy density function* $W : \mathbb{R}^{3\times 2} \to \mathbb{R}^2$ *is called frame indifferent if for all rotations* $\mathbf{R}_3 \in SO(3)$

$$W(\mathbf{R}_3\mathbf{G}) = W(\mathbf{G}). \tag{8}$$

If for all $\mathbf{R}_2 \in SO(2)$,

$$W(\mathbf{GR}_2) = W(\mathbf{G}), \tag{9}$$

then it is called isotropic.

In other words, frame indifferent energy densities are invariant against three-dimensional rotations before a deformation is applied and that isotropic energy densities are invariant against two-dimensional rotations after a deformation is applied.

Definition 6 (short (δ-short) deformation). *A deformation* $\mathbf{r} : \Omega \to \mathbb{R}^3$ *is called short (δ-short) if* $\mathbf{I}(\nabla\mathbf{r}) \leq \mathrm{Id}_{2\times 2}$ $(\leq \delta\mathrm{Id}_{2\times 2})$ *a.e. in* Ω.

Definition 7 (isometric deformation). *A deformation* $\mathbf{r} : \Omega \to \mathbb{R}^3$ *is called isometric if* $\mathbf{I}(\nabla\mathbf{r}) = \mathrm{Id}_{2\times 2}$ *a.e. on* Ω.

Short deformations result compressive stresses, while isometric deformations do not allow stretching or compression. The case $\mathbf{I} \geq \mathrm{Id}_{2\times 2}$ corresponds to tensile or, in general, non-compressive stresses. It is known that for non-compressive stresses, the membrane energy density function is already quasi-convex [41, 42].

3. Γ-convergence and Γ-limits of three-dimensional non-linear elastic energy

Rigorous derivation of two-dimensional energy functionals for thin bodies from three-dimensional functionals is of particular interest. There are several ways for dimension reduction, such as asymptotic expansion, Γ-convergence technique, and so on (for general survey, see [43]). In [44], a hierarchy of plate models is derived as Γ-limit of three-dimensional elastic energy functional when the thickness of the body $h \to 0$. It turns out that the scaling of external force in h plays an important role for Γ-limit derivation. Suppose a body occupies the domain $\Omega \times \left[-\frac{h}{2}, \frac{h}{2} \right]$, and the applied forces $\mathbf{f}^{(h)} : \Omega \to \mathbb{R}^3$ active on the outer surface of the body satisfy

$$\frac{1}{h^\alpha} \mathbf{f}^{(h)} \rightharpoonup \mathbf{f} \quad \text{in} \quad L^2 \left(\Omega, \mathbb{R}^3 \right), \tag{10}$$

and

$$E^h[\mathbf{r}] = \frac{1}{h} E[\mathbf{r}] = \int_{\Omega \times \left(-\frac{1}{2}, \frac{1}{2} \right)} W \left(\nabla_h \mathbf{r} \right) dx \tag{11}$$

denotes the rescaled elastic energy of the body, with

$$\nabla_h \mathbf{r} = \left(\frac{\partial \mathbf{r}_1}{\partial x_1}, \frac{\partial \mathbf{r}_2}{\partial x_2}, \frac{1}{h} \frac{\partial \mathbf{r}_3}{\partial x_3} \right). \tag{12}$$

The total energy of the body will be

$$E^h[\mathbf{r}] = E^h[\mathbf{r}] - \int_{\Omega \times \left(-\frac{1}{2}, \frac{1}{2} \right)} \mathbf{f}^{(h)}(x) \cdot \mathbf{r} \, dx. \tag{13}$$

The Γ-limit

$$\Gamma - \lim_{h \to 0} \frac{1}{h^\beta} E^h[\mathbf{r}] \tag{14}$$

for $\beta \geq 0$ will provide constitutive mechanical models to analyse deformed three-dimensional shape of initially flat thin bodies.

We combine the results of [44–48] in Theorem 1.

Theorem 1. *Let the stored energy density function is frame indifferent and satisfy*

$$W = 0 \quad \text{on} \quad \text{SO}(3), \tag{15}$$

$$W(\mathbf{F}) \geq c \, \text{dist}^2 (\mathbf{F}, \text{SO}(3)), \, c > 0, \tag{16}$$

and in a neighbourhood of $\text{SO}(3)$, $W \in c^2$.

Then

(i) (Membrane theory [45]). Suppose $\alpha = \beta = 0$ *and*

$$W(\mathbf{F}) \leq C\left(1 + |\mathbf{F}|^p\right), \, W(\mathbf{F}) \geq c|\mathbf{F}|^p - C, \, p \geq 2, c > 0. \tag{17}$$

Then $\left| \inf \mathcal{E}^h \right| \leq C \cdot$ *is a* β-*minimizing sequence, that is, if*

$$\limsup_{h \to 0} \frac{1}{h^\beta} \left[E^h[\mathbf{r}] - \inf E^h \right] = 0, \tag{18}$$

then $\mathbf{r}^{(h)} \rightharpoonup \bar{\mathbf{r}} \text{ in } W^{1,2} \left(\Omega \times \left(-\frac{1}{2}, \frac{1}{2} \right); \mathbb{R}^3 \right)$ *(for a subsequence). The limiting deformation* $\bar{\mathbf{r}}$ *is independent of* x_3 *and minimizes*

$$E_0^0[\mathbf{r}] = \int_\Omega \left[W_q(\nabla \mathbf{r}) - \mathbf{f} \cdot \mathbf{r} \right] dx \tag{19}$$

among all $\mathbf{r} : \Omega \to \mathbb{R}^3$.. *For derivation of* W_q *from given W see Section 4 subsequently.*

(ii) (Constrained membrane theory [46]). Suppose that $0 < \alpha < \frac{5}{3}$ *and* $\beta = \alpha$. *Then* $\left| \inf \mathcal{E}^h \right| \leq Ch^\beta$ *and every* β-*minimizing sequence* $\mathbf{r}^{(h)}$ *has a subsequence with* $\mathbf{r}^{(h)} \rightharpoonup \bar{\mathbf{r}} \text{ in } W^{1,2} \left(\Omega \times \left(-\frac{1}{2}, \frac{1}{2} \right); \mathbb{R}^3 \right)$ *in .* *The limit* $\bar{\mathbf{r}}$ *is independent of* x_3 *and minimizes*

$$E_\alpha^0[\mathbf{r}] = \int_\Omega [-\mathbf{f} \cdot \mathbf{r}] dx \tag{20}$$

among all short deformations $\mathbf{r} : \Omega \to \mathbb{R}^3$.

(iii) (Non-linear bending theory [47]). Suppose $\alpha = \beta = 2$. *Then* $\left| \inf \varepsilon^h \right| \leq Ch^2$ *and if* $\mathbf{r}^{(h)}$ *is a* β-*minimizing sequence then there is strong convergence* $\mathbf{r}^{(h)} \to \bar{\mathbf{r}} \text{ in } W^{2,2} (\Omega; \mathbb{R}^3) \cdot$ *(for a subsequence). The*

limiting deformation $\bar{\mathbf{r}}$ is isometric, independent of x_3, belongs to $W^{2,2}\left(\Omega \times \left(-\frac{1}{2},\frac{1}{2}\right);\mathbb{R}^3\right)$ *and minimizes*

$$E_2^0[\mathbf{r}] = \int_\Omega \left[\frac{1}{24}Q_2(\mathbf{II}) - \mathbf{f}\cdot\mathbf{r}\right]dx \tag{21}$$

among all isometric deformations $\mathbf{r} : \Omega \to \mathbb{R}^3$, *which belong to* $W^{2,2}(\Omega;\mathbb{R}^3)$. *The non-linear strain satisfies*

$$\frac{1}{h}\left[\left(\nabla\mathbf{r}^{(h)}\right)^T \nabla\mathbf{r}^{(h)} - \mathrm{Id}\right] \to x_3\left(\mathbf{II} + \mathrm{sym}\,a_{\min} \otimes e_3\right), \tag{22}$$

where $2\,\mathrm{sym}\,\mathbf{G} = \mathbf{G}^T + \mathbf{G}$, $a_{\min}$ *is the solution of*

$$Q_2(\mathbf{G}) = \min_{a\in\mathbb{R}^3} Q_3(\mathbf{G} + a\otimes e_3 + e_3\otimes a), \quad Q_3(\mathbf{G}) = \left.\frac{\partial^2 W}{\partial \mathbf{G}^2}\right|_{\mathbf{G}-\mathrm{Id}=0}. \tag{23}$$

In all cases, there is convergence of energy, that is,

$$\lim_{h\to 0}\frac{1}{h^\beta}E^h\left[\mathbf{r}^{(h)}\right] = \lim_{h\to 0}\frac{1}{h^\beta}\inf E^h = E_\alpha^0[\bar{\mathbf{r}}] = \min E_\alpha^0. \tag{24}$$

For $\alpha > 0$, the limiting deformation $\bar{\mathbf{r}}$ is not only isometric but is close to a rigid motion. For that reason in [44], for deformation $\mathbf{r}^{(h)} : \Omega\left(-\frac{1}{2},\frac{1}{2}\right) \to \mathbb{R}^3,$ *the deformation*

$$\tilde{\mathbf{r}}^{(h)} = \left(\mathbf{R}^{(h)}\right)^T \mathbf{r}^{(h)} - c^{(h)} \tag{25}$$

with $\widetilde{\mathbf{R}}^{(h)} \in SO(3)$ and $c^{(h)} \in \mathbb{R}^3$, is introduced and the averaged in-plane and out-of-plane displacements

$$\mathbf{U}^{(h)}(x_1,x_2) = \int_{-\frac{1}{2}}^{\frac{1}{2}}\left[\begin{pmatrix}\tilde{\mathbf{r}}_1^{(h)}\\ \tilde{\mathbf{r}}_2^{(h)}\end{pmatrix}(x_1,x_2,x_3) - \begin{pmatrix}x_1\\ x_2\end{pmatrix}\right]dx_3, \quad \mathbf{V}^{(h)}(x_1,x_2) = \int_{-\frac{1}{2}}^{\frac{1}{2}}\tilde{\mathbf{r}}_3^{(h)}dx_3 \tag{26}$$

are rescaled by

$$\mathbf{u}^{(h)} = \frac{1}{h^{\gamma}} \mathbf{U}^{(h)}, \quad \mathbf{v}^{(h)} = \frac{1}{h^{\delta}} \mathbf{V}^{(h)}, \tag{27}$$

respectively.

Then, we have

Theorem 2. *(iv) (Linearized isometry constraint). Suppose* $2 < \alpha < 3$ *and set* $\beta = 2\alpha - 2$, $\gamma = 2(\alpha - 2)$, $2\delta = \gamma$. *If* $2 < \alpha < \frac{5}{2}$, *suppose in addition that* Ω *is simply connected. Then,* $-Ch^{\beta} \leq \inf \varepsilon^h \leq 0$. *If* $\mathbf{r}^{(h)}$ *is a* β-*minimizing sequence then there exist constant* $\mathbf{R}^{(h)} \in SO(3)$ *and* $c(h, \in \mathbb{R}^3$ *such that*

$$\mathbf{R}^{(h)} \to \bar{\mathbf{R}}, \tag{28}$$

$$\nabla_h \tilde{\mathbf{r}} \to \mathrm{Id} \quad \text{in} \quad L^2\left(\Omega \times \left(-\frac{1}{2}, \frac{1}{2}\right); \mathbb{R}^{3 \times 3}\right), \tag{29}$$

$$\mathbf{u}^{(h)} \to \bar{\mathbf{u}}, \quad \mathbf{v}^{(h)} \to \bar{\mathbf{v}}, \quad \text{in} \quad W^{1,2}\left(\Omega; \mathbb{R}^2\right), \quad \bar{\mathbf{v}} \in W^{2,2}\left(\Omega; \mathbb{R}^2\right), \tag{30}$$

$$\nabla\bar{\mathbf{u}} + \left(\nabla\bar{\mathbf{u}}\right)^T + \nabla\bar{\mathbf{v}} \otimes \nabla\bar{\mathbf{v}} = 0. \tag{31}$$

Moreover, the pair $\left(\bar{\mathbf{v}}, \bar{\mathbf{R}}\right)$ *minimizes the functional*

$$\mathrm{E}_{lin}^{vK}\left(\mathbf{v}, \mathbf{R}\right) = \int_{\Omega}\left[\frac{1}{24}Q_2\left(\nabla^2\mathbf{v}\right) - \mathbf{R}_{33}\mathbf{f}_3 \cdot \mathbf{v}\right]d\mathbf{x}, \tag{32}$$

subject to $\det \nabla^2 \mathbf{v} = 0$.

(v) (von Kármán theory). Suppose that $\alpha = 3$ *and set* $\beta = 4$, $\gamma = 2$, $\delta = 1$. *Then* $-Ch^{\beta} \leq \mathcal{E}^h \leq 0$ *and for a subsequence of a* β-*minimizing sequence, (1) and (2) hold and the limit triple* $\left(\bar{\mathbf{u}}, \bar{\mathbf{v}}, \bar{\mathbf{R}}\right)$ *minimizes von Kármán functional*

$$\begin{aligned}
\mathrm{E}^{vK}\left(\mathbf{u}, \mathbf{v}, \mathbf{R}\right) &= \frac{1}{2}\int_{\Omega}\left[Q_2\left(\frac{1}{2}\left[\nabla\mathbf{u} + \left(\nabla\mathbf{u}\right)^T + \nabla\mathbf{v} \otimes \nabla\mathbf{v}\right]\right) + \frac{1}{24}Q_2\left(\nabla^2\mathbf{v}\right)\right]d\mathbf{x} - \\
&\quad - \mathbf{R}_{33}\int_{\Omega}\mathbf{f}_3 \cdot \mathbf{v} \, d\mathbf{x}.
\end{aligned} \tag{33}$$

(vi) (Linearized von Kármán theory). Suppose $\alpha > 3$ and set $\beta = 2\alpha - 2$, $\gamma = \alpha - 1$ and $\delta = \alpha - 2$. Then

$-Ch^\beta \leq \inf \varepsilon^h \leq 0$ *and for a sequence of a β-minimizing sequence. (2) holds with $\overline{\mathbf{u}} = 0$ and the pair*

$(\overline{\mathbf{v}},\overline{\mathbf{R}})$ *minimizes the linearized von Kármán functional*

$$\varepsilon^{vK}(\mathbf{v},\mathbf{R}) = \int_\Omega \left[\frac{1}{24} Q_2(\nabla^2\mathbf{v}) - \mathbf{R}_{33}\mathbf{f}_3 \cdot \mathbf{v} \right] dx. \tag{34}$$

Moreover, the non-linear strain satisfies

$$\frac{1}{h^{1-\alpha}} \left(\left[\left(\nabla_h \mathbf{r}^{(h)} \right)^T \nabla_h \mathbf{r}^{(h)} \right]^{\frac{1}{2}} - \mathrm{Id} \right) \to \mathrm{sym}\,\mathbf{G}. \tag{35}$$

In all cases, we have convergence of the rescaled energy $h^{-\beta}\varepsilon^h\left(\mathbf{r}^{(h)}\right)$ to the minimum of the limit functional ε_α^{vK}. Moreover, for $\mathbf{f}_3 \not\equiv 0$ we have $\overline{\mathbf{R}}_{33} = 1$ or -1.

Remark 1. *(i) Practically, Theorems 1 and 2 establish Γ-convergence and give the Γ-limits of three-dimensional non-linear energy functional in the range $\beta \in \left[0,\frac{5}{3}\right) \cup [2,\infty)$. The range $\beta \in \left[\frac{5}{3},2\right)$ remains unexplored.*

(ii) Even in the case $\beta = \frac{5}{3}$, it is still possible to find a sequence $\mathbf{r}_k^{(h)}$ for which the functional $h^{-\beta}\varepsilon^h\left[\mathbf{r}_k^{(h)}\right]$ is bounded when $h \to 0$. The limiting deformations $\mathbf{r}$ are composed of finitely many affine isometries separated by sharp folds and are called origami deformations [46]. It is proved ibid that the class of origami deformations is the closure of the class of short deformations with respect to the uniform convergence.

(iii) In particular, when $\alpha = \beta = 2$, for isotropic homogeneous bodies we obtain

$$Q_2(\mathbf{II}) = 2\mu|\mathbf{II}|^2 + \frac{\lambda \cdot 2\mu}{\lambda + 2\mu} \mathrm{tr}^2\mathbf{II}, \tag{36}$$

in which λ and μ are Lamé constants, coinciding with plate energy derived by Kirchhoff much earlier in [49].

4. Relaxation of epithelial elastic energy by Pipkin's procedure and by adding the bending contribution

As was mentioned in Section 1, there are two ways to relax the epithelial elastic energy. The first way is to relax the stretching energy for deformation regimes corresponding to compressive stresses. For that reason, Pipkin's procedure [41] seems to be the most common tool.

Suppose that the stretching energy density function $W = W(\nabla \mathbf{r})$ is frame indifferent, isotropic and positive except the cases

$$\nabla \mathbf{r} = \begin{pmatrix} 1 & 0 \\ 0 & 1 \\ 0 & 0 \end{pmatrix} \text{ and } \nabla \mathbf{r} = \begin{pmatrix} \delta & 0 \\ 0 & \delta \\ 0 & 0 \end{pmatrix}, \quad 1 < \delta \in \mathrm{R}, \tag{37}$$

where it turns to zero, that is, attains its minimum. On elastic energies with two minima, see [50]. This assumption is motivated by bistability of cell shapes during apical constriction (see **Figure 4**).

We restrict attention to deformations $\mathbf{r}$ with

$$\nabla \mathbf{r} = \begin{pmatrix} \sigma_1 & 0 \\ 0 & \sigma_2 \\ 0 & 0 \end{pmatrix}, \tag{38}$$

and denote $W_q(\nabla \mathbf{r}) := \widetilde{W}_q(\sigma_1, \sigma_2)$. Here $|\sigma_j| = \lambda_j$, $j \in \{1; 2\}$, are the principal stretches, the squares of which are the eigenvalues of the first fundamental form. Therefore

$$\lambda_{1,2}(\nabla \mathbf{r}) = \sqrt{\frac{1}{2}\left[\mathrm{tr}\left(\mathbf{I}(\nabla \mathbf{r})\right) \pm \sqrt{|\mathbf{I}(\nabla \mathbf{r})|^2 - 2\det\left(\mathbf{I}(\nabla \mathbf{r})\right)} \right]}. \tag{39}$$

In view of frame indifference of W, and thence, $\widetilde{W}$, we conclude that $\widetilde{W}_q(\pm\sigma_1, \pm\sigma_2) = \widetilde{W}_q(\lambda_1, \lambda_2)$.

From quasi-convexity of W_q, in particular, follows its rank-one convexity, therefore since the matrix

$$A = \begin{pmatrix} \delta_{11} & 0 \\ 0 & 0 \\ 0 & 0 \end{pmatrix}, \quad \delta_{11} \neq 0, \tag{40}$$

is rank one, we have

therefore $\widetilde{W}_q$ is convex with respect to λ_1. Repeating the argument when

$$A = \begin{pmatrix} 0 & 0 \\ 0 & \delta_{22} \\ 0 & 0 \end{pmatrix}, \quad \delta_{22} \neq 0, \tag{41}$$

we see that $\widetilde{W}_q(\lambda_1,\lambda_2)$ is separately convex.

Under assumptions made, we have $\widetilde{W}_q(\lambda_1,\lambda_2) = 0$ if $\lambda_1 = \lambda_2 = 1$ and $\lambda_1 = \lambda_2 = \delta$. Since $\delta > 1$ and $0 \leq \widetilde{W}_q$ are convex along lines parallel to $\lambda_1 = 0$ and $\lambda_2 = 0$, therefore $\widetilde{W}_q = 0$ on edges connecting the vertexes $(\pm\delta, \pm\delta)$ in the $\sigma_1\sigma_2$ plane. Repeating the argument, we conclude that $\widetilde{W}_q = 0$ inside the square $\Omega_0 = \{(\lambda_1,\lambda_2); \lambda_1 \leq \delta, \lambda_2 \leq \delta\}$. So, for δ-short maps $W_q \equiv 0$.

Since $\widetilde{W}_q(\lambda_1,\lambda_2)$ is even and convex in λ_2, it will attain its minimum with respect to λ_2 only when $\lambda_2 = 0$. Denote by $\widetilde{w}^0(\lambda_1) = \min_{\lambda_2}\widetilde{W}(\lambda_1,\lambda_2)$ when $\lambda_1 > \delta$. Suppose that $\lambda^0(\lambda_1)$ is the largest value of λ_2 for which $\widetilde{W}_q(\lambda_1,\lambda^0) = \widetilde{w}^0(\lambda_1)$, $\lambda_1 > \delta$. The convexity of $\widetilde{W}_q$ in λ_2 implies that $\widetilde{W}_q(\lambda_1,\lambda_2) = \widetilde{w}^0(\lambda_1)$ for $\lambda_2 \leq \lambda^0(\lambda_1)$, $\lambda_1 > \delta$. In the same way, using the symmetry of $\widetilde{W}_q$ in its arguments, we will arrive at $\widetilde{W}_q(\lambda_1,\lambda_2) = \widetilde{w}^0(\lambda_2)$ for $\lambda_1 \leq \lambda^0(\lambda_2)$, $\lambda_2 > \delta$. Evidently, for the rest of deformation regimes, W is convex.

If we denote by $\Omega_1 = \{(\lambda_1,\lambda_2); \lambda_1 > \delta, \lambda_2 \leq \lambda^0(\lambda_1)\}$ and $\Omega_2 = \{(\lambda_1,\lambda_2); \lambda_1 \leq \lambda^0(\lambda_2), \lambda_2 > \delta\}$, the ranges of principal stretches, corresponding to uniaxial tensions in directions of those stretches, respectively [51], we finally arrive at

$$\widetilde{W}_q(\lambda_1,\lambda_2) = \begin{cases} 0, & \text{in } \Omega_0, \\ \widetilde{w}^0(\lambda_1), & \text{in } \Omega_1, \\ \widetilde{w}^0(\lambda_2), & \text{in } \Omega_2, \\ \widetilde{W}(\lambda_1,\lambda_2), & \text{else.} \end{cases} \tag{42}$$

Besides opportunity of explicit relaxation, in [41] the derivation of criteria for convexity and quasi-convexity is described. In view of rank-one convexity, $\widetilde{W}_q$ satisfies Legendre-Hadamard inequality from which it follows

$$\tilde{W}_q^1 \geq 0, \quad \tilde{W}_q^2 \geq 0, \quad \tilde{W}_q^{11} \geq 0, \quad \tilde{W}_q^{22} \geq 0, \tag{43}$$

$$G \geq 0, \quad \sqrt{\tilde{W}_q^{11}\tilde{W}_q^{22}} - \tilde{W}_q^{12} \geq H - G, \quad \sqrt{\tilde{W}_q^{11}\tilde{W}_q^{22}} + \tilde{W}_q^{12} \geq -H - G. \tag{44}$$

For convexity of $\widetilde{W}_q$ in corresponding domain instead of the last two equalities, the stronger conditions

$$\tilde{W}_q^{11}\tilde{W}_q^{22} - \left(\tilde{W}_q^{12}\right)^2 \geq 0, G \geq | H |, \tag{45}$$

must be satisfied. Above

$$\tilde{W}_q^j = \frac{\partial \tilde{W}_q}{\partial \lambda_j}, \quad \tilde{W}_q^{jk} = \frac{\partial^2 \tilde{W}_q}{\partial \lambda_j \partial \lambda_k}, \quad G = \frac{\lambda_1 \tilde{W}_q^1 - \lambda_2 \tilde{W}_q^2}{\lambda_1^2 - \lambda_2^2}, \quad H = \frac{\lambda_2 \tilde{W}_q^1 - \lambda_1 \tilde{W}_q^2}{\lambda_1^2 - \lambda_2^2}. \tag{46}$$

The other way is the adding of pure bending contribution to the elastic energy of the tissue. Since actin-myosin network contraction leads to compressive or non-stretching stresses, we have to incorporate the elastic energy mainly for such deformations. According to Section 3 for non-stretching stresses, we have

i.   (short deformations and compressive stresses)

$$\Gamma - \lim_{h \to 0} \frac{1}{h^\beta} E^{(h)} = 0 \text{ in the range } \beta \in \left[0, \frac{5}{3}\right), \tag{47}$$

ii.   (isometric deformations, neither stretch nor compressive stresses)

$$\Gamma - \lim_{h \to 0} \frac{1}{h^2} E^{(h)} = E_b. \tag{48}$$

The deformation regime $I \geq Id$ corresponding to tensile stresses leads to $E_m[\mathbf{r}]$, which is already lower semi-continuous. In the case of uniaxial tension, there is no bending and the energy expression will look like the middle rows of W_q (42). Thence, the total energy might be given as follows:

$$E[\mathbf{r}] = -\int_\Omega \mathbf{f} \cdot \mathbf{r} \, dx + \begin{cases} 0, \ \mathbf{I} \leq \delta \text{ Id}, \\ \dfrac{1}{2}\int_\Omega \tilde{W}^0\left(\lambda_1(\nabla\mathbf{r})\right)dx, \text{ for uni-axial tension in the direction of } \lambda_1, \\ \dfrac{1}{2}\int_\Omega \tilde{W}^0\left(\lambda_2(\nabla\mathbf{r})\right)dx, \text{ for uni-axial tension in the direction of } \lambda_2, \\ \dfrac{1}{24}\int_\Omega Q_2(\mathbf{II})\,dx, \ \mathbf{I} = \text{Id}, \\ \dfrac{1}{2}\int_\Omega W_q(\nabla\mathbf{r})\,dx, \text{ otherwise.} \end{cases} \tag{49}$$

We assume that the tissue is homogeneous and isotropic, so according to Remark 1

$$Q_2(\mathbf{II}) = 2\mu|\mathbf{II}|^2 + \frac{\lambda \cdot 2\mu}{\lambda + 2\mu}\text{tr}^2\mathbf{II}. \tag{50}$$

Furthermore, the membrane energy density function we take in the following form [52, 53]:

$$W(\nabla\mathbf{r}) = \gamma_1(I_1 - 3) + \gamma_2(I_1 - 3)^2, \tag{51}$$

which is valid for large deformations of incompressible hyper-elastic membranes. Above, $I_1 = \text{tr}\,\mathbf{I}$ is the first strain invariant, $\gamma_1 > 0$ and $\gamma_2 > 0$ are material parameters, evaluated experimentally in [53]. For a neo–Hookean material $2\gamma_1 = \mu$ and $2\gamma_2 = \kappa$, in which μ is the shear modulus and κ is the bulk modulus. $\tilde{W}_q$ and $\tilde{W}^0$ are determined according to the procedure described above. For that reason, I_1 must be represented in terms of the principal stretches λ_1 and λ_2 as follows:

$$I_1(\lambda_1, \lambda_2) = \lambda_1^2 + \lambda_2^2 + \lambda_3^2 = \lambda_1^2 + \lambda_2^2 + \frac{1}{\lambda_1^2\lambda_2^2}, \tag{52}$$

in which the incompressibility condition $\lambda_1\lambda_2\lambda_3 = 1$ is taken into account.

For any fixed $\lambda_1 > 1$ (uniaxial tension in the first principal direction), the corresponding $\tilde{W}(\lambda_1,\lambda_2)$ attains its minimum with respect to λ_2 at the maximal positive root of

$$\frac{\partial\tilde{W}}{\partial\lambda_2} = 2\lambda_2\left(1 - \frac{1}{\left(\lambda_1^2 + \lambda_2^2\right)^2}\right)\left[\gamma_1 + 2\gamma_2(I_1 - 3)\right] = 0. \tag{53}$$

Since in the uniaxial tension regime $\lambda_1^2 + \lambda_2^2 > 1$, we finally get

$$\lambda^0(\lambda_1) = \frac{1}{\sqrt{\lambda_1}}. \tag{54}$$

Then,

$$W^0(\lambda_1) = \frac{1}{\lambda_1^2}(\lambda_1^3 - 3\lambda_1 + 2)\,[\gamma_1\lambda_1 + \gamma_2(\lambda_1^3 - 3\lambda_1 + 2)]. \tag{55}$$

The correspondent tension is defined by

$$\tau_1(\lambda_1) = \frac{\partial W^0(\lambda_1)}{\partial \lambda_1} = 2\frac{\lambda_1^3 - 1}{\lambda_1^3}[\gamma_1\lambda_1 + 2\gamma_2(\lambda_1^3 - 3\lambda_1 + 2)]. \tag{56}$$

Since $\widetilde{W}$ is obviously symmetric in its arguments, in the case of uniaxial tension in the second principal direction, we would have

$$W^0(\lambda_2) = \frac{1}{\lambda_2^2}(\lambda_2^3 - 3\lambda_2 + 2)[\gamma_1\lambda_2 + \gamma_2(\lambda_2^3 - 3\lambda_2 + 2)], \tag{57}$$

and

$$\tau_2(\lambda_2) = \frac{\partial W^0(\lambda_2)}{\partial \lambda_2} = 2\frac{\lambda_2^3 - 1}{\lambda_2^3}[\gamma_1\lambda_2 + 2\gamma_2(\lambda_2^3 - 3\lambda_2 + 2)]. \tag{58}$$

It is evident, that when we substitute $\lambda_1 = 1$ in the first case and $\lambda_2 = 1$ in the second case, we arrive at undeformed configuration of the membrane, so the relaxed energy is fully consistent.

Forces driving tissue deformation are strongly localized and in general are compressive. Force **f** must possess those properties.

5. Finite element analysis of three-dimensional shape of some characteristic deformations of tissues during morphogenesis

In this section, we summarize main results of finite element analysis of a single layer tissue model, the elastic energy of which is given by

$$E[\mathbf{r}] = hE_m[\mathbf{r}] + h^3 E_b[\mathbf{r}] \tag{59}$$

in which E_m and E_b are defined in Eqs. (49)–(51). Since the discretization procedure is standard, we omit the details and bring only the main results.

In **Figure 6**, we bring the model of a single-cell (element) and cell-cell junction (in red). All structures (plate and shell) considered in this section entirely consist of such cell groups. In all tissues considered below, the height of a cell $h = 4r$ and $h = 200d$, in which r is its side and d is the diameter of actin fibres. The ratio of Young's moduli of a cell and actin fibres is $E_{act} = 3E_{cell}$, and of actin fibres and cell-cell links $E_{act} = 1.5E_{link}$.

We consider

i.   initially flat rectangular plate (**Figure 7** (left)),

ii.   cylindrical shell (**Figure 9** (left)),

iii.   spherical shell (**Figure 11** (left)).

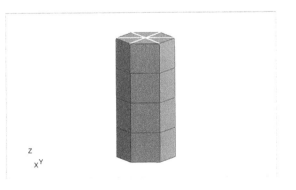 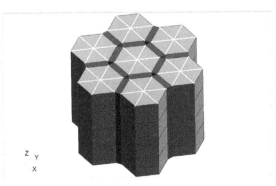

Figure 6. Single-cell model (left) and adherens junction model (right): diagonals of the top hexagon imitate actin fibres, red areas between cells imitate junction bonds.

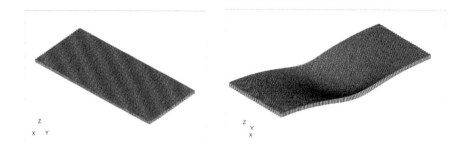

Figure 7. Apical constriction of initially flat tissue. It consists from 5050 elements or cells and has 529,245 DOFs.

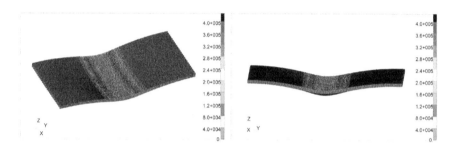

Figure 8. von Mises stress distribution in deformed configurations.

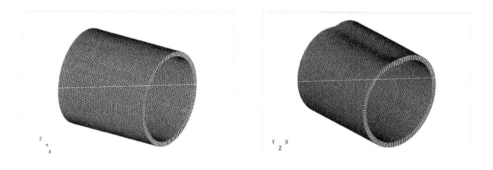

Figure 9. Apical constriction of initially cylindrical tissue. It consists from 5975 elements or cells and has 621,375 DOFs.

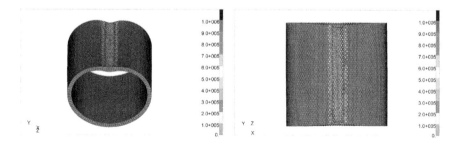

Figure 10. von Mises stress distribution in deformed configurations.

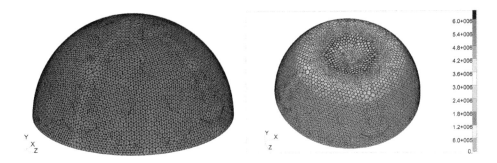

Figure 11. Apical constriction of initially spherical tissue. It consists from 3126 elements or cells and has 325,245 DOFs.

Elements of the middle part of the rectangular tissue are compressed in apical sides to imitate apical constriction in cells. Increasing the compressing stresses, the tissue is bent and a blaster-shaped pattern is formed as shown in **Figure 7** (right). The quantitative picture of the stresses arising in the tissue is drawn in **Figure 8**.

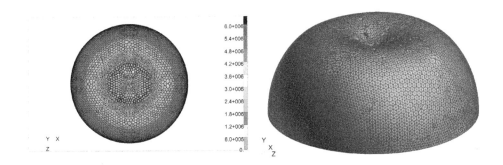

Figure 12. von Mises stress distribution in deformed configurations.

Next, we consider a cylindrical shell to imitate ventral furrow (generally all tubular patterns) formation. Elements of the top part of the cylinder are constrained in the apical sides by compressing the links standing for apical fibres (see **Figure 9**). Increasing the compressing stresses, the ventral furrow formation is simulated similar to stages presented in **Figure 1**. The quantitative picture of the stresses arising in the tissue is drawn in **Figure 10**.

Finally, a spherical shell is simulated. Cells at the top of a semi-sphere are constrained in apical sides and depending on values of compressing stresses various stages of blastopore formation in archenteron can be described (see **Figure 11** (right)). The quantitative picture of the stresses arising in the tissue is drawn in **Figure 12**.

6. Conclusions

Analysis based on lower semi-continuous energy functionals reveals real three-dimensional deformations of soft epithelial tissues. Having different forms for different deformation regimes, such as compressive stresses (short deformations), uniaxial tensions collinear to principal directions of the first fundamental form, no stretching or pure bending stresses (isometric deformations) and stretching stresses (large deformations), the resulting total energy is lower semi-continuous, so the existence of its minimizers, that is, real deformations, is ensured. Particular energy density functions are chosen and the explicit form of the total energy functional is obtained, thereby the discretization is made easy.

On the basis of obtained energy functional, a three-dimensional discretized model of epithelial tissues undergoing combined stretching and bending deformations is constructed. Discretization elements correspond to single cells forming the tissue. Actin fibres and cell-cell adhesion links, mainly contributing on the tissue energy, are explicitly embedded in elements. Deformations characteristic to specific embryonic tissues (ventral furrow, neutral tube, neurosphere) observed earlier are described quantitatively increasing contractile stresses in fibres.

Dedication

We thankfully dedicate the chapter to the blessed memory of our good fellow and colleague, a candidate of physical and mathematical sciences, Hamlet V. Hovhannisyan (1956–2016), who unexpectedly died before he could realize his best scientific ideas.

Acknowledgements

The theoretical part of the chapter is investigated under the guidance of Doctor, Professor Benedikt Wirth, Institute for Computational and Applied Mathematics, University of Münster, whom we are heartily thankful. The work of As. Kh. and S. O. was made possible in part by a research grant from the Armenian National Science and Education Fund (ANSEF) based in New York, NY, USA.

Nomenclature

$\cdot$	Inner (dot) product
λ, μ	Lamé coefficients
λ_1, λ_2	Principal stretches
E_h	Rescaled three-dimensional total energy
$\mu(\Omega)$	Measure of bounded open set Ω
∇	Gradient (nabla) operator

Ω	Midsurface of the epithelium
rank $\mathbf{F}$	Rank of the matrix $\mathbf{F}$
$\otimes$	Tensor product
dist	Usual distance in three-dimensional Euclidean space
d	Diameter of actin fibres
E	Three-dimensional elastic energy
E_b	Bending energy
E_h	Rescaled three-dimensional elastic energy
E_m	Membrane energy
E_{act}	Young's modulus of actin fibres
E_{cell}	Young's modulus of a cell
E_{link}	Young's modulus of cell-cell links
h	Thickness of the epithelium or a single cell
r	Side of a single cell
W	Membrane energy density function
W_q	The quasi-convex envelope of W
$\mathbf{II}$	The second fundamental form associated with deformation $\mathbf{r}$
$\mathbf{I}$	The first fundamental form associated with deformation $\mathbf{r}$
$\mathbf{n}$	Unit normal vector
$\mathbf{r}$	Deformation acting from $\mathbb{R}^2$ to $\mathbb{R}^3$
$\mathrm{Id}_{2\times 2}$	2×2 identity matrix
$SO(3)$	The group of all rotations about the origin of three-dimensional Euclidean space

Author details

Ara S. Avetisyan, Asatur Zh. Khurshudyan* and Sergey K. Ohanyan

*Address all correspondence to: khurshudyan@mechins.sci.am

Department of Dynamics of Deformable Systems and Connected Fields, Institute of Mechanics, National Academy of Sciences of Armenia, Yerevan, Armenia

References

[1] Rhumbler L., Zur Mechanik des Gastrulationsvorganges insbesondere der Invagination Eine entwickelungsmechanische Studie. *Archiv für Entwicklungsmechanik der Organismen*, 1902, vol. 14, issue 3, pp. 401–476.

[2] Lewis W. H., Mechanics of invagination. *The Anatomical Record*, 1947, vol. 97, issue 2, pp. 139–156.

[3] Odell G. M., Oster G., Alberch P., Burnside B., The mechanical basis of morphogenesis: I. Epithelial folding and invagination. *Developmental Biology*, 1981, vol. 85, issue 2, pp. 446–462.

[4] Polyakov O., Bing H., Michael S., Joshua W. S., Matthias K., Wieschaus E., Passive mechanical forces control cell-shape change during *Drosophila* ventral furrow formation. *Biophysical Journal*, 2014, vol. 107, issue 4, pp. 998–1010.

[5] Keller R., Developmental biology. Physical biology returns to morphogenesis. *Science*, 2012, vol. 338, pp. 201–203.

[6] Mammoto T., Ingber D. E., Mechanical control of tissue and organ development. *Development*, 2010, vol. 137, pp. 1407–1420.

[7] Martin A. C., Goldstein B., Apical constriction: themes and variations on a cellular mechanism driving morphogenesis. *Development*, 2014, vol. 141, pp. 1987–1998.

[8] Sawyer J. M., Harrell J. R., Shemer G., Sullivan-Brown J., Roh-Johnson M., Goldstein B., Apical constriction: a cell shape change that can drive morphogenesis. *Developmental Biology*, 2010, vol. 341, pp. 5–19.

[9] Martin A. C., Pulsation and stabilization: contractile forces that underlie morphogenesis. *Developmental Biology*, 2010, vol. 341, pp. 114–25.

[10] Martin A. C., Kaschube B., Wieschaus E. F., Pulse contractions of an actin-myosin network drive apical constriction. *Nature*, 2009, vol. 457, issue 22, pp. 495–501.

[11] Jones G. W., Chapman S. J., Modelling apical constriction in epithelia using elastic shell theory. *Biomechanics and Modeling in Mechanobiology*, 2010, vol. 9, issue 3, pp. 247–261.

[12] Ciarletta P., Ben Amar M., Labouesse M., Continuum model of epithelial morphogenesis during *Caenorhabditis elegans* embryonic elongation. *Philosophical Transactions of the Royal Society A: Mathematical, Physical and Engineering Sciences*, 2009, vol. 367, pp. 3379–3400.

[13] von Dassow M., Davidson L., Variation and robustness of the mechanics of gastrulation: the role of tissue mechanical properties during morphogenesis. *Birth Defects Research Part C: Embryo Today*, 2007, vol. 81, issue 4, pp. 253–269.

[14] Du. X., Osterfield M., Shvartsman S. Y., Computational analysis of three-dimensional epithelial morphogenesis using vertex models. *Physical Biology*, 2014, vol. 11, issue 6, 15 p.

[15] Fletcher A. G., Osterfield M., Baker R. E., Shvartsman S. Y., Vertex models of epithelial morphogenesis. *Biophysical Journal*, 2014, vol. 106, issue 11, pp. 2291–2304.

[16] Imai M., Furusawa K., Mizutani T, Kawabata A., Haga H., Three-dimensional morphogenesis of MDCK cells induced by cellular contractile forces on a viscous substrate. *Scientific Reports*, 2015, vol. 5, 14208.

[17] Ingber D. E., Mechanical control of tissue morphogenesis during embryological development. *International Journal of Developmental Biology*, 2006, vol.50, pp. 255–266.

[18] Inoue Y., Suzuki M., Watanabe T., Yasue N., Tateo I., Adachi T., Ueno N., Mechanical roles of apical constriction, cell elongation, and cell migration during neural tube formation in Xenopus. *Biomechanics and Modeling in Mechanobiology*, 2016, DOI 10.1007/s10237-016-0794-1.

[19] Jauvert S., Peyroux R., Richefeu V., A mechanical model for cell motility and tissue morphogenesis. *Computer Methods in Biomechanics and Biomedical Engineering*, 2013, vol. 16, pp. 13–14.

[20] Lecuit T., Lenne P.-F., Cell surface mechanics and the control of cell shape, tissue patterns and morphogenesis. *Nature Reviews Molecular Cell Biology*, 2007, vol. 8, pp. 633–644.

[21] Murisic N., et al., From discrete to continuum models of three-dimensional deformations in epithelial sheets. *Biophysical Journal*, 2015, vol. 109, issue 1, pp. 154–163.

[22] Patwari P., Lee R. T., Mechanical control of tissue morphogenesis. *Circulation Research*, 2008, vol. 103, pp. 234–243.

[23] Rauzi M., Krzic U., Saunders T. E., Krajnc M., Ziherl P., Hufnagel L., Leptin M., Embryo-scale tissue mechanics during *Drosophila* gastrulation movements. *Nature Communications*, 2015, vol. 6, Article number: 8677, doi: 10.1038/ncomms9677.

[24] Siedlik M. J., Nelson C. M., *Mechanics of tissue morphogenesis*. In *"Cell and Matrix Mechanics"* edited by Kaunas R., Zemel A., CRC Press, 2014.

[25] Vaughan B. L. Jr., Baker R. E., Kay D., Maini P. K., A modified Oster-Murray-Harris mechanical model of morphogenesis. *SIAM Journal of Applied Mathematics*, 2013, vol. 73, issue 6, pp. 2124–2142.

[26] Wyczalkowski M. A., Chen Z., Filas B. A., Varner V. D., Taber L. A., Computational models for mechanics of morphogenesis. *Birth Defects Research Part C: Embryo Today: Reviews*, 2012. vol. 96, issue 2, pp. 132–152.

[27] Hannezo E., Prost J., Joanny J.-F., Theory of epithelial sheet morphology in three dimensions. *PNAS*, vol. 111, issue 1, pp. 27–32.

[28] Dacorogna B., *Direct Methods in the Calculus of Variations*. Springer, 2009.

[29] Dal Maso G., *An Introduction to Γ-Convergence*. Birkhäuser, Boston, 1993.

[30] Steigman D. J., Pipkin A. C., Finite deformations of wrinkled membranes. *Quarterly Journal of Mechanics and Applied Mathematics*, 1989, vol. 42, pp. 427–440.

[31] Kohn R. V., Strang G., Optimal design and relaxation of variational problems I, II, III. *Communications on Pure and Applied Mathematics*, 1986, vol. 39, pp. 1–25 (I), 139–182 (II), 353-377 (III).

[32] Hilgers M. G., Pipkin A. C., Elastic sheets with bending stiffness. *Quarterly Journal of Mechanics and Applied Mathematics*, 1992, vol. 45, issue 1, pp. 57–75.

[33] Hilgers M. G., Pipkin A. C., Bending energy of highly elastic membranes. *Quarterly of Applied Mathematics*, 1992, vol. L, issue 2, pp. 389–400.

[34] Hilgers M. G., Pipkin A. C., Bending energy of highly elastic membranes II. *Quarterly of Applied Mathematics*, 1996, vol. LIV, issue 2, pp. 307–316.

[35] Hilgers M. G., Pipkin A. C., Energy–minimizing deformations of elastic sheets with bending stiffness. *Journal of Elasticity*, 1993, vol. 31, pp. 125–139.

[36] Hilgers M. G., Pipkin A. C., The Graves condition for variational problems of arbitrary order. *IMA Journal of Applied Mathematics*, 1992, vol. 48, pp. 265–269.

[37] Schmidt B., Fraternali F., Universal formulae for the limiting elastic energy of membrane networks. *Journal of the Mechanics and Physics of Solids*, 2012, vol. 60, pp. 172–180.

[38] Meyers N. G., Quasi-convexity and lower semi-continuity of multiple variational integrals of any order. *Transactions of AMS*, 1965, vol. 119, pp. 125–149.

[39] Dal Maso G., Fonseca I., Leoni G., Morini M., Higher-order quasi-convexity reduces to quasi-convexity. *Archive for Rational Mechanics and Analysis*, 2004, vol. 171, pp. 55–81.

[40] Cagnetti F., k-Quasi-convexity reduces to quasi-convexity. *Proceedings of the Royal Society of Edinburgh: Section A Mathematics*, 2011, vol. 141, issue 4, pp. 673–708.

[41] Pipkin A. C., The relaxed energy density for isotropic elastic membranes. *IMA Journal of Applied Mathematics*, 1986, vol. 36, pp. 85–99.

[42] Pipkin A. C., Relaxed energy densities for large deformations of membranes. *IMA Journal of Applied Mathematics*, 1994, vol. 52, pp. 297–308.

[43] Ciarlet P. G., *Mathematical Elasticity*, in 3 vol. Elsevier, 1993.

[44] Friesecke G., James R. D., Muller S., A hierarchy of plate models derived from nonlinear elasticity by Gamma-convergence. *Archive for Rational Mechanics and Analysis*, 2006, vol. 180, pp. 183–236.

[45] Le Dret H., Raoult A., The nonlinear membrane model as variational limit of nonlinear three-dimensional elasticity. *Journal de Mathématiques Pures et Appliquées*, 1995, vol. 74, pp. 549–578.

[46] Conti S., Maggi F., Confining thin elastic sheets and folding paper. *Archive for Rational Mechanics and Analysis*, 2008, vol. 187, pp. 1–48.

[47] Friesecke G., James R. D., Muller S., A theorem on geometric rigidity and the derivation of nonlinear plate theory from three-dimensional elasticity. *Communications on Pure and Applied Mathematics*, 2002, vol. 55, issue 11, pp. 1461–1506.

[48] Friesecke G., James R. D., Mora M. G., Muller S., Derivation of nonlinear bending theory for shells from three-dimensional nonlinear elasticity by Γ-convergence. *Comptes Rendus de l'Académie des Sciences. Series I Mathematics*, 2003, vol. 336, pp. 697–702.

[49] Kirchhoff G., Über das Gleichgeweicht und die Bewegung einer elastischen Scheibe. *Journal für die reine und angewandte Mathematik*, 1850, vol. 40, pp. 51–88.

[50] Pipkin A. C., Elastic materials with two preferred states. *Quarterly Journal of Mechanics and Applied Mathematics*, 1991, vol. 44, issue 1, pp. 1–15.

[51] Cesana P., Plucinsky P., Bhattacharya K., Effective behavior of nematic elastomer membranes. *Archive for Rational Mechanics and Analysis*, 2015, vol. 218, issue 2, pp. 863–905.

[52] Chagnon G., Rebouah M., Favier D., Hyperelastic energy densities for soft biological tissues: a review. *Journal of Elasticity*, 2015, vol. 120, pp. 129–160.

[53] Raghavan M.L., Vorp D. A., Toward a biomechanical tool to evaluate rupture potential of abdominal aortic aneurysm: Identification of a finite strain constitutive model and evaluation of its applicability. *Journal of Biomechanics*, 2000, vol. 33, issue 4, pp. 475–482.

4

Simulating Contact Instability in Soft Thin Films through Finite Element Techniques

Jayati Sarkar, Hemalatha Annepu and

Satish Kumar Mishra

Additional information is available at the end of the chapter

Abstract

When a thin film of soft elastic material comes in contact with an external surface, contact instability triggered by interaction forces, such as van der Waals, engenders topologically functionalized surfaces. Innumerable technological applications such as adhesives; microelecromechanical systems (MEMS), and nanoelectromechanical systems (NEMS) demand understanding of the physics behind the mechanical contact, relationship between the morphologies, and detachment forces in such films. Indentation tests are important experimental approach toward this; there also exist many simulation procedures to model the mechanical contact. Both atomistic level and analytical continuum simulations are computationally expensive and are restricted by the domain geometries that can be handled by them. Polymeric films also particularly demonstrate a rich variety of nonlinear behavior that cannot be adequately captured by the aforementioned methods. In this chapter we show how finite element techniques can be utilized in crack opening and in contact-instability problems.

Keywords: ABAQUS, thin films, patterned substrate, VDLOAD, contact instability

1. Introduction

In nature, there are several examples such as lotus leaves, peacock's feathers, butterfly wings, gecko feet, and moths' eyes where meso-nano-scaled physical patterns on the surface impart characteristic properties such as hydrophobicity, structural color, adhesiveness, and optical properties, which are absent otherwise, to the surfaces. To engineer such surfaces artificially and to fabricate such features, there are mainly two most commonly used approaches: one a top-down approach and the other a bottom-up approach. The top-down approach consists of the various lithographic techniques such as electron beam lithography, dip-pen lithography, embossing lithography, laser lithography [1], laser photoablation [2], ion implantation [3], micromachining [4], etc. The bottom-up approach, on the other hand, consists of self-assembly of molecules to produce bigger building blocks to a growing structure as in chemical vapor deposition [5]. While the self-assembly procedure involves numerous steps, lithographic methods such as dip-pen lithography, which are used for creating patterns on hard silicon surfaces, are time-consuming, involve great cost and may not at all be suitable to create patterns on soft surfaces such as polymers. Self-organization methods, on the other hand, are for bulk production of desired structures involving lower cost and therefore are more potentially applicable fabrication techniques on soft surfaces. In self-organization technique, materials such as polymeric films, which have highly tunable mechanical properties, can be used to obtain a desired mesoscopic structure due to the influence of internal or external forces. The mechanical and interaction properties of these films can be controlled by the amount of cross-linker added during the synthesis step itself. The instabilities during self-organization can be harnessed to engineer desired periodic arrangements of sub-micron features in technological applications such as in flexible electronics [6], optoelectronics [7], functional coatings [8], sensors [9], microfluidic devices, microelecromechanical systems (MEMS) and nanoelectromechanical systems (NEMS) [10], pressure-sensitive adhesives [11], high-efficiency light-emitting diodes, thin-film transistors, etc. Thus, these thin films are model-mesoscopic systems for understanding physical phenomena such as tunable adhesion, adhesion debonding, pattern formation, wetting dewetting and friction at soft interfaces, etc.

When a thin elastic film (shear modulus of <1 MPa) is brought in contact proximity of an external contactor, it forms miniaturized surface patterns because of a competition between the destabilizing interaction forces between the film and the contactor and the restoring elastic forces present in the bulk of the elastic film. The wavelengths of instabilities scale as 4 h in the case of peeling geometry [12–14] (whereas glass slide rests on a rigidly bonded film in cantilever configuration) and application of normal force at the end of the glass slide leads to well-defined one-dimensional (1D) finger-like patterns at the crack opening and 3 h in the case of adhesive geometry [15–26]. In the adhesive-contact geometry, the free surface of the film in contact proximity with an external contactor spontaneously roughens to form a two-dimensional (2D) labyrinthic pattern when the stiffness of the attractive forces due to van der Waals (VDW) interactions (arising because of the contactor) exceeds the elastic stiffness of the film. This pattern remained unchanged in experiments either when the upper glass slide was silanized with a chemisorbed layer of fluorinated monochlorodecyl silane [15] or when the interactions were switched to electrostatic ones [21, 24, 25]. In recent past, much effort has been devoted to understand how further miniaturization of length scales and hence enhanced functional properties can be made technologically feasible in these already short wavelength exhibiting adhesive soft elastic thin films in contact geometry. From a fabrication point of view, the smallest patterns realized till date at such soft interfaces are ~ 0.1 h and are obtained with elastic bilayers when the surface energies of the films are very low and the top film is considered to be much thinner and of very small shear modulus compared to the bottom film [27, 28]. But pattern formation in elastic bilayers through squeezing modes of instabilities has the disadvantage of delaminating at the film-film interface. To alleviate this problem, one has found that films cast on patterned substrates can give rise to surface patterns, which are at length scales that are about an order of magnitude less than that found in films cast on flat substrates [29–31].

Apart from direct experiments, these systems are well analyzed both theoretically and numerically. In both cases, atomistic scale models can be considered but are computationally expensive and are restricted by the domain geometries that can be handled by them. For elastic films, linear stability analysis is generally carried out to understand the critical length scales at the incipience of instability by perturbing Navier's equations with bifurcation modes and obtaining the nontrivial solutions [16, 17]. In nonlinear analysis [18–20], on the other hand, it is possible to find the surface morphology by trying to find the equilibrium displacements that minimize the total energy, which is composed of the interaction, and the elastic energies. Finding the optimized Fourier coefficients, which define the top surface, with the help of conjugate-gradient method, does this. However, for elastic films cast on generally patterned substrates the obtained equations show highly nonlinear behavior, which cannot be solved by the simplistic analytical methods or even by the energy-minimizing schemes developed for the base case. On top of these, polymeric films particularly demonstrate a rich variety of nonlinear behavior ranging from viscoelasticity to plasticity that cannot be adequately captured by the aforementioned methods. Finite element analysis (FEA) methods can be used to alleviate these problems. FEA methods have been used extensively in recent years to study crack opening, crack propagation [32–34], delamination [35], film instability over soft substrates, and bifurcation analysis of elastic contact instability [36–39].

In this chapter we show how to implement cohesive-zone modeling (CZM) for simple shear and normal modes of crack opening in the finite element software and how to simulate contact instability and adhesion debonding in soft thin films cast on complex geometries.

2. Cohesive-zone modeling

Most of the failures in engineering structures are the result of cracks that are preexisting (during production) or the cracks that are formed in service. Continuum mechanics calculations fail to handle such cracks and these are handled by fracture mechanics, which primarily studies resistance of a material to fracture. When a crack is formed, stress is usually not transmitted between the two "virtual" surfaces that form the following crack formation. We can consider a cohesive zone, of zero thickness, to bridge these two virtual surfaces and it can be suggested that fracture happens when material strength in this zone decays. The basic premise for cohesive-zone model is that infinite stresses (stress singularity) at crack tip are unrealistic. Dugdale [40] and Barenblatt [41] developed the first models to address this shortcoming and model brittle fracture. Their models divide the crack tip into stress-free region and cohesively stressed regions. More than a decade later, Hillerborg [42] was the first one to use finite element analysis for cohesive-zone modeling of brittle fracture. Tvergaard's [43–44] modification to Dugdale and Barenblatt's model ensured that continuum elements remain intact in the cohesive model. It is their first decohesion model where traction is dependent on both normal and tangential separation, whereas in Barenblatt's model, it is dependent on the distance from the crack tip. They do this by defining the cohesive elements between the continuum elements such that damage initiation is characterized by opening of the cohesive elements (and governed by some material law) and at failure these elements lose their stiffness, resulting in the continuum elements disjointing from each other. This model is also called the cohesive-zone model or damage zone model (DZM). The initiation and evolution of the damage are defined according to material-softening law/cohesive law/bridging law/traction-separation law (TSL). TSL can be defined based on the properties of the cohesive zone. Traction-separation laws are not universal, and these are not physical laws to characterize fracture at bonded interfaces. Rather, they are highly material dependent. We can define the TSLs in many ways but all separation laws have one thing in common: they all suggest that the traction initially increases with separation and beyond a critical separation distance it diminishes to zero (material softening) at which point these cohesive surfaces detach from each other and a real crack tip is defined.

For implementing TSL in CZM, two constitutive relations are considered: one for the continuum or the "bulk behavior" of the blocks and another for the gap between the surfaces that is defined by the traction-displacement relationships. If the cohesive zone is a thin adhesive layer bonding the blocks, we can define the TSL as the traction at this interface with respect to the separation at the interface. In the modeling by commercial finite element software ABAQUS, the cohesive zone is represented by a single layer of elements that connect the two blocks/surfaces and is constrained by one of the blocks as can be seen from **Figure 1**. Each element on the surface of one block is "tied" with its corresponding neighboring element in the other block through a series of "inelastic springs" which govern the interaction between these two surfaces. This tie constraint prevents the propagation of singular modes in deformation that can arise due to lack of membrane stiffness. The debonding/crack-opening process is akin to the failure of these springs.

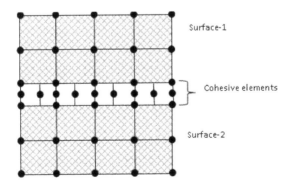

Figure 1. Meshing with tie constraints for cohesive elements in ABAQUS.

2.1. Cohesive zone implementation in ABAQUS with an example problem

To show the implementation of cohesive zone model with traction-separation law in ABAQUS, we have provided an example problem [43] below. In this, we study the propagation of a crack in a material block. A debonding model is taken from Tvergaard's work [43] and is described in brief below. This model does not consist of a debonding potential, but is designed to address the effect of fiber debonding from a metal-matrix composite on the tensile properties (as this requires one to consider both normal and tangential separations in the debonding). For this, first, a function $F(\lambda)$ was chosen such that

$$F(\lambda) = \frac{27}{4}\sigma_{max}\left(1 - 2\lambda + \lambda^2\right) \text{ and } 0 \le \lambda \le 1 \tag{1}$$

The nondimensional parameter λ is defined as

$$\lambda = \sqrt{\left(\frac{u_n}{\delta_n}\right)^2 + \left(\frac{u_t}{\delta_t}\right)^2} \tag{2}$$

For a monotonically increasing value of λ the tractions are $T_n = \frac{u_n}{\delta_n}F(\lambda)$ and $T_t = \alpha\frac{u_t}{\delta_t}F(\lambda)$. Here, the normal and tangential tractions are T_n and T_t respectively, normal and tangential displacements are u_n and u_t respectively, δ_n and δ_t are the maximum separation distances in normal and traction modes, respectively. Here, we have considered that the two virtual surfaces that form after a crack growth are of unit dimension. For solving this, we have developed our own code using MATLAB and ABAQUS. MATLAB is excellent to call external commands to run the PYTHON scripts for generating the input files for ABAQUS.

ABAQUS has vast libraries of constitutive material models but this library is neither a complete one nor a completely flexible one. However, fortunately, user-defined constitutive material models can be implemented in ABAQUS through either UMAT or VUMAT. UMAT is an implicit time integration method (used with ABAQUS/Standard) and it requires the material stiffness matrix as input for forming the consistent Jacobian (C), which is also called algorithmic tangential stiffness or ATS, of the nonlinear equations. For linearly elastic materials, it is defined as

$$C = \frac{\partial\Delta\sigma}{\partial\Delta\varepsilon} \tag{3}$$

where $\Delta\sigma$ is the increment in Cauchy stress and $\Delta\varepsilon$ is the increment in strain.

VUMAT, on the other hand, uses explicit time integration and hence does not require Jacobian matrix. It is implemented in ABAQUS/Explicit and is easier to write. In the case of cohesive zone modeling, we can include element failure and progressive damage failure in the VUMAT subroutine. The VUMAT subroutine consists of the strain decomposition of the total strain into elastic (computed from a linear elastic or hyperelastic constitutive model) and plastic components and flow rule to define the material's plastic behavior. A sample of the input file (filename.inp) and VUMAT subroutine (vumat.f) are annotated and provided at the end of this section. These are run in ABAQUS through the following command:

abaqus job=*filename.inp* user=*vumat.f*

There are a minimum of five parameters that have to be prescribed for the CZM. They are as follows:

1. Cohesive strength (T_n and T_t, the peak values of the traction-separation curve).

2. Cohesive energy (area under the traction-separation curve).

3. Characteristic length (u_n and u_t, usually the separation value corresponding to the cohesive strength).

Cohesive strength (related to yield stress) and cohesive energy signify the maximum resistance to fracture and dissipation following material separation, respectively. For the cohesive zone modeling with traction-separation law, we need to specify the initial elastic stiffness (K).

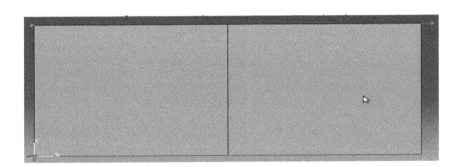

Figure 2. Cohesive zone model (CZM) in ABAQUS. Loads and boundary conditions for the case of purely normal traction (T_t= 0).

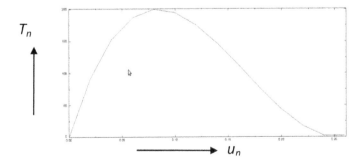

Figure 3. Normal traction (T_n) versus separation (u_n) obtained after CZM in ABAQUS.

We cannot use the exact value of the material's Young's modulus (E) for this as this stiffness here refers to a "penalty stiffness," that is, we are free to choose a value that is necessary to prevent interpenetration of the surfaces and for the convergence of our model. One rule of thumb is to take a value of K that is equal to E/h (h is the cohesive layer thickness). Hence, K can be taken to be a very large value as the cohesive elements are considered to be a layer of zero thickness. Also, for simplification, identical values of K are taken for the crack-opening mode (mode I) and crack-shearing modes (mode II). The chosen damage initiation and damage evolution criteria affect how these two modes of crack opening interact with each other.

The variables we output (stress, strain, etc.) depend on the kind of problems being modeled by the cohesive elements. This is indicated in the .inp file itself in the definition of the section properties by specifying the response type required. The stress components are as follows:

σ_{11}—Direct membrane stress

σ_{22}—Direct through-thickness stress

σ_{12}—Transverse shear stress

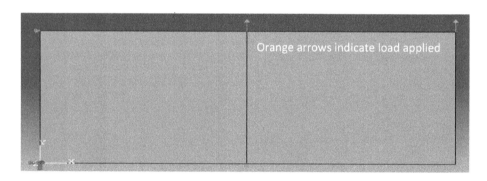

Figure 4. Cohesive zone model (CZM) in ABAQUS. Loads and boundary conditions shown for the case of purely shear traction ($T_n = 0$).

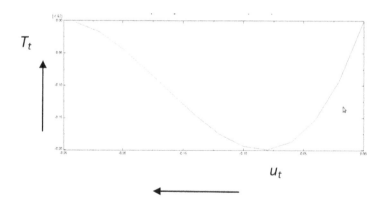

Figure 5. Tangential traction (T_t) versus shear separation (u_t) obtained from CZM in ABAQUS.

During a purely normal crack opening ($u_t = 0$), according to our TSL, the normal traction T_n initially increases with the normal separation u_n, reaches a maximum value σ_{max} and reduces to 0 when $u_n = \delta_n$ that is, when the final separation occurs (see **Figures 2** and **3**). Similarly, during a purely shear crack opening ($u_n = 0$), the shear traction T_t initially increases with tangential separation u_t, reaches a maximum value $\alpha\sigma_{max}$ and then at $u_t = \delta_t$ the final separation occurs (see **Figures 4** and **5**). The negative values in **Figure 5** indicate compressive stresses.

2.2. Writing ABAQUS .inp file and VUMAT subroutine

2.2.1. Snippet of input file

Snippet of input file (filename.inp) containing the geometry, meshing, material parameters, and output variables

*Heading

** Job name: cohesive-zone Model name: Model-1

** Generated by: Abaqus/CAE 6.9-1

*Preprint, echo=NO, model=NO, history=NO, contact=NO

** PARTS

*Part, name=Part-1

*End Part

**

** ASSEMBLY

**

*Assembly, name=Assembly

**

*Instance, name=Part-1-1, part=Part-1 ***(two unit blocks/surfaces, each with 4 nodes)

*Node

⋮

*Element, type=CPE4R***(4 noded continuum plane-strain elements for the blocks)

⋮

*Element, type=COH2D4 ***(4 noded cohesive elements for the cohesive zone)

⋮

*Nset, nset=_PickedSet$_i$, internal, generate

⋮

*Elset, elset=_PickedSet$_i$, internal

⋮

** Section: Section-1

*Solid Section, elset=_PickedSet$_i$, material=steel

,

** Section: Section-2

*Cohesive Section, elset=_PickedSet$_i$, material=coh, response=TRACTION SEPARATION ***(*specifying response as TRACTION SEPARATION to implement TSL*)

*End Instance

**

⋮

*Surface, type=ELEMENT, name=_PickedSurf21, internal

__PickedSurf21_S3, S3

*End Assembly

*Amplitude, name=Amp-1 ***(*time dependent loading conditions*)

0., 0., 0.5, 0.5, 1., 1.

t=0 amp_at_t=0 t=0.5 amp_at_t=0.5 t=1 amp_at_t=1

**

** MATERIALS

**

*Material, name=coh ***(*cohesive zone parameters*)

*User material, Constants = 5 ***(*user defined subroutine with 5 parameters*)

200.0,0.25,0.25,1.0,0.5 * * * (σ_{max}, δ_n, δ_t, α. *these are read through props( ) matrix in vumat.f*)

*Density

5.4e-7

*Depvar

*7, ***(number of solution-dependent variables SDVs)*

*Initial conditions, type=solution

Part-1-1._PickedSet4,0.0,0.0,0,0.0,0.0,0.0,0.0 ***(*initial values of the 7 SDVs*)

*Material, name=material-1 ***(*material properties of the continuum surfaces*)

*Density

7.8e-06,

*Elastic

2.5e+8, 0.25***(Young's modulus E and Poisson's ratio of Material-1)*

** ---*

** STEP: Step-1

**

*Step, name=Step-1

*Dynamic, Explicit

, 1.

*Bulk Viscosity

0.06, 1.2

** Mass Scaling: Semi-Automatic

** Whole Model

*Fixed Mass Scaling, factor=50.

**

** BOUNDARY CONDITIONS

**

** Name: BC-2 Type: Displacement/Rotation

*Boundary

_PickedSet17, 2, 2

** Name: BC-3 Type: Displacement/Rotation

*Boundary

_PickedSet18, 1, 1

** Name: BC-4 Type: Displacement/Rotation

*Boundary, amplitude=Amp-1

_PickedSet19, 2, 2, 1.

**

** LOADS

**

** Name: Load-1 Type: Pressure

*Dsload, amplitude=Amp-3

_PickedSurf21, P,50. ***(Surface-2 of and permitted to have maximum displacement 0.5 in x-direction i.e. =0.5)*

**

** OUTPUT REQUESTS

**

*Restart, write, number interval=1, time marks=NO

**

** FIELD OUTPUT: F-Output-2

**

*Output, field,op=new,number interval=50

*Node Output

RF, U ***(output variables at the nodes: reaction forces and displacements)*

*Element Output, directions=YES

S, SDV ***(output variables over the elements: stresses and SDVs which are defined in the .f file of VUMAT)*

**

** FIELD OUTPUT: F-Output-1

**

*Output, field, variable=PRESELECT

**

** HISTORY OUTPUT: H-Output-1

**

*Output, history, variable=PRESELECT

*End Step

2.2.2. Snippet of vumat.f subroutine

The headers of this subroutine are common to every VUMAT and can be obtained from ABAQUS documentation. We have listed below only portions of the user-defined calculations for the properties.

! Reading material properties specified in abaqus input file through props() array

σ_{max} = props(1) *! max nominal stress at which damage is initiated*

δ_n = props(2) *! max normal displacement at which the material fails and T_n=0*

δ_t = props(3) *! max tangential displacement at which the material fails and T_t=0*

α = props(4) *!parameter in* $T_t = \alpha\dfrac{u_t}{\delta_t}F(\lambda)$

mu = props(5)

do ii = 1,nblock

! Reading the old state variables or SDVs.

u_n = stateOld(ii,1) *! normal displacement*

u_n = stateOld(ii,2) *!tangential displacement*

counter = stateOld(ii,3)

T_t = stateOld(ii,4)*!tangential traction*

T_n = stateOld(ii,5)*!normal traction*

! Reading the strain Increments.

! In VUMAT shear components are stored as tensor components and not as engineering components.

! so Δu_t will be twice of tensorial shear strain.

Δu_n = strainInc(ii,1)

Δu_t = 2.0*strainInc(ii,2)

!Depending on pure normal traction or pure shear traction or mixed mode of debonding, calculate the following:

$$\lambda \quad = \quad \dots\dots$$

$$T_{n,\text{new}} \quad = \quad \frac{u_n}{\delta_n}F(\lambda)$$

$$T_{t,\text{new}} \quad = \quad \alpha\frac{u_t}{\delta_t}F(\lambda)$$

$$\sigma_{11} = \left(\frac{1}{\delta_n} \right) \left(F(\lambda) + u_n \frac{\partial F(\lambda)}{\partial u_n} \right); \frac{\partial F(\lambda)}{\partial u_n} = \frac{\partial F(\lambda)}{\partial \lambda} \frac{\partial \lambda}{\partial u_n}$$

$$\sigma_{12} = \left(\frac{u_n}{\delta_n} \right) \frac{\partial F(\lambda)}{\partial u_t}; \frac{\partial F(\lambda)}{\partial u_t} = \frac{\partial F(\lambda)}{\partial \lambda} \frac{\partial \lambda}{\partial u_t}$$

$$\sigma_{13} = \alpha \left(\frac{u_t}{t} \right) \frac{\partial F(\lambda)}{\partial u_n}$$

$$\sigma_{14} = \left(\frac{\alpha}{\delta_t} \right) \left(F(\lambda) + u_t \frac{\partial F(\lambda)}{\partial u_t} \right)$$

!*Increment in stress*

$$\Delta T_n = (\sigma_{11} * \Delta u_n) + (\sigma_{12} * \Delta u_t)$$
$$\Delta T_t = (\sigma_{21} * \Delta u_n) + (\sigma_{22} * \Delta u_t)$$

! *stress update*

stressNew(ii,1) = stressOld(ii,1)+ ΔT_n

stressNew(ii,2) = stressOld(ii,2)+ ΔT_t

! *state variable update*

stateNew(ii,1) = stateOld(ii,1) + Δu_n

stateNew(ii,2) = stateOld(ii,2) + Δu_t

stateNew(ii,3) = stateOld(ii,3) + 1

stateNew(ii,4) = 1

stateNew(ii,5) = $T_{t,new}$

enddo

return

end

3. Elastic contact instability through FEM simulations

Figure 6A and **B** shows the schematic setup of a soft incompressible initially stress-free elastic film of shear modulus μ <1 MPa, mean thickness h, and lateral length L. It is cast over a rough substrate. To demonstrate the effect of roughness here, we have chosen a substrate with a uniform sawtooth profile characterized by its amplitude βh and wavelength $\lambda_s = L/n$ where n

is the number of substrate troughs or crests. In the asymptotic case when $\beta h \rightarrow 0$ or $L/n \rightarrow \infty$, we get the classical case of a smooth substrate, though in real systems it is almost impossible to come across a substrate that is atomistically smooth and almost all surfaces have inherent roughness. Again in real situations mechanical/thermal noises and vibrations almost always disturb the film surface at the air interface. To incorporate them for numerical simulations, the film surface is perturbed by sinusoidal disturbances having different frequencies and random amplitudes of the order of 10^{-3} nm. The mean distance from the free surface of the film and the contactor is termed the gap distance and is represented by the symbol d (refer to **Figure 6A**). In simulations, the contactor, as in experiments, is brought near the film surface from a finite distance at an approach velocity v_a (~ 1 nm/s) maintained below the critical distance where the instabilities first initiate (adhesion) for around ~ 15 s. This is necessary to allow the film to have sufficient time to arrange itself under the interplay of imposed force and elasticity of the film. Once the patterns get mature, the debonding phase is started. In the debonding phase, the contactor is pulled off at different velocities (debonding: v_d). The contactor positions at different times can be visualized from **Figure 6B**. The thickness of the film considered for the simulations is 500 nm and length L of the film considered is $8h$. The β is varied from 0.1 to 0.7 and n is varied from 1 to 12 (for $L = 8h$) in the simulations. Though in reality the film is three-dimensional (3D) as shown in **Figure 6A**, for ease of computation the simulations are carried out considering a plane-strain model (as because of normal traction from the contactor the displacements can be considered to be confined in the plane of the paper) and a 2D geometry as shown in **Figure 6B** has been mostly considered. To understand the morphology in greater detail, 3D simulations are also carried out in certain cases with the 3D geometry.

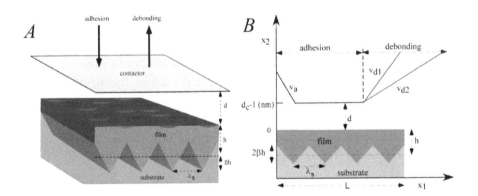

Figure 6. Schematic diagram of an elastic thin film case on a (A) 3D sawtooth and (B) 2D sawtooth-patterned substrate and in contact proximity to an external contactor. The position of the contactor at different time is also shown.

If one considers an infinitesimal control volume inside the elastic film, a force balance will give rise to the following governing thin-film (Navier's) equation:

$$\vec{\nabla} \cdot \overset{=}{\sigma} + \vec{f} = 0 \tag{4}$$

where, $\bar{\bar{\sigma}} = pI + \mu\left(\vec{\nabla}\vec{u} + \vec{\nabla}\vec{u}^{T}\right)$ is the stress developed inside the film, $\vec{u}$ is the displacement vector, p is the pressure across the film, and **I** is the identity matrix. The second term, $\vec{f}$, represents the body force (per unit volume) that the film experiences because of the contactor. The equation as can be seen is a partial differential equation in the unknown $\vec{u}$ and does not yield an analytical solution in the case when the substrate is patterned or when the film material displays geometric or material nonlinearity. A numerical solution can, however, be obtained when the differential equation is discretized by considering a trial/shape function for the displacement and converted into a set of algebraic equations. In the Galerkin finite element formulation, the residual obtained because of the trial function can now be minimized in a weighted fashion according to

$$\int_{\Omega}\left(\bar{\nabla}.\bar{\bar{\sigma}} + \vec{f}\right)\phi d\Omega = 0 \tag{5}$$

where Ω is the discretized domain inside the film and Φ is the shape function. The desired discretization and subsequent simulations to realize the film deformation and morphology due to influence of the external contactor are carried out with the help of the commercial finite element software ABAQUS

3.1. Geometry and mesh creation

To mimic the physical geometry and to simulate several cases of substrates (having varying frequency and amplitudes) and to incorporate different perturbation conditions at the film-contactor interface, the graphical user interface in the software proves to be difficult. Python scripting was used instead to generate the multitude of geometries. For the film's lateral edges and the substrate boundary, straight lines are used, while for achieving the perturbed top surface cubic splines are fitted to get a continuous line out of the random sinusoidal fluctuations at the film-contactor interface. Meshing forms an integral part of the preprocessing steps, which helps in discretizing the geometry. The accuracy that can be obtained from any finite element analysis is directly related to the finite element mesh that is used. Generally, for the large deformations in 2D, eight node elements are used but those are computationally intensive. In 2D as discussed earlier for the present scenario one can consider a plain-strain condition, therefore, continuum plain-strain 4 node-reduced integration elements (CPE4R) are used in 2D. For 3D geometry, continuum three-dimensional eight-node-reduced integration (C3D8R) elements are used. To circumvent the problem of artificial stiffness due to shear locking that can arise due to four node elements, a large number of elements are used while maintaining the aspect ratio of the elements close to 1, which also helps in avoiding problems associated with skewness. Further, for the large deformation problem, reduced integration elements are shown to be successfully implemented without impacting the results and reduce the computational load. On the top of the film, the force is much higher and decreases drastically with depth in the film due to the highly nonlinear dependence of force on distance. Thus, it becomes necessary to have high density of mesh toward the top of the film. The geometry of the film in case of a smooth substrate is seeded with a bias ratio to have smaller elements toward the top as shown in **Figure 7A** and **B** (for 2D and 3D geometries, respectively). For sawtooth profile, the geometry is divided into two blocks. The top block has similar seeding as in case of smooth substrate and the bottom is meshed as shown in **Figure 7C** and **D** (for 2D and 3D geometries, respectively). Since the force applied depends on the amplitude of substrate roughness as well, the meshed geometry is tested with the grid independence test for every case and the finalized meshes are then chosen.

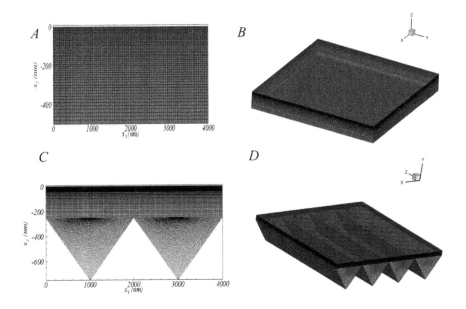

Figure 7. The meshing done inside the film geometry for (A)&(B) a planar substrate, (C)&(D) for a sawtooth substrate, respectively. Figures on the left and right represent meshing in 2D and 3D respectively.

3.2. Boundary conditions

To imitate the rigid boundary conditions of the base in the simulations, the bottom edge of the film is pinned to the substrate and movement toward either direction is restricted with the help of an Encastre boundary condition. To incorporate periodic boundary conditions on the lateral sides of the film, x-symmetric boundary conditions are applied.

3.3. Force calculations

As discussed earlier, so far the failure at the interfaces was captured via a cohesive zone model. In the model, the contactor (a rigid body) and the elastic film were considered to be in intimate contact separated only by a very thin layer of cohesive zone. In the cohesive zone, a traction-separation law (inbuilt in ABAQUS) is defined in such a way that the traction initially increases with separation and beyond a critical separation distance it diminishes to zero (material softening) at which point these cohesive surfaces detach from each other. The energy release rate at debonding is given by the area under the curve. The problem with the method is except for the energy all the other parameters are not well characterized and the traction-separation law is not based on any physical law. Also, while the model is good for peeling/debonding experiments and almost always considers the initial stage as one where the rigid contactor and the film is in intimate contact, it fails to capture the essential morphologies at critical separation distance.

Thus, to capture both the adhesion and debonding of an elastic film due to the interaction between the film and the contactor, a body-force approach has been considered, where each node in the film experiences a varying magnitude body force depending on its relative position with the contactor. The most generic interaction between two different materials when it comes in contact proximity is given by van der Waals type of potential. The attractive potential of VDW prevalent between two atoms or molecules separated at a distance r can be described as [45]

$$\Psi(r) = -M / r^6 \tag{6}$$

where M is the coefficient of attraction. However, a molecule in the film experiences attraction from all the molecules in the contactor. Thus, if one considers a ring-like element in the contactor as shown in **Figure 8A**, the total number of atoms/molecules present in the ring will be $2\pi\rho_c dx_1 dx_2$ where ρ_c denotes the number density of atoms/molecules of the contactor. Hence, the total effective potential that a molecule in the film will experience due to a contactor that is semi-infinitely thick is laterally unbounded and is situated at a surface-to-surface separation distance of D which is given by

$$w(D) = -2\pi\rho_c M \int_{x_2=D}^{x_2=\infty} dx_2 \int_{x_1=0}^{x_1=\infty} \frac{x_1 dx_1}{\left(\sqrt{x_1^2 + x_2^2}\right)^6} = -\frac{\pi M \rho_c}{6D^3} \tag{7}$$

If the single molecule of the film is now replaced by a solid body of unit volume having number density of atoms/molecules ρ_f, the body force that the elastic film will experience is given by

$$f(D) = -\rho_f \frac{dw}{dD} = -\frac{\pi M \rho_f \rho_c}{2D^4} = -\frac{A}{2\pi D^4} \tag{8}$$

where A is known as the Hamaker constant and has the value of 10^{-19} J for the present simulations. In the simulations, the above body-force term is modified and a born-repulsion term is also added to avoid extremely high forces at total contact such that

$$f(D) = -\frac{A}{2\pi D^4} + \frac{9B}{D^{10}} \tag{9}$$

where $B = Al_e{}^6/18\pi$ Jm^6 (l_e is an equilibrium distance and has a value of 0.138 nm for the present case). The nature of the body force can be seen in **Figure 8B**.

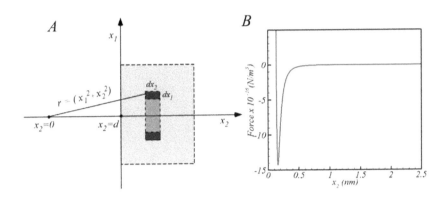

Figure 8. (A) Schematic diagram of the calculation of force between a contactor surface and a molecule inside the elastic film. (B) It shows the van der Waals body force present between the contacting surface and any nodal point in the mesh inside the film geometry.

The contactor in the simulations is virtual in nature, and its presence is felt only through the body-force term f. Since the contactor position keeps on changing with time (refer to **Figure 6B**) so also does the body force. Hence, the gap distance ξ between a particular node and the surface of the contactor keeps on changing with time as per the following:

During adhesion: $\xi = \left(D_{\text{initial}} - v_a \times t\right) - u_2(t)$ for $0 \le t \le t_1$ where $t_1 = (d_c + 1)/v_a$

During resting: $\xi = \left(D_{\text{initial}} - (d_c + 1)\right) - u_2(t)$ for $t_1 \le t \le t_2$ where $t_2(d_c + 1)/v_a + 15$

During debonding phase:

$$\xi = \left(D_{\text{initial}} - (d_c + 1)\right) + v_d \times (t - t_2) - u_2(t) \text{ For } t_2 \le t \tag{10}$$

In the above set of equations, D_{initial} denotes the initial gap distance, $u_2(t)$ the normal position of the particular node at time t, d_c the critical distance at which the film begins to experience substantial force due to the contactor and starts deforming. Its value can be roughly estimated analytically from linear stability analysis on sinusoidal substrates according to [30]

$$\frac{hA}{2\pi\mu d_c^4} = \frac{6.22}{(1-\beta)} \tag{11}$$

In VDLOAD subroutine of ABAQUS, the body force for a particular node is thus calculated according to

$$f(\xi) = -\frac{A}{2\pi\xi^4} + \frac{9B}{\xi^{10}}$$

(12)

The morphological evolution of the film due to the presence of the contactor is thus dependant on the dynamic contactor position and thus is a time-dependent problem. The solution is obtained by marching forward in time using an explicit scheme such that the body force calculated at a particular time t is given by

$$f(t) = f(t - \Delta t) + \frac{\partial \xi}{\partial t} \times \frac{\partial f}{\partial \xi}\bigg|_{(t - \Delta t)}$$

(13)

3.4. Structure of VDLOAD subroutine

The headers of this subroutine are common to every VDLOAD and can be obtained from ABAQUS documentation. We have listed below only portions of the user-defined load subroutine

*** **Declare new variables used (if any)**

*** **Declare the values of contactor approach velocity, retracting velocity, van der Waals potential/force parameters, initial separation distance, cutoff distance**

do k = 1, nblock

u2= curCoords (k,2) *** **curCoords(k,1) and curCoords(k,2) represent the updated coordinates in x_1 and x_2 direction respectively)**

** **Calculate gap distance according to Eq. 10**

*** **Calculate forces according to Eq. 12**

** **Calculate force update according to Eq. 13 and input the magnitude in** the array value (k), which is the prescribed **ABAQUS declared array to contain forces**

end do

The FE results displaying the effect of the substrate roughness on the morphologies formed, the work of adhesion exhibited, are discussed next in "Results" section.

3.5. Results

Linear stability analysis performed with the help of a single Fourier mode [16, 17] and energy-minimizing nonlinear analysis [18–20] has already been able to identify the nontrivial bifurcation modes for which instability is possible. For critical conditions at which instability first initiates, it has been observed that the critical wave length $\lambda \sim 2.96$ h is at par with the experimental observations. In FEM to obtain the critical wave mode, the geometry is created with the help of a series of cosine waves having random amplitudes and frequencies in the vicinity of a mean value j. When the particular geometries are simulated using VDLOAD, only in the adhesive branch, the displacements at the corner-most node, which has the highest amplitude (because of the cosine nature of the waves), is tracked. The displacement of the node thus obtained at any generic time near critical separation distance is plotted against the average wave modes in **Figure 9A**. It can be seen that the curve has a bell shape indicating that near a particular mean surface wave mode the deformation of the surface is highest. This marks the dominant wave mode, whose value matches with those from Linear stability analysis (LSA) and experiments involving flat substrates.

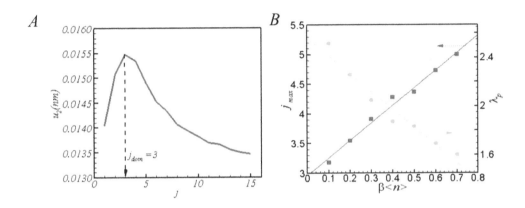

Figure 9. (A) The displacement of the top-most corner node of the film for different perturbed film surfaces at a particular time near critical. The dominant wave mode is ~3 for flat substrate. (B) The dominant wave mode and the wavelength for different substrate amplitude averaged over the substrate wavelength. With increased roughness in substrate miniaturization of the surface patterns occurs.

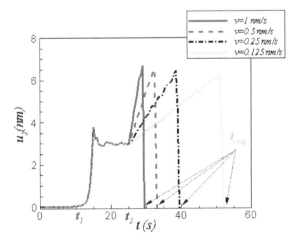

Figure 10. The trajectory of the corner-most point with time.

To study whether the substrate roughness has any influence on the emerging surface patterns, similar studies have been conducted for sawtooth-profiled substrates having different substrate parameters of β and n. The results reveal that though the substrate wavelengths have negligible effect, the substrate amplitudes have a profound influence on the emerging wavelengths. The surface wave mode/wave lengths are found to be an increasing/decreasing function of the substrate amplitude averaged over the different substrate wave modes considered, indicating that the patterned substrates do engender miniaturized length scales as can be seen from **Figure 9B**.

The displacement profile of the corner node at different time is shown in **Figure 10**. It can be seen that at initial time $t = 0$ since the initial gap is much greater than the critical value, the film surface remains planar with zero displacement. Near critical distance (near t_1), the displacements start to have nonzero values and at t just greater than t_1 when the contactor is in resting position the film comes in total contact. The node continues to be in contact with the contactor even in the debonding phase when the contactor is pulled up and it gets detached only at snap-off distance d_{snap}. The trajectory of the corner node arising due to different debonding velocity is found to be different in the debonding phase. It can be seen that the snap-off also occurs at different times. Though the snap-off time t_{snap} for the lower velocity is found to be highest, the snap-off distance $d_{snap} = v_d \times t_{snap}$ is in reverse order ($\sim 30,\ 16, 5,\ 10, 6.6$ nm) showing that in case of lower debonding velocity the detachment occurs at the lowest snap-off distance.

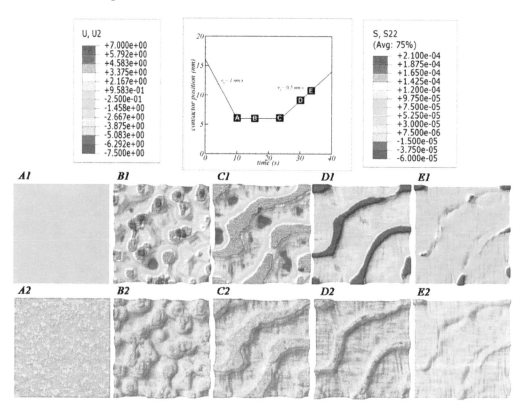

Figure 11. (A1-E1) Morphologies at different contactor positions. (A2-E2) Stresses in the film at different contactor positions for a film cast on a sawtooth-profiled substrate of amplitude $\beta = 0.1$ and $n = 4$.

In ABAQUS, not only a single node but the whole evolution of the film can be traced throughout adhesion-debonding. In **Figure 11**, the labels A1-E1 indicate the morphologies and A2-E2 the stress profiles that develop across a film cast on a sawtooth-profiled substrate (of amplitude $\beta = 0.1$ and $n = 4$) for the different contactor positions. In the inset, a contactor displacement graph is provided for easy understanding of the positions. At position A1 where the contactor is just near critical distance the surface is seen to begin destabilizing where the structures formed have very less asperities. At stage B1, the film surface comes in physical contact with the contactor and the top surface takes the shape of columns bridging the gap with intervening cavities (which form the dispersed phase). At C1, the end of resting phase, the columnar structures mature to form continuous ridges, which upon withdrawal to D1 shrinks in size due to peeling from the edges. Continuous peeling ultimately gives rise to isolated columns (which now forming the dispersed phase) as shown in E1 leading to snap-off. Thus, from adhesion to debonding, the morphologies at the surface go through a phase inversion. The corresponding stress profiles can be seen from **Figure 11** A2-E2. It can be seen that the stresses lie concentrated at the column edges. Thus, more number or greater width of columns (B2 and C2) are seen to have higher stresses at the edges which are responsible for subsequent peeling and stress release as seen in **Figure 11** D2 and E2.

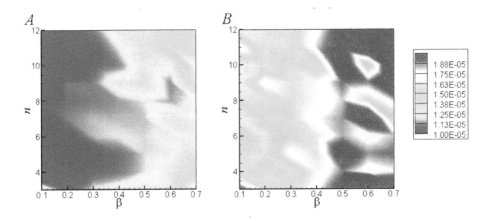

Figure 12. Contour plots of the work of adhesion (J/m²) for different substrate parameters for a film cast on a rough (sawtooth-profiled) substrate. *(A) For debonding velocity* $v_d = 0.125$ nm/s. *(B) For debonding velocity,* $v_d = 0.25$ nm/s.

The sum of the stresses across the total top surface area is a signature of the forces required by the contactor to pull the film up to a certain pull-off distance. The area under the force displacement curve from the beginning of debonding phase to snap-off yields the work of adhesion, which is required to separate the two surfaces of the film and the contactor. **Figure 12** reveals the work of adhesion exhibited by films cast on substrates having various degrees of roughness. It can be seen vividly that while the effect of the wavelength of the substrate is negligible, the higher the substrate amplitude, more is the substrate roughness more is the work of adhesion and better is the performance of the elastic film as an adherent. The work of adhesion is also seen to be a function of the debonding velocity.

For a higher debonding velocity (**Figure 12B**), it can be seen that the work of adhesion is also high (compared to **Figure 12A**). The fact is intuitive considering in band-aids when we pull at higher velocity higher adhesiveness is felt compared to that felt at lower velocities [46].

4. Conclusions

Opening of crack surfaces through traction-separation laws in cohesive-zone modeling is demonstrated for cohesive blocks. In the case of adhesion-debonding of elastic films, simulations are performed for topologically rough substrates to demonstrate the ability of the method to resolve complex geometries, which these analytical methods are incapable of. At incipience of instability when the film surface is perturbed by random fluctuations at the vicinity of prescribed wavelengths, the displacements made by those contacting surface nodes are found highest near the dominant wavelength. These dominant perturbations grow into columnar structures at contact. A thorough FE study reveals that film cast on rough substrate is ideal for fabrication of features/columns at miniaturized length scales and exhibits high work of adhesion. Thus, these films can act as better adhesives and can produce enhanced functional surfaces.

Nomenclature

F	Function related to traction
λ	Nondimensional parameter related to displacements
σ_{max}	Maximum value of normal traction
T_n	The normal traction
T_t	The tangential traction
α	Ratio of maximum values of normal to shear traction
C	Algorithmic tangential stiffness
$\Delta\sigma$	Increment in Cauchy stress
$\Delta\varepsilon$	Increment in strain
K	Elastic stiffness
E	Young's modulus
σ_{11}	Direct membrane stress
σ_{22}	Direct through-thickness stress
σ_{12}	Transverse shear stress
μ	Shear modulus
h	Mean film thickness

L	Lateral length
β	Nondimensional substrate amplitude
λ_s	Substrate wavelength
n	Substrate wave mode
d	Film-contactor gap distance
v_a	Approach velocity
v_d	Debonding velocity
$\bar{\bar{\sigma}}$	Stress tensor in the film
$\vec{u}$	Displacement vector
P	Pressure across the film
I	The identity matrix
$\vec{f}$	Body force (per unit volume)
Ω	The discretized domain inside the film
Φ	The shape function
x_1-x_2	Cartesian coordinate system
Ψ	Attractive van der Waals potential
r	Separation distance between two atoms or molecules
M	The coefficient of attraction
ρ_c	The number density of atoms/molecules of the contactor
D	Surface-to-surface separation distance of D
w	Modified interaction potential
ρ_f	The number density of atoms/molecules of the film
A	The Hamaker constant
B	Born-repulsion coefficient
l_e	An equilibrium distance
ξ	Gap distance between a particular node and the surface of the contactor
D_{intial}	The initial gap distance
t	Time
t_2	Adhesive phase end time
t_2	Resting phase end time of contactor
d_c	Critical gap distance
u_2	Normal displacement
λ	Surface wavelength
j	Mean wave mode of surface

Acknowledgements

Funding from the Department of Science & Technology, New Delhi, India, is highly acknowledged.

Author details

Jayati Sarkar[1*], Hemalatha Annepu[2] and Satish Kumar Mishra[3]

*Address all correspondence to: jayati@chemical.iitd.ac.in

1 Department of Chemical Engineering, Indian Institute of Technology Delhi, New Delhi, India

2 Institute of Advanced Simulations-2, Forschungszentrum Gmbh, Jülich, Germany

3 Department of Chemical Engineering, Mississippi State University, MS, USA

References

[1] G. V. Shivashankar and A. Libchaber. Biomolecular recognition using submicron laser lithography. Appl. Phys. Lett. 1998; 73:417–419.

[2] R. Vaidya, L. M. Tender, G. Bradley, M. J. O'Brien II, M. Cone, and G. P. Lopez. Computer-controlled laser ablation: a convenient and versatile tool for micropatterning biofunctional synthetic surfaces for applications in biosensing and tissue engineering. Biotechnol. Prog. 1998;14:371–377.

[3] J. –S. Lee, M. Kaibara, M. Iwaki, H. Sasabe, Y. Suzuki. and M. Kusakabe. Selective adhesion and proliferation of cells on ion-implanted polymer domains. Biomaterials. 1993;14:958–960.

[4] G. P. Lopez, H. A. Biebuyck, R. Harter, A. Kumar, and G. M. Whitesides. Fabrication and imaging of two-dimensional patterns of proteins adsorbed on self-assembled monolayers by scanning electron microscopy. J. Am. Chem. Soc. 1993;115:10774–10781 .

[5] N. L. Jeon and R. G. Nuzzo. Patterned self-assembled monolayers formed by micro-contact printing direct selective metalization by chemical vapor deposition on planar and nonplanar substrates. Langmuir. 1995;21:3024–3026.

[6] M. Watanabe, H. Shirai, and T. Hirai. Wrinkled polypyrrole electrode for electroactive polymer actuators. J. Appl. Phys. 2002;92:4631–4637.

[7] F. Zhang, T. Nyberg, and O. Inganäs. Conducting polymer nanowires and nanodots made with soft lithography. Nano Lett. 2002;2(12):1373–1377.

[8] D. Yoo, A. Wu, J. Lee, M. F. Rubner. New electro-active self-assembled multilayer thin films based on alternately adsorbed layers of polyelectrolytes and functional dye molecules. Synth. Metals. 1997;85:1425–1426.

[9] Z. Li, P. Dharap, S. Nagarajaiah, E. V. Barrera, and J. D. Kim. Carbon nanotube film sensors. Adv. Mater. 2004;16:640–643.

[10] H. G. Craighead. Nanoelectromechanical systems. Science. 2000;290:1532–1535.

[11] R. A. Chivers. Easy removal of pressure sensitive adhesives for skin applications. Int. J. Adhes. Adhes. 2001;21:381–388.

[12] A. Ghatak, L. Mahadevan, J. Y. Chung, M. K. Chaudhury, and V. Shenoy. Peeling from a biomimetically patterned thin elastic film. Proc. R. Soc. Lond. A. 2004;460:2725–2735.

[13] A. Ghatak, M. K. Chaudhury, V. Shenoy, and A. Sharma. Meniscus instability in a thin elastic film. Phys. Rev. Lett. 2000;85: 4329–4332.

[14] A. Ghatak and M. K. Chaudhury. Adhesion-induced instability patterns in thin confined elastic film. Langmuir. 2003;19:2621– 2631.

[15] W. Mönch and S. Herminghaus. Elastic instability of rubber films between solid bodies. Europhys. Lett. 2001;53:525–531.

[16] V. Shenoy and A. Sharma. Pattern formation in a thin solid film with interactions. Phys. Rev. Lett. 2001;86:119–122.

[17] J. Sarkar, V. Shenoy, and A. Sharma. Spontaneous surface roughening induced by surface interactions between two compressible elastic films. Phys. Rev. E. 2003;67:031607 (11).

[18] J. Sarkar, V. Shenoy, and A. Sharma. Patterns, forces, and metastable pathways in debonding of elastic films. Phys. Rev. Lett. 2004;93:018302 (4).

[19] J. Sarkar, A. Sharma, and V. Shenoy. Adhesion and debonding of soft elastic films: crack patterns, metastable pathways, and forces. Langmuir. 2005;21:1457–1469.

[20] J. Sarkar, A. Sharma, and V. Shenoy. Adhesion and debonding of soft elastic films on rough and patterned surfaces. J. Adhes. 2005;81:271–295.

[21] N. Arun, A. Sharma, V. B. Shenoy, and K. S. Narayan. Electric-field-controlled surface instabilities in soft elastic films. Adv. Mater. 2006;18:660–663.

[22] M. Gonguntla, A. Sharma, J. Sarkar, S. A. Subramanian, M. Ghosh, and V. Shenoy. Contact instability in adhesion and debonding of thin elastic films. Phys. Rev. Lett. 2006;97:018303(4).

[23] J. Y. Chung, K. Kim, M. K. Chaudhury, J. Sarkar, and A. Sharma. Confinement-induced instability and adhesive failure between dissimilar thin elastic films. Eur. Phys. J. E. 2006;20:47–53.

[24] N. Arun, J. Sarkar, A. Sharma, V. B. Shenoy, and K. S. Narayan. Electric-field induced morphological transitions in elastic contact instability of soft solid films. J. Adhes. 2007;83:513–534.

[25] J. Sarkar, A. Sharma, and V. B. Shenoy. Electric-field induced instabilities and morphological phase transitions in soft elastic films. Phys. Rev. E. 2008;77:031604 (10).

[26] J. Sarkar and A. Sharma. A unified theory of instabilities in viscoelastic thin films: From wetting to confined films, from viscous to elastic films, and from short to long waves. Langmuir. 2010;26:8464–8473.

[27] G. Tomar, A. Sharma, V. Shenoy, and G. Biswas. Surface instability of confined elastic bilayers: Theory and simulations. Phys. Rev. E. 2007;76:011607(8).

[28] H. Annepu and J. Sarkar. Squeezing instabilities and delamination in elastic bilayers: A linear stability analysis. Phys. Rev. E. 2012;86:051604 (12).

[29] R. Mukherjee, R. C. Pangule, A. Sharma, and I. Banerjee. Contact instability of thin elastic films on patterned substrates. J. Chem. Phys. 2007;127:064703 (6).

[30] H. Annepu, J. Sarkar, and S. Basu. Pattern formation in soft elastic films cast on periodically corrugated surfaces—a linear stability and finite element analysis. Model Simul. Mater. Sci. Eng. 2014;22:055003 (20).

[31] H. Annepu and J. Sarkar. Miniaturized pattern formation in elastic films cast on sinusoidally patterned substrates. Langmuir. 2014;30:12278–12286.

[32] F. Rabold and M. Kuna. Automated finite element simulation of fatigue crack growth in three-dimensional structures with the software system ProCrack. Procedia Mater. 2014;3:1099–1104.

[33] J. Shi, D. Chopp, J. Lua, N. Sukumar, and T. Belytschko. ABAQUS implementation of extended finite element method using a level set representation for three-dimensional fatigue crack growth and life predictions. Eng. Fract. Mech. 2010;77:2840–2863.

[34] X. Su, Z. Yang, and G. Liu. Finite element modelling of complex 3D static and dynamic crack propagation by embedding cohesive elements in ABAQUS. Acta. Mech. Solida Sin. 2010;23:271 –282.

[35] S. M. Xia, Y. F. Gao, A. F. Bower, L. C. Lev, and Y. T. Cheng. Delamination mechanism maps for a strong elastic coating on an elastic-plastic substrate subjected to contact loading. Int. J. Solids. Struct. 2007;44:3685–3699.

[36] S. Q. Huang, Q. Y. Li, X. Q. Feng, and S. W. Yu. Pattern instability of a soft elastic thin film under van der Waals forces. Mech. Mater. 2006;38:88–99.

[37] Q. Wang and X. Zhao. Phase diagrams of instabilities in compressed film-substrate systems. J. Appl. Mech. 2014;81:510041–5100410.

[38] F. Xu, M. Potier-Ferry, S. Belouettar, and Y. Cong. 3D finite element modeling for instabilities in thin films on soft substrates. Int. J. Solids Struct. 2014;51:3619–3632.

[39] F. Xu, Y. Koutsawa, M. Potier-Ferry, and S. Belouettar. Instabilities in thin films on hyperelastic substrates by 3D finite elements. Int. J. Solids Struct. 2015;69:7–1-85.

[40] D. S. Dugdale, Yielding of steel sheets containing slits. J. Mech. Phys. Solids. 1960;8:100–104.

[41] G. I. Barenblatt, The mathematical theory of equilibrium cracks in brittle fracture. Adv. Appl. Mech. 1962;7:55–129.

[42] A. Hillerborg, M. Modeer, and P. E. Petersson. Analysis of crack formation and crack growth in concrete by means of fracture mechanics and finite elements. Cem. Concr. Res. 1976;6:773–781.

[43] V. Tvergaard. Effect of fibre debonding in a whisker-reinforced metal. Mater. Sci. Eng. A. 1990;125:203–213.

[44] A. Needleman and V. Tvergaard. An analysis of ductile rupture in notched bars. J. Mech. Phys. Solids. 1984;32:461–490.

[45] J. N. Israelachvili. Intermolecular and Surface Forces, New York, NY: Academic, 2011.

[46] S. Kundu and E. P. Chan. Adhesion Behavior of Soft Materials in Engineering Biomaterials for Regenerative Medicine, Springer, 2012.

5

On Finite Element Vibration Analysis of Carbon Nanotubes

Ishan Ali Khan and Seyed M. Hashemi

Additional information is available at the end of the chapter

Abstract

In this chapter, a finite element formulation is proposed to study the natural frequencies of double-walled carbon nanotubes modeled as, both, local and nonlocal Euler-Bernoulli beams, coupled with van der Waals interaction forces. The formulation uses Galerkin-weighted residual approach and employs Hermite cubic polynomial function to derive the linear eigenvalue problem. Natural frequencies are found for clamped-free, clamped-clamped and simply supported-simply supported boundary conditions. The results are in good agreement with the formulations found in the literature. The effect of nonlocal factor on the natural frequencies of the system is found out by comparing local and nonlocal results. Additionally, the universality of the proposed model is proven by application to a double-elastic Euler-Bernoulli beam. This formulation paves way for Finite Element Method (FEM) analysis of multi-walled CNTs—either locally or nonlocally.

Keywords: carbon nanotubes, Euler-Bernoulli beam, DWCNTs, finite element analysis, nonlocal continuum mechanics, vibrations

1. Introduction

Carbon nanotubes are tubules of carbon, in the dimensional range of *nanometre* (in the order of 10e−9 m), with atoms arranged in a way that gives them exceptional properties. The high aspect ratio, the ratio of length to its diameter, and chirality are the factors that contribute to the same. Carbon nanotubes are classified as single- and multi-walled depending on the number of tubes held concentrically. A considerable amount of research has been dedicated to the study of mechanical properties of both these types using experimental or theoretical methods. Theoretical methods involve the representation of C—C bonds as is, conveniently named as atomistic modelling methods, or as continuous structures such as bar, beam and shell. The latter is usually employed to study the vibrational properties as the use of atomistic models require comparatively large computational time and effort, and are often accurate for a particular time period in the loading cycle. The laws of continuum structures have been found to be at the nanometre scale as well [1].

Continuum structures, by definition, consider the model to be continuous and ignore the inter-atomic forces. Eringen and Edelen [2] and Eringen [3, 4] proposed a model that would connect the lattice mechanics with the continuum mechanics, named as nonlocal continuum mechanics. This is achieved by introducing nonlocal factors in the governing equations [5]. As will be seen in the following sections, the introduction of these nonlocal factors have shown improved description of the model. Peddieson et al. [6] extended the nonlocal continuum models to nanotechnology and hence paved the way for these theoretical models to represent the properties of nanomaterials with greater accuracy.

Finite element methods have been employed for analysis of continuum structures since 1950s, as the numerical technique is very adaptable in terms of complex geometries and boundary conditions. The method involves the division of the structure into number of 'elements' and using appropriate interpolations functions to express the approximate solutions. The eigen-value problem hence achieved is solved for system's natural frequencies and mode shapes.

The study of vibrations of carbon nanotubes, modeled as continuum models has gained considerable attention with beams and shells being used extensively. The elastic model has been presented by Ru [7] to study the column buckling of multi-walled carbon nanotubes, where the adjacent tubes were presented to be interacting through van der Waals interaction forces. Ru [8] also studied the transverse vibrations of single- and multi-walled carbon nanotubes by considering them as Euler-Bernoulli beams. Sufficient attention was given to the effect of van der Waals interaction forces on the vibrational frequency. Yoon et al. [9] studied the non-coaxial vibrational modes of multi-walled carbon nanotubes embedded in an elastic medium and deduced that the concentric geometry of carbon nanotubes will be distorted at ultrahigh frequencies. Nonlinear free vibrations of multi-walled carbon nanotubes embedded in an elastic medium were studied by Fu et al. [10]. The relation between nonlinear free vibration frequency, stiffness of the surrounding medium and van der Waals interaction forces was discussed and amplitude curves presented. Vibrational characteristic analysis of double-walled carbon nanotube (DWCNT) with simply supported boundary condition using multiple Euler-Bernoulli beam model was investigated by Natsuki et al. [11]. It was seen that the amplitudes of inner and outer tubes are non-coaxial and in opposite direction. Natsuki also studied DWCNTs embedded in elastic medium, represented by Winkler spring model, for free supported boundary condition [12] and DWCNTs with different lengths for inner and outer tubes [13]. Xu et al. [14] studied the vibrations of DWCNTs with nonlinear van der Waals interaction forces and concluded that it does not affect the coaxial free vibrations. Elishakoff and Pentaras [15, 16] studied the natural frequencies of DWCNTs and TWCNTs using approximate methods, like Bubnov-Galerkin and Petrov-Galerkin and exact solutions. The coupling between the concentric tubes is considered as van der Waals interaction forces, in both the cases.

Nonlocal continuum mechanics approach has also been used extensively in the recent years. Constitutive relations of nonlocal elasticity to be used in analysis of carbon nanotubes for Euler-Bernoulli, Timoshenko beams and cylindrical shells were presented by Wang and Wang [17]. Extensive attention was given to the shear stress and strain relation for the Timoshenko beams. Wang [18] also studied the wave propagation in carbon nanotubes using nonlocal Euler-Bernoulli and nonlocal Timoshenko beams and concentrated on the effect of nonlocal factor on the mechanical behaviour of carbon nanotubes. Yoon et al. [19] also performed a similar study concluded that the rotary inertia and shear deformation play a significant role when the measured natural frequency is much closer to the critical frequency. One more such study was performed by Wang and Varadan [20], who developed explicit frequency solutions for both single-walled carbon nanotubes (SWCNTs) and double-walled carbon nanotube (DWCNTs) on the basis of nonlocal continuum mechanics and employed both the beam theories. The ratio of local and nonlocal frequencies is used to study the effect of nonlocal factor. Arash and Wang [21] reviewed various studies on the nonlocal continuum theory for carbon nanotubes and graphene sheets. They also compared the nonlocal models to the local equivalents. Reddy [22] reformulated governing equations, based on nonlocal theory, and presented analytical solutions for bending, buckling and vibrations of Euler-Bernoulli, Timoshenko, Reddy and Levinson beams. Further, Reddy and Pang [23] also presented the governing equations of Euler-Bernoulli and Timoshenko beams, based on nonlocal theory, specifically for carbon nanotubes and used these equations to study the vibrations, buckling and static bending. Murmu and Pradhan [24] employed the differential quadrature (DQ) method to study the thermo-mechanical vibration of SWCNT embedded in an elastic medium, represented as Winkler-type elastic foundation, using nonlocal elasticity theory. It was found that the difference between local and nonlocal frequencies is particularly high for low temperature changes. Narendar et al. [25] studied the wave propagation in SWCNTs, under magnetic field, using nonlocal Euler-Bernoulli beam theory. De Rosa and Lippiello [26] analysed the free vibration of DWCNTs, modeled as nonlocal Euler-Bernoulli beams, using cell-discretization method (CDM) and a semi-analytical Rayleigh-Schmidt method. A rare study of forced vibrations of carbon nanotubes was performed by Karaoglu and Aydogyu [27] using both local and nonlocal Euler-Bernoulli beam models, for both SWCNTs and DWCNTs. Khosrozadeh and Hajabasi [28] studied the free vibrations of DWCNTs embedded in an elastic medium with nonlinear interlayer van der Waals interaction forces using nonlocal Euler-Bernoulli beam model. Fang et al. [29] performed a similar study for DWCNTs embedded in elastic medium considering it to be Winkler model.

Timoshenko models have also been used extensively as it considers the rotational inertia and transverse shear. Wang et al. [30] considered it and studied the free vibration of MWCNTs using differential quadrature (DQ) method to solve the governing equations. It is seen that the frequencies are over-predicted by Euler-Bernoulli model when the aspect ratio is small. Yang et al. [31] studied the nonlinear free vibration of SWCNT with the von Karman geometric nonlinearity considering them as nonlocal Timoshenko beams. Nonlinear free vibration of embedded DWCNTs modeled as nonlocal Timoshenko beams was presented by Ke et al. [32] where again differential quadrature (DQ) technique was employed, and the surrounding elastic medium was represented by spring-based Winkler model. Pradhan [33] presented a finite element model using nonlocal Timoshenko beams and Galerkin weighted residual technique. The buckling of carbon nanotubes using Timoshenko model was studied by Zhang et al. [34], and various studies on buckling were extensively reviewed by Wang et al. [35] and Shima [36].

A theory similar to nonlocal theory was presented by Park and Gao [37] using modified couple stress theory where internal material length parameter is considered and a variational model is presented basing on minimum total energy potential for Euler-Bernoulli beam model. It found a relation between deflections and beam thickness. Another nonlocal theory, for nanobeams, was presented by Thai [38] in which the governing equations were derived using Hamilton's principle and analytical solutions were presented. The results were found to be comparable to Timoshenko and Reddy beam theories even though the formulation is similar to that of Euler-Bernoulli theory. A generalized nonlocal beam theory, to study properties of nanobeams, was presented by Aydogdu [39]. Various beam models were studied as a special case of this beam theory for simply supported nanobeams, and the numerical results were found to be stand valid. Lu et al. [40] compared various nonlocal beam models that are used for carbon nanotubes and made some interesting observations.

Various variational techniques have also been employed with nonlocal theories to study the vibrational behaviour of carbon nanotubes. Adali [41] employed a semi-inverse method and presented one such model. Alshorbagy et al. [42] developed a nonlocal finite element for static analysis of nanobeams. Eltaher et al. [43] analysed the vibrations of nonlocal Euler-Bernoulli nanobeams using finite element method. A similar study was performed by Phadikar and Pradhan [44], where finite element analysis of nanoplates and nanobeams was presented. All these models are found to be efficient for SWCNTs. Ansari and Hemmatnezhad [45] studied the nonlinear vibrations of MWCNTs embedded in an elastic medium using variational iteration method. A finite element analysis of embedded Timoshenko beam was also performed by Hemmatnezhad and Ansari [46], where carbon nanotubes were modeled as nonlocal beam using statically exact shape functions to achieve an eigenvalue problem. Shakouri et al. [47] studied the transverse vibrations of DWCNTs modeled as nonlocal Euler-Bernoulli beams using Galerkin method. Dinçkal [48], more recently, proposed a finite element model that uses exact dynamic shape functions (trigonometric in nature) to form the frequency-dependant dynamic stiffness matrix and hence study the free vibrations of carbon nanotubes, modeled as both nonlocal Euler-Bernoulli and Timoshenko beams. Ehteshami and Hajabasi [49] and Zhang et al. [50] performed an analytical study and presented exact solutions for finding natural frequencies of DWCNTs modeled as nonlocal Euler-Bernoulli beams. The results of both these studies have been considered as benchmark to verify the results obtained in the current study. This chapter exploits the generality of the FEM technique to obtain the natural frequencies of DWCNTs, coupled with van der Waals interaction forces. The model has been proposed and applied to both local (classical) Euler-Bernoulli and nonlocal Euler-Bernoulli beam cases. The results are compared with the values presented in the literature.

2. Formulation

This section gives the formulation for the proposed models. Section 2.1 would present the formulation for local Euler-Bernoulli beam and Section 2.2 for nonlocal Euler-Bernoulli beam. As will be seen ahead, the formulation uses Galerkin weighted residual method and Hermite cubic polynomial functions, in both the cases in interest of generality.

2.1. DWCNTs based on local Euler-Bernoulli beam

Euler-Bernoulli beam, also known as the classical beam, is known to efficiently represent a carbon nanotube, in the case when the aspect ratio (L/d ratio) is sufficiently high. The governing equation for an Euler-Bernoulli beam is given by [51]:

$$EIw''' + \rho A\ddot{w} = p(x)$$

(1)

where EI is the bending rigidity, w is the displacement, ρ is the mass density, A is the cross-sectional area, and the derivatives of transverse displacement with respect to beam length and time are represented by prime (') and a dot (.), respectively. Ru [8] used the multiple beam model to derive the governing equations for DWCNTs. It is taken as two single-walled carbon nanotubes coupled by an interaction force, represented by van der Waal's coefficient, which is estimated as:

$$c = \frac{\pi \varepsilon R_1 R_2 \sigma^6}{a^4}\left[\frac{1001\sigma^6}{3}H^{13} - \frac{1120}{9}H^7\right]$$

(2)

where σ and ε are the van der Waal's radius and Lennard-Jones potential's well depth, $a = 0.142$ — the C—C bond length and R_1 and R_2 are the inner and outer radius, respectively, whereas

$$H^m = (R_1 + R_2)^{-m}\int_0^{\frac{\pi}{2}}\frac{d\theta}{\left(1 - K\cos^2\theta\right)^{\frac{m}{2}}}(m = 7,13)$$

(3)

and

$$K = \frac{4R_1 R_2}{(R_1 + R_2)^2}$$

(4)

The governing equations for a DWCNT are [8]:

$$E_1 I_1 w_1''' + \rho_1 A_1 \ddot{w}_1 = cw_2 - cw_1$$

(5)

$$E_2 I_2 w_2''' + \rho_2 A_2 \ddot{w}_2 = -cw_2 + cw_1$$

where the subscripts 1, 2 for E, I, w, ρ, A represent the inner and outer tubes, respectively. Simple harmonic motion is assumed, i.e., $w_j(x,t) = W_j e^{i\omega t}$ is assumed to remove time dependency from Eq. (5) and $i = 1,2$ to represent inner and outer carbon nanotube, respectively, and ω and t represent the circular frequency and time. Using simple harmonic motion in governing equations modifies them as:

$$E_1 I_1 W_1''' + \left(c - \rho_1 A_1 \omega^2\right) W_1 - cW_2 = 0$$
$$E_2 I_2 W_2''' + \left(c - \rho_2 A_2 \omega^2\right) W_2 - cW_1 = 0$$

(6)

Following Galerkin weighted residual method, weight functions are introduced as $\delta W_{1,2}$ and the transverse displacements continue to be represented by $W_{1,2}$. The weighted-integral form of the governing equations is given as:

$$\bar{W}_1^k = \int_0^L \left(E_1 I_1 W''' \delta W_1 + \left(c - \rho_1 A_1 \omega^2\right) W_1 \delta W_1 - cW_2 \delta W_1 \right) dx = 0$$

(7)

$$\bar{W}_2^k = \int_0^L \left(E_2 I_2 W''' \delta W_2 + \left(c - \rho_2 A_2 \omega^2\right) W_2 \delta W_2 - cW_1 \delta W_2 \right) dx = 0$$

The weak integral form of the governing equations is eliminated by performing integration by parts, twice on Eq. (7), as given below:

$$\bar{W}_2^k = \int_0^L \left(E_2 I_2 W_2'' \delta W_2'' + \left(c - \rho_2 A_2 \omega^2\right) W_2 \delta W_2 - cW_1 \delta W_2 \right) dx + \left[(E_2 I_2 W''') \delta W_2 \right]_0^L$$
$$- \left[(E_2 I_2 W'') \delta W_2' \right]_0^L = 0$$

$$\overline{W}_2^k = \int_0^L \left(E_2 I_2 W_2^{''} \delta W_2^{''} + \left(c - \rho_2 A_2 \omega^2 \right) W_2 \delta W_2 - c W_1 \delta W_2 \right) dx + \left[(E_2 I_2 W_2^{'''}) \delta W_2 \right]_0^L$$

$$- \left[(E_2 I_2 W_2^{''}) \delta W_2^{'} \right]_0^L = 0$$

(8)

The boundary terms in Eq. (8) which vanish with the application of system boundary conditions, represent the shear force and moment of the beams are given by $V = E_i I_i W_i^{'''}$ and $M = E_i I_i W''$ and remain similar to those of a classical Euler-Bernoulli beam. The domain length of the DWCNT is now discretized with four nodes and two Degrees of Freedom (DOF) per node (one transverse displacement and one slope per node) such that:

$$\overline{W}_{w_1}^k = \int_0^{l^k} \delta W_1^{''} \left(E_1 I_1 W_1^{''} \right) dx + \int_0^{l^k} \delta W_1 \left(c - \rho_1 A_1 \omega^2 \right) W_1 - \int_0^{l^k} \delta W_1 c W_2 = 0$$

$$\overline{W}_{w_2}^k = \int_0^{l^k} \delta W_2^{''} \left(E_2 I_2 W_2^{''} \right) dx + \int_0^{l^k} \delta W_2 \left(c - \rho_2 A_2 \omega^2 \right) W_2 - \int_0^{l^k} \delta W_2 c W_1 = 0$$

(9)

The present work uses Hermite type polynomial approximations to derive the finite element formulation such that the interpolation function is given as:

$$\overline{W}(x) = \sum_1^4 N_i(x_i) W_i$$

(10)

where $\langle N_i(x_i) \rangle$ is a row vector of cubic shape functions, of the beam elements given by:

$$N_1 = \frac{1}{L^3} \left(2x^3 - 3x^2 L + L^3 \right) \quad N_2 = \frac{1}{L^3} \left(x^3 L - 2x^2 L + xL \right)$$

$$N_3 = \frac{1}{L^3} \left(-2x^3 + 3x^2 L \right) \quad N_4 = \frac{1}{L^3} \left(x^3 L - x^2 L^2 \right)$$

(11)

2.2. DWCNTs based on nonlocal Euler-Bernoulli beam

The concept of nonlocality, which is accounted for with the introduction of a nonlocal or a small scale factor was extended to the field of nanotechnology by Peddieson et al. [6] where the author applied it to Euler-Bernoulli beam model. The small scale effect or the nonlocal parameter is given as $\mu = e_0 a$ to consider the stress at one point of the system as the function of strain at all points of the system. This is achieved with e_0 being the material constant (to be determined for each material) and a being the length of C—C bond. Subsequently, researchers like Ehteshami and Hajabasi [49], Zhang et al. [50] and Wang and Varadan [20] developed the model for DWCNTs using nonlocal Euler-Bernoulli beam model. The derivation of governing equations requires the classic Hooke's law for uniaxial stress state to be modified, taking nonlocal elasticity into consideration, as:

$$\sigma - \left(e_0 a\right)^2 \frac{\partial^2 \sigma}{\partial x^2} = E\varepsilon \tag{12}$$

with σ and ε being axial stress and strain, respectively. The equations of motion, perpendicular to x axis, are given by:

$$\frac{\partial S}{\partial x} - \rho A \frac{\partial^2 w}{\partial t^2} = 0; V - \frac{\partial M}{\partial x} = 0 \tag{13}$$

where ρ is the mass density of material, A is the cross-sectional area, w is deflection of the beam and M and S denotes the bending moment and shear force, respectively. Using these in the moment equilibrium conditions, results in the governing equation for nonlocal Euler-Bernoulli beam, given as:

$$p = EI \frac{\partial^4 w}{\partial x^4} + \rho A \frac{\partial^2 w}{\partial t^2} - \mu^2 \left(\rho A \frac{\partial^4 w}{\partial x^4} - \frac{\partial^2 p}{\partial x^2} \right) \tag{14}$$

For nonlocal DWCNTs, the governing equations are derived to be [20, 49, 50]:

$$E_1 I_1 \frac{\partial^4 w_1}{\partial x^2} + \rho_1 A_1 \frac{\partial^2 w_1}{\partial t^2} - \mu^2 \rho_1 A_1 \frac{\partial^4 w_1}{\partial x^2 \partial t^2} - c(w_2 - w_1) + \mu^2 c \left(\frac{\partial^2 w_2}{\partial x^2} - \frac{\partial^2 w_1}{\partial x^2} \right) = 0$$

$$E_2 I_2 \frac{\partial^4 w_2}{\partial x^2} + \rho_2 A_2 \frac{\partial^2 w_2}{\partial t^2} - \mu^2 \rho_2 A_2 \frac{\partial^4 w_2}{\partial x^2 \partial t^2} - c(w_1 - w_2) + \mu^2 c \left(\frac{\partial^2 w_1}{\partial x^2} - \frac{\partial^2 w_2}{\partial x^2} \right) = 0 \tag{15}$$

The solution of the equations is in the form $w_j(x, t) = W_j e^{i\omega t}$, similar to the local Euler-Bernoulli formulation. The time dependency is removed by considering the transverse displacement with respect to time as circular frequency, ω^2:

$$E_1 I_1 W_1''' - m_1 \omega^2 W_1 - \mu^2 m_1 \omega^2 W_1'' - cW_2 + cW_1 + \mu^2 cW_2'' - \mu^2 cW_1'' = 0$$
$$E_2 I_2 W_2''' - m_2 \omega^2 W_2 - \mu^2 m_2 \omega^2 W_2'' - cW_1 + cW_2 + \mu^2 cW_1'' - \mu^2 cW_2'' = 0 \tag{16}$$

To maintain uniformity in mathematical modelling with the formulation proposed for local Euler-Bernoulli model, Galerkin weighted residual model is used for FEM, with δW_i taken as weighted residual. The weak integral form of governing equations takes the form:

$$\int_0^L (E_1 I_1 W_1''' \delta W_1 - m_1 \omega^2 W_1 \delta W_1 - \mu^2 m_1 \omega^2 W_1'' \delta W_1 - cW_2 \delta W_1 + cW_1 \delta W_1 + \mu^2 cW_2'' \delta W_1$$
$$- \mu^2 cW_1'' \delta W_1) dx = 0$$
$$\int_0^L (E_2 I_2 W_2''' \delta W_2 - m_2 \omega^2 W_2 \delta W_2 - \mu^2 m_2 \omega^2 W_2'' \delta W_2 - cW_1 \delta W_2 + cW_2 \delta W_2 + \mu^2 cW_1'' \delta W_2 \tag{17}$$
$$- \mu^2 cW_2'' \delta W_2) dx = 0$$

Integration by parts is performed on the above set of equations once, and the weak form vanishes with the application of system boundary conditions,

$$\int_0^L \left(\begin{array}{c} \left(\delta W_1' \left(-E_1 I_1 W_1''\right)\right) - \left(\delta W_1 \left(m_1 \omega^2 W_1\right)\right) - \left(\delta W_1' \left(\mu^2 m_1 \omega^2 W_1'\right)\right) \\ + \left(\delta W_1 \left(cW_1\right)\right) - \left(\delta W_1 \left(cW_2\right)\right) - \left(\delta W_1' \left(\mu^2 cW_2'\right)\right) + \left(\delta W_1' \left(\mu^2 cW_1'\right)\right) \end{array} \right) dx = 0$$
$$\int_0^L \left(\begin{array}{c} \left(\delta W_2' \left(-E_2 I_2 W_2''\right)\right) - \left(\delta W_2 \left(m_2 \omega^2 W_2\right)\right) - \left(\delta W_2' \left(\mu^2 m_2 \omega^2 W_2'\right)\right) \\ + \left(\delta W_2 \left(cW_2\right)\right) - \left(\delta W_2 \left(cW_1\right)\right) - \left(\delta W_2' \left(\mu^2 cW_1'\right)\right) + \left(\delta W_2' \left(\mu^2 cW_2'\right)\right) \end{array} \right) dx = 0 \tag{18}$$

The resulting internal shear forces for both the beams are given as:

$$V_1 = E_1 I_1 W_1'' + \mu^2 \left(m_1 \omega^2 W_1' + c\left(W_2' - W_1'\right)\right)$$
$$V_2 = E_2 I_2 W_2'' + \mu^2 \left(m_2 \omega^2 W_2' + c\left(W_1' - W_2'\right)\right) \tag{19}$$

and the resultant bending moments are given as:

$$M_1 = E_1 I_1 W_1^{"} - \mu^2 \left(m_1 \omega^2 W_1 - c(W_2 - W_1) \right)$$

$$M_2 = E_2 I_2 W_2^{"} - \mu^2 \left(m_2 \omega^2 W_2 - c(W_1 - W_2) \right) \tag{20}$$

Integration by parts is performed once again on the first terms in Eq. (18) and after rearranging for clarity, the following set of equations is obtained:

$$\bar{W}_{w_1}^k = E_1 I_1 \int_0^{l^k} \left(W_1^{"} \delta W_1^{"} \right) dx - m_1 \omega^2 \left(\int_0^{l^k} (W_1 \delta W_1) + \mu^2 \int_0^{l^k} (W_1' \delta W_1') \right) dx$$

$$+ c \left(\int_0^{l^k} (W_1 \delta W_1) + \mu^2 \int_0^{l^k} (W_1' \delta W_1') \right) dx - c \left(\int_0^{l^k} (W_2 \delta W_1) + \mu^2 \int_0^{l^k} (W_2' \delta W_1') \right) dx$$

$$\bar{W}_{w_2}^k = E_2 I_2 \int_0^{l^k} \left(W_2^{"} \delta W_2^{"} \right) dx - m_2 \omega^2 \left(\int_0^{l^k} (W_2 \delta W_2) + \mu^2 \int_0^{l^k} (W_2' \delta W_2') \right) dx \tag{21}$$

$$+ c \left(\int_0^{l^k} (W_2 \delta W_2) + \mu^2 \int_0^{l^k} (W_2' \delta W_2') \right) dx - c \left(\int_0^{l^k} (W_1 \delta W_2) + \mu^2 \int_0^{l^k} (W_1' \delta W_2') \right) dx$$

Using Hermite cubic polynomial functions, given in Eq. (11), the finite element model is developed. The element mass and stiffness matrices for both the local and nonlocal scenarios are explicitly presented in the Appendix A. An FEM code in MATLAB solves the linear eigenvalue problem which is given as:

$$\det \left(K - \omega^2 M \right) = 0 \tag{22}$$

where K represents global stiffness matrix and M represents the global mass matrix, respectively, and is achieved after assembly. **Table 1** gives the element matrices K_e and M_e, which are to be assembled to form the global matrices for both local and nonlocal cases.

Local Euler-Bernoulli beam	Nonlocal Euler-Bernoulli beam
$K_e = \begin{pmatrix} k_1 + k_3 & -k_4 \\ -k_3 & k_2 + k_4 \end{pmatrix}$	$K_e = \begin{pmatrix} k_1 + k_3 + k_5 & -(k_4 + k_6) \\ -(k_3 + k_5) & k_2 + k_4 + k_6 \end{pmatrix}$
$M_e = \begin{pmatrix} m_1 & 0 \\ 0 & m_2 \end{pmatrix}$	$M_e = \begin{pmatrix} m_1 + m_3 & 0 \\ 0 & m_2 + m_4 \end{pmatrix}$

Table 1. Elemental matrices for local and nonlocal DWCNTs modeled as Euler-Bernoulli beams.

3. Results and discussion

The robustness and generality of proposed FEM model is demonstrated by its application to a double-elastic Euler-Bernoulli beam and then to carbon nanotubes modeled as Euler-Bernoulli beam, both locally and nonlocally. Natural frequencies are calculated for clamped-free, clamped-clamped and simply supported-simply supported boundary conditions. The parameters of the local double elastic Euler-Bernoulli beam are taken as:

$$\rho_1 = \rho_2 = 1\,kg/m^3 \quad E_1 = E_2 = 1\,N/m^2 \quad A_1 = 1\,m^2 \quad A_2 = 2\,m^2$$
$$I_1 = 1\,m^4 \quad I_2 = 2\,m^4 \quad c = 10;\,\mu = 0.1 \quad L = 1\,m$$

Boundary conditions	[14]	Present study	Error percentage
C–F	3.52	3.52	0.01
C–C	22.37	22.37	0
S–S	9.87	9.87	0

Table 2. Non-dimentionalized natural frequencies of a local double-elastic Euler-Bernoulli beam.

These parameters are so selected that the double beam replicates the geometry of carbon nanotubes, i.e., both are concentric and are coupled with an interaction forces between the walls. The natural frequencies of the double-elastic system, in this chapter, are normalized using $\bar{\omega} = \omega L^2 \sqrt{\rho A/EI}$ where $E = E_1 + E_2$ and $I = I_1 + I_2$. The values presented by the proposed model converge at about five elements, but the data tabulated, for all cases, are taken for 10 elements, unless mentioned otherwise. The non-dimentionalized natural frequencies for three classic boundary conditions are given in **Table 2**.

Boundary conditions	[50]	Present study	Error percentage
C–F	3.45	3.44	−0.54
C–C	20.23	21.10	4.38
S–S	9.42	9.42	0

Table 3. Non-dimentionalized natural frequencies of a nonlocal double-elastic Euler-Bernoulli beam.

The percentage error has been calculated by ((approximate−exact)/exact) × 100 in this study. These values are compared to the first natural frequency obtained using the analytical solutions found in Xu et al. The values are in good agreement and hence the proposed model is found to be efficient to find the natural frequencies of local double-elastic Euler-Bernoulli beam. The applicability of the proposed nonlocal model is demonstrated by the values in **Table 3**. It is to be noted that the values are presented for a single value nonlocal factor, where $\mu = 0.1$, and it can be confirmed that $\mu = 0$ would give the same values as presented in **Table 1** as that would reduce the nonlocal formulation to local one. The values presented in **Table 1** are compared to the values obtained using the beam parameters in analytical solutions provided by Zhang et al. [50]. It can be seen the error percentages are small hence validating the proposed model.

Table 4 gives the error percentage between local and nonlocal double-elastic Euler-Bernoulli beam when $L/d = 10$. This error helps to measure the effect of nonlocal factor on the natural frequencies of double-elastic Euler-Bernoulli beams. It is seen that the values obtained using nonlocal model is less than that obtained using local double-elastic Euler-Bernoulli model. This can be attributed to the presence of a nonlocal factor that considers the strain at one point to be function of all the points in the body.

Boundary conditions	Local	Nonlocal	Error percentage
C–F	3.52	3.44	2.25
C–C	22.37	21.10	5.65
S–S	9.87	9.42	4.60

Table 4. Error percentage between natural frequencies of local and nonlocal double-elastic Euler-Bernoulli beam.

It is concluded that a novel double-elastic Euler-Bernoulli beam FEM model has been proposed, and its veracity established for both local and nonlocal cases, the same model will now be applied to carbon nanotubes with the parameters used in Xu et al. [14] and Elishakoff and Pentaras [15], given below:

$$\rho_1 = \rho_2 = 2.3 \text{ g/cm}^3 \qquad\qquad E_1 = E_2 = 1 \text{ Tpa}$$
$$c = 71.11 \text{ GPa} \qquad\qquad e_0 \approx 0.82; a = 0.142 \text{ nm}$$
$$r_{1,i} \text{(inner radius, inner tube)} = 0.18 \text{ nm} \quad r_{1,o} \text{(outer radius, inner tube)} = 0.52 \text{ nm}$$
$$r_{2,i} \text{(inner radius, outer tube)} = 0.53 \text{ nm} \quad r_{2,o} \text{(outer radius, outer tube)} = 0.87 \text{ nm}$$

Boundary conditions	[14]	Present study	Error percentage
C–F	0.16	0.16	0.01
C–C	1.06	1.06	0
S–S	4.67	4.67	0

Table 5. Natural frequencies of a local DWCNTs modeled as Euler-Bernoulli beam (10^{12} rads/s).

The natural frequencies of a local DWCNT, modeled as Euler-Bernoulli beams, are presented in **Table 5**. The nonlocal factor μ is introduced as a product of material constant and characteristic length. Zhang et al. calculated the material constant as the ratio of local result to nonlocal result for axial buckling strain of SWCNT and arrived at a value $e_0 \approx 0.82$, and the characteristic length is taken to be the length of C–C bond i.e., $a = 0.142$ nm. The natural frequencies calculated using the proposed model are compared to the values obtained using the analytical formulation presented in Xu et al. [14]. The error percentages in **Table 5** confirm that the proposed formulation holds valid even at nanoscale level. Further, negative error percentage denotes that the values obtained using the present FEM model are a little higher than those presented by Ehteshami and Hajabasi [49] (see **Table 6**).

Boundary conditions	[49]	[50]	Present study	Error percentage 1	Error percentage 2
C—F	0.166	0.16	0.16	0	0.01
C—C	1.06	1.06	1.06	−0.04	0.04
S—S	0.467	0.46	0.46	−0.03	0

Table 6. Natural frequencies of a nonlocal DWCNT modeled as Euler-Bernoulli beam (10^{12} rads/s).

Boundary conditions	Local	Nonlocal	Error percentage
C—F	0.16	0.16	0.02
C—C	1.06	1.06	0.04
S—S	0.46	0.46	0.03

Table 7. Error percentage between natural frequencies of local and nonlocal DWCNTs modeled as Euler-Bernoulli beam (10^{12} rads/s).

1	L/d	Local	Nonlocal	Error percentage
C—F	20	0.41	0.41	0
C—C		2.65	2.65	0.01
S—S		1.17	1.17	0
C—F	40	0.10	0.10	0
C—C		0.66	0.66	0
S—S		0.29	0.29	0
C—F	60	0.04	0.04	0
C—C		0.29	0.29	0
S—S		0.13	0.13	0
C—F	80	0.02	0.02	0
C—C		0.16	0.16	0
S—S		0.07	0.07	0

Table 8. Error percentage between natural frequencies of local and nonlocal DWCNTs modeled as Euler-Bernoulli beam with different L/d ratios (10^{12} rads/s).

Employing the FEM model proposed in Section 1.2, the natural frequencies of nonlocal DWCNTs modeled as Euler-Bernoulli beam are given in **Table 6**. The natural frequencies thus obtained are compared to the values obtained using the analytical formulations given by Ehteshami and Hajabasi [49] Zhang et al. [50]. The error percentages, between present study and these two studies, are presented as error percentage 1 and 2, respectively. The effect of nonlocal factor on the natural frequencies is best understood when the error percentage between local results and nonlocal results are compared, presented in **Table 7**. It will be noted that the error percentage is very small compared to the error percentage reported in **Table 4**. This difference is attributed to the value of nonlocal factor—the double-elastic beam model considers it to be between 1 and 2 and DWCNTs have it in the order of e−10, to be exact 1.1644e − 10. It is also seen (**Table 8**) that as L/d ratio is increased, the natural frequency and the error percentage, between local and nonlocal results, decrease, i.e., as the aspect ratio increases, the effect of nonlocal factor decreases.

It is noted that though many tables in this chapter may have identical values in the columns that are being compared, the indicated percentage error is a nonzero number, or on the contrary, the columns being compared might not have identical values, but the indicated error percentage is zero. A justification for these values stems from the large magnitude of the numbers reported. For the sake of uniformity, we have rounded off the numbers to 2 decimal points.

4. Conclusion

This chapter proposed FEM formulations to find the natural frequencies of DWCNTs modeled as, both, local and nonlocal Euler-Bernoulli beams, coupled with van der Waals interaction forces. It uses Galerkin weighted residual approach and Hermite cubic polynomial functions to form the stiffness and mass matrices. The formulation is applied to double-elastic Euler-Bernoulli beam and to DWCNTs, to check its generality. The natural frequencies thus obtained are in agreement with those of the formulations found in the literature. It is seen that as the L/d ratio of the system increases, the difference between local and nonlocal formulations reduces. It has also been observed that difference between local and nonlocal system is dependent on the magnitude of the nonlocal factor considered. These formulations would let researchers apply FEM to multi-walled CNTs in order to better understand their behaviour.

Nomenclature

a, length of the C—C bond

A, cross-sectional area

c, van der Waal's interaction coefficient

E, Young's Modulus

I, second area moment of inertia

M, bending moment

N, shape functions

t, time

V, shear force

w, lateral displacement

W, amplitude

x, length of the beam

δW, weighting function

μ, nonlocal factor

ρ, mass density

ω, circular frequency

e_0, material constant

Appendix A. Element matrices

$$k_1 = \begin{pmatrix} \dfrac{12E_1 I_1}{l^3} & \dfrac{6E_1 I_1}{l^2} & \dfrac{-12E_1 I_1}{l^3} & \dfrac{6E_1 I_1}{l^2} \\ & \dfrac{4E_1 I_1}{l} & \dfrac{-6E_1 I_1}{l^2} & \dfrac{2E_1 I_1}{l} \\ & Sym & \dfrac{12E_1 I_1}{l^3} & \dfrac{-6E_1 I_1}{l^2} \\ & & & \dfrac{4E_1 I_1}{l} \end{pmatrix} \begin{pmatrix} w_{11} \\ \theta_{11} \\ w_{12} \\ \theta_{12} \end{pmatrix}$$

$$k_3 = \begin{pmatrix} \dfrac{156c}{420} & \dfrac{22lc}{420} & \dfrac{54c}{420} & \dfrac{-13lc}{420} \\ & \dfrac{4l^2 c}{420} & \dfrac{13lc}{420} & \dfrac{-3l^2 c}{420} \\ & Sym & \dfrac{156c}{420} & \dfrac{-22lc}{420} \\ & & & \dfrac{4l^2 c}{420} \end{pmatrix} \begin{pmatrix} w_{11} \\ \theta_{11} \\ w_{12} \\ \theta_{12} \end{pmatrix}$$

$$k_2 = \begin{pmatrix} \dfrac{12E_2 I_2}{l^3} & \dfrac{6E_2 I_2}{l^2} & \dfrac{-12E_2 I_2}{l^3} & \dfrac{6E_2 I_2}{l^2} \\ & \dfrac{4E_2 I_2}{l} & \dfrac{-6E_2 I_2}{l^2} & \dfrac{2E_2 I_2}{l} \\ & Sym & \dfrac{12E_2 I_2}{l^3} & \dfrac{-6E_2 I_2}{l^2} \\ & & & \dfrac{4E_2 I_2}{l} \end{pmatrix} \begin{pmatrix} w_{21} \\ \theta_{21} \\ w_{22} \\ \theta_{22} \end{pmatrix}$$

$$k_4 = \begin{pmatrix} \dfrac{156c}{420} & \dfrac{22lc}{420} & \dfrac{54c}{420} & \dfrac{-13lc}{420} \\ & \dfrac{4l^2 c}{420} & \dfrac{13lc}{420} & \dfrac{-3l^2 c}{420} \\ & Sym & \dfrac{156c}{420} & \dfrac{-22lc}{420} \\ & & & \dfrac{4l^2 c}{420} \end{pmatrix} \begin{pmatrix} w_{21} \\ \theta_{21} \\ w_{22} \\ \theta_{22} \end{pmatrix}$$

$$k_5 = \begin{pmatrix} \dfrac{6\mu^2 c}{5l} & \dfrac{\mu^2 c}{10} & \dfrac{-6\mu^2 c}{5l} & \dfrac{\mu^2 c}{10} \\[2mm] & \dfrac{2l\mu^2 c}{15} & \dfrac{-\mu^2 c}{10} & \dfrac{-\mu^2 cl}{30} \\[2mm] & Sym & \dfrac{6\mu^2 c}{5l} & \dfrac{-\mu^2 c}{10} \\[2mm] & & & \dfrac{2l\mu^2 c}{15} \end{pmatrix} \begin{pmatrix} w_{11} \\ \theta_{11} \\ w_{12} \\ \theta_{12} \end{pmatrix}$$

$$k_6 = \begin{pmatrix} \dfrac{6\mu^2 c}{5l} & \dfrac{\mu^2 c}{10} & \dfrac{-6\mu^2 c}{5l} & \dfrac{\mu^2 c}{10} \\[2mm] & \dfrac{2l\mu^2 c}{15} & \dfrac{-\mu^2 c}{10} & \dfrac{-\mu^2 cl}{30} \\[2mm] & Sym & \dfrac{6\mu^2 c}{5l} & \dfrac{-\mu^2 c}{10} \\[2mm] & & & \dfrac{2l\mu^2 c}{15} \end{pmatrix} \begin{pmatrix} w_{21} \\ \theta_{21} \\ w_{22} \\ \theta_{22} \end{pmatrix}$$

$$m_1 = \begin{pmatrix} \dfrac{156m_1 l}{420} & \dfrac{22l^2 m_1}{420} & \dfrac{54m_1 l}{420} & \dfrac{-13l^2 m_1}{420} \\[2mm] & \dfrac{4l^3 m_1}{420} & \dfrac{13l^2 m_1}{420} & \dfrac{-3l^3 m_1}{420} \\[2mm] & Sym & \dfrac{156m_1 l}{420} & \dfrac{-22l^2 m_1}{420} \\[2mm] & & & \dfrac{4l^3 m_1}{420} \end{pmatrix} \begin{pmatrix} w_{11} \\ \theta_{11} \\ w_{12} \\ \theta_{12} \end{pmatrix}$$

$$m_3 = \begin{pmatrix} \dfrac{6\mu^2 m_1}{5l} & \dfrac{\mu^2 m_1}{10} & \dfrac{-6\mu^2 m_1}{5l} & \dfrac{\mu^2 m_1}{10} \\[2mm] & \dfrac{2l\mu^2 m_1}{15} & \dfrac{-\mu^2 m_1}{10} & \dfrac{-\mu^2 m_1 l}{30} \\[2mm] & Sym & \dfrac{6\mu^2 m_1}{5l} & \dfrac{-\mu^2 m_1}{10} \\[2mm] & & & \dfrac{2l\mu^2 m_1}{15} \end{pmatrix} \begin{pmatrix} w_{11} \\ \theta_{11} \\ w_{12} \\ \theta_{12} \end{pmatrix}$$

$$m_2 = \begin{pmatrix} \dfrac{156m_2 l}{420} & \dfrac{22l^2 m_2}{420} & \dfrac{54m_2 l}{420} & \dfrac{-13l^2 m_2}{420} \\[2mm] & \dfrac{4l^3 m_2}{420} & \dfrac{13l^2 m_2}{420} & \dfrac{-3l^3 m_2}{420} \\[2mm] & Sym & \dfrac{156m_2 l}{420} & \dfrac{-22l^2 m_2}{420} \\[2mm] & & & \dfrac{4l^3 m_2}{420} \end{pmatrix} \begin{pmatrix} w_{21} \\ \theta_{21} \\ w_{22} \\ \theta_{22} \end{pmatrix}$$

$$m_4 = \begin{pmatrix} \dfrac{6\mu^2 m_2}{5l} & \dfrac{\mu^2 m_2}{10} & \dfrac{-6\mu^2 m_2}{5l} & \dfrac{\mu^2 m_2}{10} \\[2mm] & \dfrac{2l\mu^2 m_2}{15} & \dfrac{-\mu^2 m_2}{10} & \dfrac{-\mu^2 m_2 l}{30} \\[2mm] & Sym & \dfrac{6\mu^2 m_2}{5l} & \dfrac{-\mu^2 m_2}{10} \\[2mm] & & & \dfrac{2l\mu^2 m_2}{15} \end{pmatrix} \begin{pmatrix} w_{21} \\ \theta_{21} \\ w_{22} \\ \theta_{22} \end{pmatrix}$$

Author details

Ishan Ali Khan and Seyed M. Hashemi[*]

*Address all correspondence to: smhashem@ryerson.ca

Department of Aerospace Engineering, Ryerson University, Toronto, Canada

References

[1] Yakobson BI, Smalley RE. Fullerene nanotubes: C 1,000,000 and beyond: Some unusual new molecules—long, hollow fibers with tantalizing electronic and mechanical properties—have joined diamonds and graphite in the carbon family. American Scientist. JSTOR; 1997;85(No. 4):324–37.

[2] Eringen AC, Edelen D. On nonlocal elasticity. International Journal of Engineering Science (Elsevier); 1972;10(3):233–248.

[3] Eringen AC. Nonlocal polar elastic continua. International Journal of Engineering Science (Elsevier); 1972;10(1):1–16.

[4] Eringen AC. On differential equations of nonlocal elasticity and solutions of screw dislocation and surface waves. Journal of Applied Physics (AIP); 1983;54(9):4703–4710.

[5] Eringen AC. Nonlocal continuum mechanics based on distributions. International Journal of Engineering Science (Elsevier); 2006;44(3):141–147.

[6] Peddieson J, Buchanan GR, McNitt RP. Application of nonlocal continuum models to nanotechnology. International Journal of Engineering Science (Elsevier); 2003;41(3): 305–312.

[7] Ru C. Column buckling of multiwalled carbon nanotubes with interlayer radial displacements. Physical Review B (APS); 2000;62(24):16962.

[8] Ru C. Elastic models for carbon nanotubes. Encyclopedia of nanoscience and nano-technology. Stevenson Ranch, CA: American Scientific Publishers; 2004. p. 731–44.

[9] Yoon J, Ru C, Mioduchowski A. Vibration of an embedded multiwall carbon nanotube. Composites Science and Technology. Elsevier; 2003;63(11):1533–1542.

[10] Fu Y, Hong J, Wang X. Analysis of nonlinear vibration for embedded carbon nanotubes. Journal of Sound and Vibration (Elsevier); 2006;296(4):746–756.

[11] Natsuki T, Ni Q-Q, Endo M. Analysis of the vibration characteristics of double-walled carbon nanotubes. Carbon (Elsevier); 2008;46(12):1570–1573.

[12] Natsuki T, Lei X-W, Ni Q-Q, Endo M. Free vibration characteristics of double-walled carbon nanotubes embedded in an elastic medium. Physics Letters A (Elsevier); 2010;374(26):2670–2674.

[13] Natsuki T, Lei X-W, Ni Q-Q, Endo M. Vibrational analysis of double-walled carbon nanotubes with inner and outer nanotubes of different lengths. Physics Letters A (Elsevier); 2010;374(46):4684–4689.

[14] Xu K, Guo X, Ru C. Vibration of a double-walled carbon nanotube aroused by nonlinear intertube van der Waals forces. Journal of Applied Physics (AIP Publishing); 2006;99(6): 064303.

[15] Elishakoff I, Pentaras D. Fundamental natural frequencies of double-walled carbon nanotubes. Journal of Sound and Vibration (Elsevier); 2009;322(4):652–664.

[16] Pentaras D, Elishakoff I. Free vibration of triple-walled carbon nanotubes. Acta mechanica (Springer); 2011;221(3–4):239–249.

[17] Wang Q, Wang C. The constitutive relation and small scale parameter of nonlocal continuum mechanics for modelling carbon nanotubes. Nanotechnology (IOP Publishing); 2007;18(7):075702.

[18] Wang Q. Wave propagation in carbon nanotubes via nonlocal continuum mechanics. Journal of applied physics. 2005;98:124301.

[19] Yoon J, Ru C, Mioduchowski A. Timoshenko-beam effects on transverse wave propagation in carbon nanotubes. Composites Part B: Engineering (Elsevier); 2004;35(2):87–93.

[20] Wang Q, Varadan V. Vibration of carbon nanotubes studied using nonlocal continuum mechanics. Smart Materials and Structures (IOP Publishing); 2006;15(2):659.

[21] Arash B, Wang Q. A review on the application of nonlocal elastic models in modeling of carbon nanotubes and graphenes. Computational Materials Science (Elsevier); 2012;51(1):303–313.

[22] Reddy J. Nonlocal theories for bending, buckling and vibration of beams. International Journal of Engineering Science (Elsevier); 2007;45(2):288–307.

[23] Reddy J, Pang S. Nonlocal continuum theories of beams for the analysis of carbon nanotubes. Journal of Applied Physics (AIP); 2008;103(2):023511–023511.

[24] Murmu T, Pradhan S. Thermo-mechanical vibration of a single-walled carbon nanotube embedded in an elastic medium based on nonlocal elasticity theory. Computational Materials Science (Elsevier); 2009;46(4):854–859.

[25] Narendar S, Gupta S, Gopalakrishnan S. Wave propagation in single-walled carbon nanotube under longitudinal magnetic field using nonlocal Euler-Bernoulli beam theory. Applied Mathematical Modelling (Elsevier); 2012;36(9):4529–4538.

[26] De Rosa MA, Lippiello M. Free vibration analysis of DWCNTs using CDM and Rayleigh-Schmidt based on nonlocal Euler-Bernoulli beam theory. The Scientific World Journal (Hindawi Publishing Corporation); 2014;2014.

[27] Karaoglu P, Aydogdu M. On the forced vibration of carbon nanotubes via a non-local Euler−Bernoulli beam model. Proceedings of the Institution of Mechanical Engineers, Part C: Journal of Mechanical Engineering Science (SAGE Publications); 2010;224(2):497–503.

[28] Khosrozadeh A, Hajabasi M. Free vibration of embedded double-walled carbon nanotubes considering nonlinear interlayer van der Waals forces. Applied Mathematical Modelling (Elsevier); 2012;36(3):997–1007.

[29] Fang B, Zhen Y-X, Zhang C-P, Tang Y. Nonlinear vibration analysis of double-walled carbon nanotubes based on nonlocal elasticity theory. Applied Mathematical Modelling (Elsevier); 2013;37(3):1096–1107.

[30] Wang C, Tan V, Zhang Y. Timoshenko beam model for vibration analysis of multi-walled carbon nanotubes. Journal of Sound and Vibration (Elsevier); 2006;294(4):1060–1072.

[31] Yang J, Ke L, Kitipornchai S. Nonlinear free vibration of single-walled carbon nanotubes using nonlocal Timoshenko beam theory. Physica E: Low-dimensional Systems and Nanostructures (Elsevier); 2010;42(5):1727–1735.

[32] Ke L, Xiang Y, Yang J, Kitipornchai S. Nonlinear free vibration of embedded double-walled carbon nanotubes based on nonlocal Timoshenko beam theory. Computational Materials Science (Elsevier); 2009;47(2):409–417.

[33] Pradhan S. Nonlocal finite element analysis and small scale effects of CNTs with Timoshenko beam theory. Finite Elements in Analysis and Design (Elsevier); 2012;50:8–20.

[34] Zhang Y, Wang C, Tan V. Buckling of multiwalled carbon nanotubes using Timoshenko beam theory. Journal of Engineering Mechanics (American Society of Civil Engineers); 2006;132(9):952–958.

[35] Wang C, Zhang Y, Xiang Y, Reddy J. Recent studies on buckling of carbon nanotubes. Applied Mechanics Reviews (American Society of Mechanical Engineers); 2010;63(3): 030804.

[36] Shima H. Buckling of carbon nanotubes: a state of the art review. arXiv preprint arXiv: 11124839. 2011.

[37] Park S, Gao X. Bernoulli-Euler beam model based on a modified couple stress theory. Journal of Micromechanics and Microengineering (IOP Publishing); 2006;16(11):2355.

[38] Thai H-T. A nonlocal beam theory for bending, buckling, and vibration of nanobeams. International Journal of Engineering Science (Elsevier); 2012;52:56–64.

[39] Aydogdu M. A general nonlocal beam theory: its application to nanobeam bending, buckling and vibration. Physica E: Low-dimensional Systems and Nanostructures (Elsevier); 2009;41(9):1651–1655.

[40] Lu P, Lee H, Lu C, Zhang P. Application of nonlocal beam models for carbon nanotubes. International Journal of Solids and Structures (Elsevier); 2007;44(16):5289–5300.

[41] Adali S. Variational principles for multi-walled carbon nanotubes undergoing non-linear vibrations by semi-inverse method. Micro & Nano Letters (IET); 2009;4(4):198–203.

[42] Alshorbagy AE, Eltaher M, Mahmoud F. Static analysis of nanobeams using nonlocal FEM. Journal of Mechanical Science and Technology (Springer); 2013;27(7):2035–2041.

[43] Eltaher M, Alshorbagy AE, Mahmoud F. Vibration analysis of Euler-Bernoulli nano-beams by using finite element method. Applied Mathematical Modelling (Elsevier); 2013;37(7):4787–4797.

[44] Phadikar J, Pradhan S. Variational formulation and finite element analysis for nonlocal elastic nanobeams and nanoplates. Computational Materials Science (Elsevier); 2010;49(3):492–499.

[45] Ansari R, Hemmatnezhad M. Nonlinear vibrations of embedded multi-walled carbon nanotubes using a variational approach. Mathematical and Computer Modelling (Elsevier); 2011;53(5):927–938.

[46] Hemmatnezhad M, Ansari R. Finite element formulation for the free vibration analysis of embedded double-walled carbon nanotubes based on nonlocal Timoshenko beam theory. Journal of Theoretical and Applied Physics (Springer); 2013;7(1):1–10.

[47] Shakouri A, Lin R, Ng T. Free flexural vibration studies of double-walled carbon nanotubes with different boundary conditions and modeled as nonlocal Euler beams via the Galerkin method. Journal of Applied Physics (AIP Publishing); 2009;106(9): 094307.

[48] Dinçkal Ç. Free vibration analysis of carbon nanotubes by using finite element method. Iranian Journal of Science and Technology, Transactions of Mechanical Engineering (Springer); 2016;40(1):43–55.

[49] Ehteshami H, Hajabasi MA. Analytical approaches for vibration analysis of multi-walled carbon nanotubes modeled as multiple nonlocal Euler beams. Physica E: Low-dimensional Systems and Nanostructures (Elsevier); 2011;44(1):270–285.

[50] Zhang Y, Liu G, Xie X. Free transverse vibrations of double-walled carbon nanotubes using a theory of nonlocal elasticity. Physical Review B (APS); 2005;71(19):195404.

[51] Timoshenko S. History of strength of materials: with a brief account of the history of theory of elasticity and theory of structures. New York: McGraw-Hill; 1953.

6

Micromechanical Analysis of Polymer Fiber Composites under Tensile Loading by Finite Element Method

Ezgi Günay

Additional information is available at the end of the chapter

Abstract

In this chapter, the critical stress transfer factors of interface material have been studied under tensile loading. The polypropylene (PP) short fiber was embedded into the polypropylene co-ethylene (PPE) cylindrical interface first and then into the matrix material. Modified interface PPE material with lower elastic constant value than matrix material was used in our study. In this chapter, interface parameters affecting the stress transfer mechanism have been investigated. Finite element analysis (FEA) package (Ansys) has been used in the numerical modeling by using representative volume element (RVE). Tensile load was applied on one side of the composite cylinder as the other side of the composite is fixed. The critical stress-strain distributions are determined and presented by curves and tables for different fiber and interface diameters. For verification, the equivalent elastic material constants have been compared with the analytical solution and the results have been appropriate.

Keywords: FEA, representative volume element, fiber composite, stress transfer, interface, polymer

1. Introduction

There was considerable work on the determination of equivalent elastic constants of fiber-reinforced composites in the literature survey. The methods used in these studies can be summarized as follows: (i) numerical methods: finite difference and finite element method; (ii) analytical methods: semi-empirical Halpin-Tsai equation, rule of mixtures (ROM); and (iii) experimental studies in macro-, micro-, and nanoscales.

In the literature survey, studies proposing finite difference modeling and equivalent elastic properties of fiber composite structures were calculated in the consideration of the effect of fiber modulus E_f and aspect ratio (l/d) [1–6]. These studies were performed on the representative models according to both the multiple and single-fiber-reinforced material compositions.

Finite element method (FEM) is one of the most useful numerical methods in engineering problem-solving. Other methods such as the sublevel numerical procedures were additionally developed and used with FEM in solution phases. One of the main methods used was representative volume element (RVE) that used to predict the mechanical properties of unidirectional fiber composites. By using finite element analysis of RVE, effective elastic modulii of the composite were determined [7]. Experimental studies were also performed to support the numerical results [8]. Two-dimensional (unit cell method) and three-dimensional finite element analysis (FEA) with RVE was performed, and results were compared with the results of experimental studies in the literature [9–23]. Researchers often used the following FE commercial codes: ABAQUS [11, 12, 16, 19], ANSYS [17, 20], NASTRAN [13], and ALGOR-FEAS [9]. The numerically obtained results were compared and discussed with the analytical [2, 5, 14, 15, 21, 23] and experimental data in the literature survey [10, 14, 15, 18].

The aim of this study was to determine the stress and strain distributions in fiber, matrix, and fiber-matrix-interface in discontinuous fiber-matrix composite by using FEA. Each of the FE model consists of a polypropylene co-ethylene (PPE) matrix which contains a polypropylene fiber (PP) in it. In this study, 18 models were used and nine of them had also an interface volume. In this research, following six main concepts were presented by examining the single short fiber cylindrical bar within the matrix material under tensile loading for mechanical response.

1. By using RVE, testing the effectiveness of the finite element modeling procedures on the results, that is, mesh element types, meshing, definition and implementation of the boundary conditions, application of the tensile loading.

2. Considering the different volume fractions, testing the effectiveness of the various volume fraction of the fiber on the stress transfer mechanism from matrix to fiber material.

3. In terms of three-dimensional analysis, to investigate the influence of definition and modeling of interface volume between fiber and matrix in 3D.

4. In terms of three-dimensional analysis, examining the effects of fiber surface area on the stress transfer mechanism.

5. Establishing the explanations and curves for clarification the stress and strain localization at the ends of the fiber.

6. Calculating the equivalent elastic constant E_1.

2. The fiber-reinforced composite material with interface volume: modeling by representative volume element (RVE) method

Cylindrical RVE was used to represent the matrix and fiber all together. The different material properties of fiber, matrix, and interface were selected. The elastic constants of the polymer material were expressed as $E_m = 1.05$ GPa, $v_m = 0.33$, $E_f = 4.5$ GPa, $v_f = 0.2$, $E_i = 0.1 \times E_m = 0.105$ GPa [4], $v_i = 0.33$. Here, E_m, v_m, E_f, v_f, E_i, v_i reflected the Young's modulus and Poisson's ratio of the matrix, fiber, and interface materials, respectively. While the fiber material was composed of elastic polyethylene (PE), the matrix and interface materials were composed of bilinear material (PPE). The thickness t_i of the interface region was defined as $t_i = 0.025d$. Here, d was the diameter of the fiber. The shear modulus of the interface region was defined as $G_i = 0.1\ G_m$ [4]. In 3D composite modeling steps, nine different geometrical properties were used with variable thickness t_i, diameter d_i, and fiber volume fraction V_f as shown in **Table 1**. According to these different geometric values, fiber composite RVE was modeled by FEM and the stress-strain transmission conditions from fiber to interface and stress transfer from interface to matrix of the three types of materials were examined.

Fiber interface thickness $t_i (\mu m)$	Fiber diameter d (μm)	Fiber volume fraction V_f (%)	Rule of mixtures (L = ℓ), E_1 (GPa)
1	40	4.98	1.222
1.125	45	5.87	1.283
1.25	50	6.75	1.283
1.375	55	7.63	1.313
1.5	60	8.51	1.344
1.625	65	9.37	1.373
1.75	70	10.22	1.403
1.875	75	11.06	1.432
2	80	11.87	1.459

Table 1. PPE/PP single-fiber-matrix modeling according to the various interface geometric properties and analytical results of continuous $(L = \ \ell)$ fiber-matrix composite.

Fiber volume fraction values and the size of the material models were obtained by using the following equation [13];

$$V_f = \frac{\pi \ell d^2}{4 L S^2}$$

(1)

Here, ℓ, L, and S correspond to the fiber spacing, fiber length, and longitudinal fiber spacing, respectively, as shown in **Figure 1**.

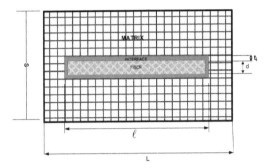

Figure 1. 2D geometrical parameters of the matrix/interface/fiber combination of PPE/PP microcomposite.

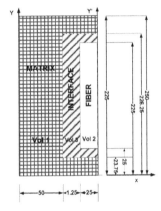

Figure 2. One of the typical geometrical descriptions of the polymer composite (matrix/interface/fiber, d = 50 μm) and generated volume numbers.

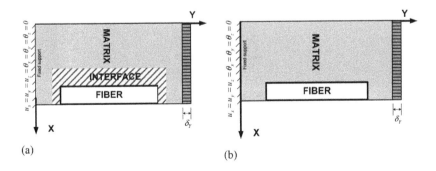

(a)

(b)

Figure 3. Two different RVE fiber composite geometries and applied displacement boundary conditions: (a) fiber, interface, and matrix combination; (b) fiber and matrix combination.

By rotating the 2D model 360° around the Y'-axis, 3D material models were obtained as shown in **Figure 2**. Cylindrical geometry was divided into two segments and one segment was used to demonstrate the results (**Figures 2** and **3**). In general, the cylindrical geometry was defined in cylindrical coordinates (r, θ, z). In Ansys, modeling (x, y, z) Cartesian coordinate axes refers to the (r, θ, z) in the cylindrical coordinate system. However, in this study, all of the results and Ansys code screen outputs were demonstrated only on the x-y plane of the projected surface for one half of the cylindrical geometry.

2.1. Analytical formulation.

The aim of the micromechanical approaches was to determine the equivalent elastic constants of composite material considering individual elastic constants constituting the composite material. The equivalent elastic constants $\left(E_1, E_2, G_{12}, v_{12}\right)$ of the fiber-reinforced-composite have been determined analytically in terms of the relative volume fractions $\left(V_f, V_m\right)$ and elastic constants $\left(E_f, E_m, G_f, G_m, v_f, v_m\right)$ of fiber and matrix. It may be mentioned two basic analytical approaches in micromechanics of continuous fiber-matrix composite materials in obtaining the equivalent elastic constants. The first one was the rule of mixtures (ROM), and the second one was the Halpin-Tsai semi-empirical model [24, 25]. The first model "rule of mixtures" defined as the mathematical expressions that give the elastic properties of the continuous fiber composite material in terms of original material properties, volume fiber fraction, and arrangement of its constituents: (a) the apparent Young's modulus in the same direction as the fibers (E_1) (Eq. (2)), (b) the apparent Young's modulus in the direction perpendicular to the fibers (E_2) (Eq. (3)), (c) the major Poisson's ratio (v_{12}) (Eq. (4)), and (d) the in-plane shear modulus (G_{12}) of a lamina (Eq. (5)). Rule of mixtures (ROM) equations have been listed and shown as the formulas below:

$$E_1 = E_f V_f + E_m \left(1 - V_f\right) \tag{2}$$

$$E_2 = \frac{E_f E_m}{V_m E_f + V_f E_m} \tag{3}$$

$$v_{12} = V_f v_f + v_m \left(1 - V_f\right) \tag{4}$$

$$G_{12} = \frac{G_m G_f}{V_m G_f + V_f G_m} \tag{5}$$

The second model "Halpin-Tsai" included the expressions obtained by curve fitting as: (a) the apparent Young's modulus in the same direction as the fibers (E_1) (Eq. (6)), (b) the apparent

Young's modulus in the direction perpendicular to the fibers (E_2) (Eq. (7)), (c) the major Poisson's ratio (v_{12}) (Eq. (8)), and (d) the in-plane shear modulus (G_{12}) (Eq. (9)) of a single layer of layered composite "ply." These related equations have been listed and shown below:

$$E_1 = E_f V_f + E_m V_m \tag{6}$$

$$\frac{E_2}{E_m} = \left[\frac{1 + \xi \eta V_f}{1 - \eta V_f}\right] \quad \eta = \frac{\left[\dfrac{E_f}{E_m}\right] - 1}{\left[\dfrac{E_f}{E_m}\right] + \xi} \tag{7}$$

$$v_{12} = V_f v_f + v_m V_m \tag{8}$$

$$\frac{G_{12}}{G_m} = \frac{1 + \xi \eta V_f}{1 - \eta V_f} \quad \eta = \frac{\left[\dfrac{G_f}{G_m}\right] - 1}{\left[\dfrac{G_f}{G_m}\right] + \xi} \tag{9}$$

The reinforcing factor (ξ), measuring reinforcement of the composite, is variable depending on the fiber geometry, packing geometry, and loading condition. It is a measure of reinforcement of the composite. The values of ξ have been obtained by comparing the Eqs. (7) and (8) with exact elasticity solutions, and corresponding curve fitting results. The generalized Hooke's law equation is as follows:

$$\sigma_i = C_{ij} \varepsilon_j \tag{10}$$

In this equation, σ_i is the stress vector, C_{ij} is the stiffness matrix, and ε_i is the strain vector components. In functional form, C_{ij} has been represented by Eq. (11) in terms of the elastic properties of the fiber, matrix, relative volume fractions of fiber and matrix.

$$C_{ij} = C_{ij}\left(E_f, v_f, V_f, E_m, v_m, V_m\right) \tag{11}$$

In most literature studies, the basic analytical approaches have been presented without taking into account the adhesion of the interface across the end faces of the fibers and the stress concentration effects at the fiber ends [2, 26, 27].

3. Finite element modeling of short fiber in microcomposite and analyses results

In the literature survey, a detailed examination on fiber-reinforced polymer matrix composites was observed in determining the most suitable fiber-matrix combination model. In the literature, different studies were found about tension/compression and shear loading to the different modeling types of fiber/interface/matrix combinations, and in these studies, the strength of the applied tensile/compression and shear loading types have been investigated. In this research, the stress transfer mechanism and equivalent elastic constants of short fiber composites were tried to be obtained by using new modeling. In FE modeling, the design criteria were as follows: the dimensions of fiber and matrix, the material types of fiber and matrix, the dimensions and material types of interface volume and the application of the tensile load. In the first stage of the study, a single short fiber was studied with ANSYS code in determining the optimum interface thickness by comparing the results obtained. In this step, two different models were tested. The first one was fiber-matrix microcomposite with interface (**Figure 3a**); the second model was fiber-matrix microcomposite without interface (**Figure 3b**). In the second stage of the study, the effects of interface volumes on the values of stress distributions around the tip points of the fiber were attempted to explain. In the calculation of the single-fiber modeling, nine different interface thicknesses t_i and nine different fiber diameters d_i were used $t_i = 0.025\ d_i$, $(d_i = 40, 45, ..., 80\ \mu m)$. In this study, the interface volume was defined around all of the faces of the fiber. In the literature, the studies were performed by defining the interface surface or volume along the longitudinal surface (**Figure 3**).

Fiber diameter d (μm)	Number of mesh elements and nodes in the fiber-interface-matrix model (SHELL93)	Elastic constant E_1 (GPa) (fiber-interface-matrix model)	Number of mesh elements and nodes in the fiber-matrix model (SHELL93)	Elastic constant E_1 (GPa) (fiber-matrix model)
40	31,776/93,823	1.472	2271/6680	1.054
45	16,520/48,859	1.465	2475/7238	1.056
50	11,503/33,926	1.459	2474/7237	1.057
55	33,190/98,585	1.449	2543/7438	1.081
60	33,155/98,478	1.446	2559/7486	1.063
65	21,104/62,686	1.415	2957/8668	1.066
70	14,298/42,267	1.428	2998/8795	1.065
75	15,029/44,458	1.441	3103/9110	1.035
80	15,604/46,171	1.411	3229/9480	1.047

Table 2. The used geometric parameters, mesh elements, node numbers, and obtained elastic constants of discontinuous $(L)\ell$ fiber-matrix microcomposite.

In this study, the short single-fiber composite polymer (PPE/PP) material was modeled in microlevel by finite element method (FEM). Single-fiber arrangement in matrix under the axial loading was adequate to explain the overall characteristics of the fiber composite structures. SHELL93 as ANSYS element type was used. This element has 6 degree of freedom per node $\left(u_x, u_y, u_z, \theta_x, \theta_y, \theta_z\right)$. The generated FE models for nine different geometries have different total number of mesh elements and node numbers. Exact number of elements and nodes corresponding to the composite models has been summarized in **Table 2**.

Composite model consists of three volume sections representing the fiber matrix and interface (**Figure 4**). The first boundary condition of the model was applied by fixing one end of the geometry, and this was performed by setting the 6 degree of freedom of each node to zero (BC_1).

The second boundary condition of the model was related with the loading condition. The second end of the composite cylinder was pulled with a constant load. The loading magnitude applied to the nodes was $P = 0.1$ N. In this application, because of the unsymmetrical meshing system, the resultant deformation of the bar was obtained as unsymmetrical. In order to overcome this difficulty, second boundary condition was applied to the second end of the cylinder. On this face along the loading application thickness or level $\left(t_{app}\right)$, the "unit displacement" $U_y = 0.1$ μm was adopted to each node to obtain the symmetric displacement condition over the whole body $\left(1\ \mu m \le t_{app} \le 2\ \mu m\right)$ (BC_2) (**Figure 3**). The stress concentration regions were developed between the fiber and matrix at the sharp edge corners as shown in **Figures 5–8**. Fiber-matrix model showed higher stress concentrations than fiber-matrix-interface model. In order to give more explanation to the developing stress distributions on these faces, the third boundary condition was applied (BC_3). The previously defined first- and second-type boundary conditions were applied over the extremely large sections of the body $\left(20\ \mu m \le t_{app} \le 26\ \mu m\right)$, and new stress distribution results were obtained (**Figures 9** and **10**).

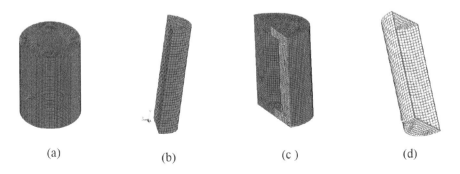

(a)   (b)   (c)   (d)

Figure 4. FEA meshing with SHELL93 element (a) RVE of fiber cylindrical composite model, (b) fiber, (c) matrix, and (d) interface.

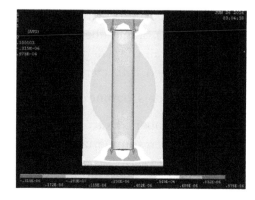

Figure 5. Stress (σ_y) distribution on the matrix section obtained from FEA nodal solution without interface region ($d = 40$ μm).

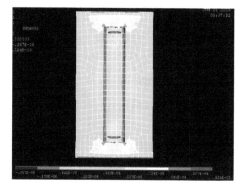

Figure 6. Stress (σ_y) distribution on the matrix section obtained from FEA element solution without interface region ($d = 40$ μm).

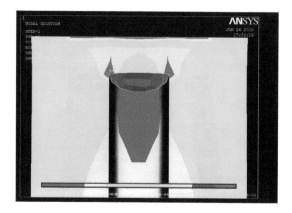

Figure 7. Stress (σ_y) intensity on the matrix section obtained from FEA element solution without interface region ($d = 40$ μm).

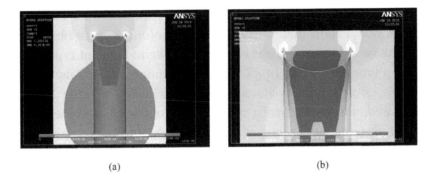

(a)   (b)

Figure 8. Stress (σ_y) intensity developing on the matrix section (a) with interface region, (b) without interface region ($d = 80\ \mu m$).

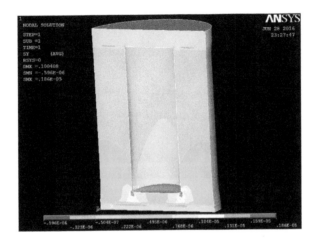

Figure 9. FE results for the BC_2, $\left(\sigma_y\right)$ stress localization which is parallel to the applied displacement loading δ_y and generated around the sharp corners of the fiber–matrix model without interface region ($d = 80\ \mu m$).

Figures 5–7 have been represented the σ_y distribution developing within the composite model in matrix segment with noninterface case for the fiber diameter $d = 40\ \mu m$ [2]. The stress distributions were defined for both nodal and elemental solutions. The developing stress localizations appeared around the tip sections of the fiber in matrix. The developing maximum stress distributions were intensified around the fiber end sections. At the same region around the neighborhood sections of the fiber segment, stress levels reached to relatively lower stress localizations in comparison with maximum. This stress distribution was wide spread around the maximum stress localization in a definite region. Normal stress value reached to their secondarily largest value around the middle section of the fiber in matrix material. Additionally, nodal solution curves gave better results than elemental solution. In nodal solution, stress localizations appeared in a narrower region with longer segments. In finite element analysis, element solutions were obtained by Gauss quadrature integration points. Nodal solution results were determined at the coordinates of the nodal points by interpolation functions.

Gauss integration points have been defined at the inner section of the elements which were not coincided with nodal coordinates. These element solutions were obtained by using the interpolating functions in the curvilinear coordinate system. Element types varied according to the interpolation functions used. In the generated composite models, the generated total number of elements, nodes, and the obtained results were listed in **Table 2**. When the number of elements increased, the most correct results were obtained. For these processes, high-capacity computer systems were required. Stress distributions developing on the fiber and matrix sections without interface volume were presented in **Figures 11** and **12**. In these figures, stress localizations were developed on both matrix and fiber surfaces.

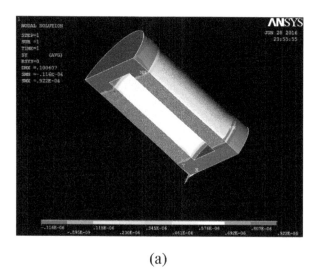

(a)

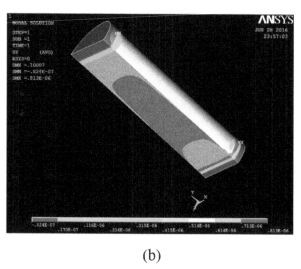

(b)

Figure 10. FE results for the BC_3, $\left(\sigma_y\right)$ stress localization on the (a) matrix and (b) fiber which are parallel to the applied displacement loading δ_y and generated above the sharp corners of the fiber–matrix model without interface region ($d = 75\mu m$).

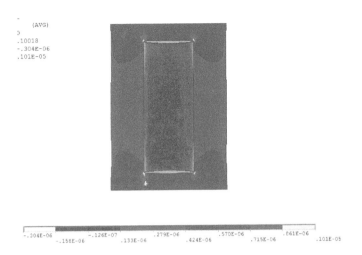

Figure 11. FEA stress $\left(\sigma_y\right)$ distribution developing on the matrix section of the fiber-matrix model without interface region ($d = 80~\mu$m).

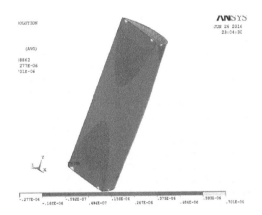

Figure 12. Stress (σ_y) distribution on the fiber section obtained from the FEA without interface region ($d = 80~\mu$m).

As the fiber diameter decreased, the stress distributions collected at the end surface of the cylindrical fiber material grown locally. When the stress localizations reduced in the interface region between matrix and fiber at the same time, higher stresses in fiber section has emerged. As it has shown by **Figures 13** and **14**, in the polymer fiber model with an interface region, the maximum stress value was $\sigma_y = 0.952 \times 10^{-6}$ N/μm^2, and in the polymer fiber model without interface, maximum stress developing on the fiber was equal to $\sigma_y = 0.732 \times 10^{-6}$ N/μm^2($d = 40~\mu$m). On the other hand, in the model with an interface, matrix sections near to the fiber had the value $\sigma_y = 0.265 \times 10^{-6}$ N/μm^2, and in the noninterface model, stress value was $\sigma_y = 0.429 \times 10^{-6}$ N/μm^2 (**Figures 15** and **16**) ($d = 40~\mu$m).

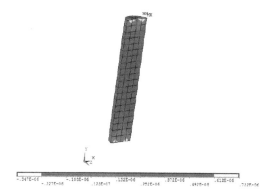

Figure 13. FEA stress $\left(\sigma_y\right)$ distribution developing on the fiber section of the fiber-matrix model without interface region ($d = 40\ \mu$m).

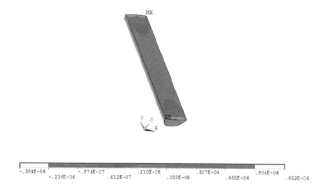

Figure 14. FEA (σ_y) distribution developing on the fiber section of the fiber-matrix model with interface region ($d = 40\ \mu$m).

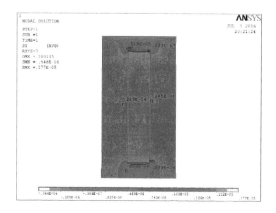

Figure 15. Stress $\left(\sigma_y\right)$ distribution developing on the matrix section of the fiber-matrix model with interface ($d = 40\ \mu$m).

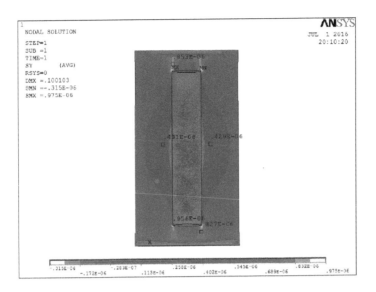

Figure 16. Stress $\left(\sigma_y\right)$ distribution developing on the matrix section of the fiber-matrix model without interface $(d = 40\ \mu m)$.

When the models were analyzed in terms of interface thicknesses, in the models with thicker interface, the stress was found to be more. The interface region with the largest diameter had the largest stress σ_y and Von Mises stress σ_2 distributions relative to the smallest one. These were equal to $\sigma_y = 0.130 \times 10^{-5}\ N/\mu m^2$ (**Figure 17**) and $\sigma_2 = 0.132 \times 10^{-5}\ N/\mu m^2$ (**Figure 18**) for $d = 40\ \mu m$ and $\sigma_y = 0.08967\ N/\mu m^2$ (**Figure 19**) and $\sigma_2 = 0.233 \times 10^{-5}\ N/\mu m^2$ (**Figure 20**) for $d = 80\ \mu m$. Having studied the **Figures 21** and **22**, it was seen that the maximum stress distributions are developed at the tip corner sections of the interface geometries. Nodal solution results of $\sigma_y = 0.149 \times 10^{-5}\ N/\mu m^2$ for $d = 40\ \mu m$ and $\sigma_y = 0.154 \times 10^{-5}\ N/\mu m^2$ for $d = 80\ \mu m$ were obtained.

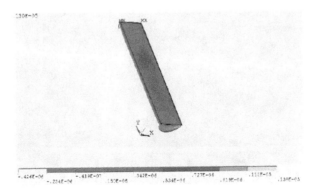

Figure 17. FEA $\left(\sigma_y\right)$ distribution developing on the interface section of the fiber–matrix model $(d = 40\ \mu m)$.

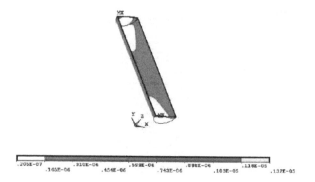

Figure 18. FEA Von Mises $\left(\sigma_2\right)$ distribution developing on the interface section ($d = 40\ \mu$m).

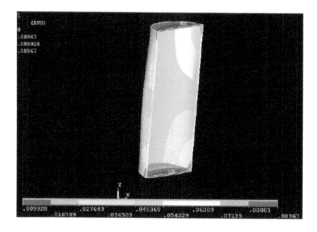

Figure 19. Stress (σ_y) distribution on the interface section obtained from FEA nodal solution ($d = 80\ \mu$m).

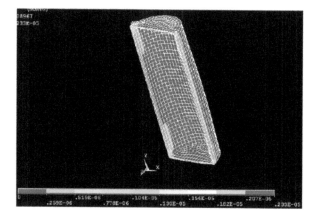

Figure 20. Von Mises $\left(\sigma_2\right)$ stress distribution on the interface section obtained from FEA nodal solution ($d = 80\ \mu$m).

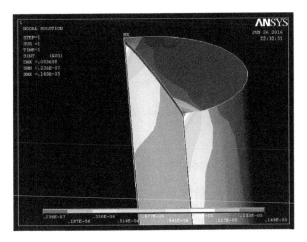

Figure 21. Stress intensity on the interface section ($d = 40 \ \mu$m).

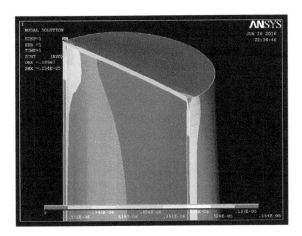

Figure 22. Stress intensity on the interface section ($d = 80 \ \mu$m).

For nine different interface geometries, FEA results were represented by curves. These curves included the results for the fiber diameters between 40 and 80 μm, and corresponding thicknesses were $t_i = 0.025(40) = 1, ..., t_i = 0.025(80) = 2$ (**Table 1**). The overall stress-strain distributions developed in the composite were affected by the thicknesses of the interface region, and these were proportional to the fiber diameter. As it has shown by **Figure 23**, the largest interface stresses were developed in the models with the diameters $d = 40 \ \mu$m and $d = 55 \ \mu$m. As the interface grew in diameter, the interface stresses became diminished from 6.9×10^{-7} to 5.5×10^{-7} N/μm^2. **Figure 23** presents the suddenly changed stress intensity values at the tip points of the fiber. Shear stress distributions τ_{xy} and τ_{yz} along the main axis Y' (**Figure 2**) were shown with curves. In **Figures 24** and **25**, shear stresses were found to be changed suddenly around the corner sections of the fiber end portion. The largest shearing stresses in fiber-reinforced microcomposites have been developed with the largest diameters. In summary,

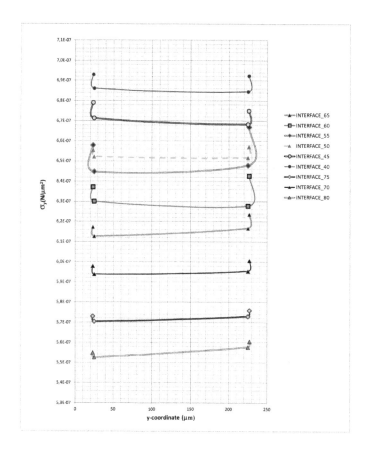

Figure 23. FEA results for σ_y stress distributions on nine different interface regions of the fiber-matrix (RVE) under tensile load.

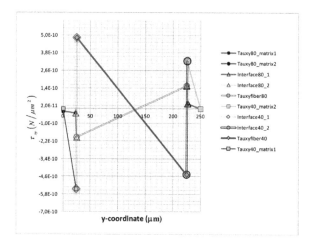

Figure 24. Comparison of stress $\left(\tau_{xy}\right)$ distributions along the main y-axis of the fiber composite in microscale for the fiber diameters $d = 40\ \mu$m and $d = 80\ \mu$m.

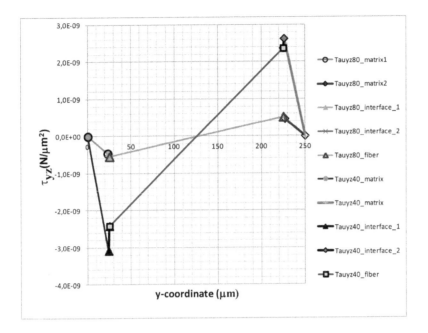

Figure 25. Comparison of stress $\left(\tau_{yz}\right)$ distributions along the main y-axis of the fiber composite in microscale for the fiber diameters $d = 40\ \mu m$ and $d = 80\ \mu m$.

$$\left|\tau_{xy}\right|_{max} = 5.8 \times 10^{-10}\ \text{N}/\mu m^2 \quad d = 40\ \mu m \tag{12}$$

$$\left|\tau_{xy}\right|_{max} = 3.5 \times 10^{-10}\ \text{N}/\mu m^2 \quad d = 80\ \mu m \tag{13}$$

$$\left|\tau_{yz}\right|_{max} = 3.0 \times 10^{-9}\ \text{N}/\mu m^2 \quad d = 40\ \mu m \tag{14}$$

$$\left|\tau_{yz}\right|_{max} = 0.5 \times 10^{-9}\ \text{N}/\mu m^2 \quad d = 80\ \mu m \tag{15}$$

The stress-strain $\sigma_y - \varepsilon_y$ curves were plotted in FE models for diameters $d = 40\ \mu m$, $d = 70\ \mu m$, and $d = 80\ \mu m$. These are presented in **Figure 26**. From the slopes of these curves, the elastic constant values parallel to the fiber and loading direction $\left(E_1\right)$ were obtained and results are listed in **Table 2** for both fiber-matrix and fiber-interface-matrix models. These models have provided an opinion to the resultant data for $\left(E_1\right)$. FE model for the short fiber composite without interface case gave the value as $\left(E_1\right)_{avg} = 1.058$ GPa, and for the short fiber composite with interface case, it was $\left(E_1\right)_{avg} = 1.446$ GPa.

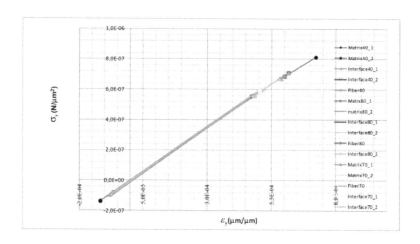

Figure 26. Stress-strain curves of FE-RVE models for fiber diameters $d = 40\ \mu$m, $d = 75\ \mu$m and $d = 80\ \mu$m.

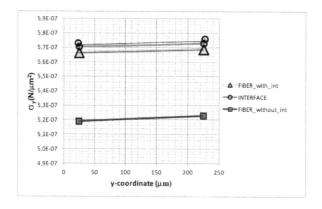

Figure 27. Comparison of stress distributions $\left(\sigma_y\right)$ obtained from the interface segment of the RVE-FE model ($d = 75\ \mu$m): (a) fiber with interface, (b) interface, (c) fiber without interface.

Figure 27 presented the comparison of σ_y distribution for (a) fiber without interface, (b) interface, and (c) fiber with interface regions. As it has shown in the curve for $d = 75\ \mu$m, fiber with interface and also interface region stresses were near to each other in magnitudes 5.7×10^{-7} N/μm^2. In case, fiber without interface showed the σ_y distribution around 5.2×10^{-7} N/μm^2. The difference between them was equal to 0.5×10^{-7} N/μm^2.

4. Discussion and conclusion

The effectiveness of the imposed interface volume and its geometric properties on the homogeneously distributed stress components in the polymer type fiber composites have been shown in this study by using finite element method.

The results obtained from this study were summarized as below::

1. The developing stress concentrations at the fiber-interface and interface-matrix common surfaces showed that the increase in fiber content was inversely proportional to the reduction in stress values.

2. Fiber volume fraction range from 4.98 to 11.87 was examined. Although the generated number of elements was different in the FE modeling of fiber composite structures, the obtained results of analysis were converged to the definite values. In the examined fiber volume fractions, the numerically calculated elastic constant values changed in small degree. The distribution of all values obtained from FEM was calculated in terms of polynomials, so that all resultant values were followed the polynomial properties.

3. In the FE modeling, the thickness of the interface region was changed in proportional to the fiber diameter and then obtained resultant elastic constant remained in a stable range. The total changes for fiber-interface-matrix and fiber-matrix models were obtained as 0.046 and 0.061 GPa mutually.

4. The application of the mechanical load per node $\left(P = 0.1 \times 10^{-4}\,\text{N}\right)$ gave the elastic constants 1.39 and 1.18 GPa for fiber and matrix sections of the $d = 80\ \mu m$ microcomposite by Ansys code FE analysis. While the applied load affected the entire combined structure, some portions of the stress were transferred to the other sections of the composite body. Therefore, the original individual material properties of the composite material could not be measured after loading stage.

5. The maximum developing stress distribution was seen on the composite fiber section while the maximum developing y-displacement u_y was developed on the composite matrix section.

6. The generated mesh system was not symmetric in composite cylinder transverse cross sections. The developing displacement distribution u_y on the composite fiber section showed symmetric configuration in the center of the main axis $\left(P = 0.1 \times 10^{-4} N\right)$ (**Figure 28**). The developing displacement distribution u_y in the composite matrix section localized at the end portions of the matrix portion of the cylinder.

7. In the analysis, the fiber in the matrix material was moved along the y-axis under tensile loading. The fiber material was deformed by the help of stress transmission from matrix to fiber. The role of the difference in Young's modulus and Poisson's ratio of the fiber and matrix material on deformation analysis should be considered (**Figure 29**).

8. In this study, it was determined that the fiber content of fiber/interface/matrix composition was significant in the stress distribution in all PPE/PP composite models and this was confirmed by using FEA. With less fiber content ($V_f\%$), stress concentration at the fiber-matrix interface was found to be larger.

9.   When three layers of the composite compared, the fiber material carried higher stresses than the interface and the interface material carried higher stresses than the matrix. This was displayed as $\left(\sigma_y^{fiber} \geq \sigma_y^{interface} \geq \sigma_y^{matrix}\right)$.

10. According to our study, when high fiber content in the matrix material was present, the matrix material decreased and the stress transfer mechanism in this case was broken (**Table 2**).

11. In our analysis work, the obtained results of stress distributions were applied for all models of discontinuous fiber embedded into the matrix material. The stress distribution results obtained from discontinuous fiber were compared with continuous fiber analytical results for the commercial engineering applications (**Tables 1** and **2**).

12. In this research, the end-face effect of the fiber was considered by placing interface in the ends.

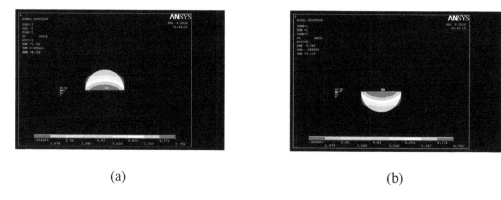

(a)   (b)

Figure 28. Comparison of stress distributions $\left(\sigma_y\right)$ obtained from the cross section of the RVE FE model for mechanical load ($d = 80\ \mu$m): (a) fiber without interface volume 1, (b) fiber without interface volume 2.

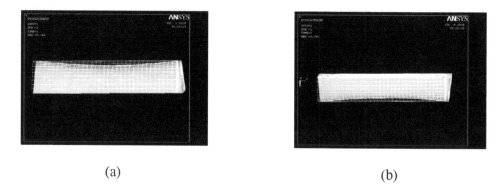

(a)   (b)

Figure 29. Comparison of displacement distributions (deformed/undeformed shapes) of the fiber obtained from the cross section of the RVE FE model ($d = 80\ \mu$m): (a) fiber without interface volume 1, (b) fiber without interface volume 2 (force loading $Force/Node = 0.1$ N).

Three main conclusions obtained from this research were evaluated for the values of the matrix/fiber diameters and their effect on the equivalent elastic constant.

The first conclusion was presented by the comparison curve that plotted by the "linear trendline curve" representing the average differences between two FE models. The relative percentage change of the equivalent elastic constant value E_1 in the two main models was decreased as the diameter increased proportionally (**Table 2** and **Figure 30**). Adding the interface with the small diameter fiber into the cylinder strengthens the composite structure.

The second conclusion was described in the fiber-matrix models. The diameter of the fiber increased from 40 to 55 μm in an order. As a result of this application, the equivalent elastic constant of the composite cylinder E_1 was increased from 1.054 to 1.081 GPa in proportion. The decrease in elastic modulus value E_1 was obtained from 1.063 to 1.047 GPa in a nonlinear manner for the diameter ranges from 60 to 80 μm.

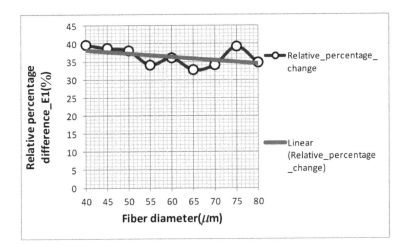

Figure 30. Comparison E_1 between fiber-matrix and fiber-interface-matrix FE models.

The third conclusion was explained for the fiber-interface-matrix model. As the diameter increased from 40 to 65 μm, the equivalent elastic constant E_1 of the microcomposite decreased from 1.472 to 1.415 GPa linearly. However, the decrease in elastic modulus value E_1 between the diameters 70 and 80 μm was obtained as 1.428 and 1.411 GPa in a nonlinear manner.

These results explained us that within the limits of 4.98–9.37% fiber volume fraction, proportionally increased interface volume caused the linearly decreasing elastic modulus value E_1.

Within the same limits, the fiber-matrix microcomposite had a linearly increasing value. The interface volume worked as a brake in the composite system. The interface volume reduced the stresses passing from matrix to fiber, and this region worked as a damper in a spring-damper mechanical system. For the fiber volume, fraction ranges from 1022 to 11.87%, the interface volume caused a nonlinear decreasing in the equivalent elastic modulus values, and similarly, the fiber-matrix microcomposite had a decreasing value as nonlinear.

In other words, the physical meaning of the fiber matrix interaction behaviors was dependent on the interface volume. Interface volume caused a general linearity between the dimensions of the fiber, matrix, and the calculated equivalent elastic constant value (**Table 1**).

As a future work,, the effects of dimensional properties of composite models obtained in this study can be introduced into semi-empirical model (Halpin-Tsai) based on elasticity equations by curve fitting.

Acknowledgements

Thanks for the great supports of FIGES and BAP project under grant no. 06/2011-57. This study was performed in Department of Mechanical Engineering, Gazi University, Ankara, Turkey.

Nomenclature

Symbols

C_{ij} elastic constants matrix $\left(\mathrm{N/m}^2\right)$

d diameter of the fiber $(\mu\mathrm{m})$

$E_1,\left(E_1\right)_{avg}$ equivalent Young's modulus and average equivalent Young's modulus parallel to fiber direction $\left(\mathrm{N/m}^2\right)$

E_2 Young's modulus perpendicular to the fiber $\left(\mathrm{N/m}^2\right)$

E_f, E_m, E_i Young's modulus of fiber, matrix, and interface materials $\left(\mathrm{N/m}^2\right)$

G_f, G_m, G_i Shear modulus of fiber, matrix, and interface materials $\left(\mathrm{N/m}^2\right)$

G_{12} in-plane shear modulus $\left(\mathrm{N/m}^2\right)$

ℓ length of the fiber $(\mu\mathrm{m})$

L length of the matrix $(\mu\mathrm{m})$

P force loading (N)

S diameter of cylindrical matrix segment $(\mu\mathrm{m})$

t_i thickness of the interface tubular volume $(\mu\mathrm{m})$

t_{app} loaded thickness of the composite cylinder $(\mu\mathrm{m})$

U_y displacement type loading $(\mu\mathrm{m})$

| u_x, u_y, u_z | displacements parallel to the x, y, z directions in an order (μm) |
| V_f, V_m | fiber and matrix volume fractions |

Greek symbols

ν_f, ν_m	Poisson's ratio of fiber and matrix
ν_{12}	major in-plane ratio
ξ	reinforcing factor
σ_i	stress vector $\left(N/\mu m^2\right)$
σ_y, y	-directional stress component $\left(N/\mu m^2\right)$
σ_2	Von Mises stress component $\left(N/\mu m^2\right)$
ε_i	strain vector
$\theta_x, \theta_y, \theta_z$	displacements parallel to the x, y, z directions in an order (rad).

Author details

Ezgi Günay

Address all correspondence to: ezgigunay@gazi.edu.tr

Department of Mechanical Engineering, Gazi University, Maltepe, Ankara, Turkey

References

[1] Termonia Y. Computer model for the elastic properties of short fibre and particulate filled polymers. Journal of Materials Science. 1987;22:1733–1736.

[2] Termonia Y. Theoretical study of the stress transfer in single fibre composites. Journal of Materials Science. 1987;22:504–508.

[3] Termonia Y. Fibre coating as a means to compensate for poor adhesion in fiber-reinforced materials. Journal of Materials Science. 1990;25:103–106.

[4]   Termonia Y. Effect of strain rate on the mechanical properties of composites with a weak fibre/matrix interface. Journal of Materials Science. 1992;27:4878–4882.

[5]   Termonia Y. Tensile strength of discontinuous fibre-reinforced composites. Journal of Materials Science. 1990;25:4644–4653.

[6]   Termonia Y. Dependence of fibre critical length on modulus in single-fibre composites. Journal of Materials Science Letters. 1993;12:732–733.

[7]   Sun CT, Vaidya RS. Prediction of composite properties from a representative volume element. Composites Science and Technology. 1996;56:171–179.

[8]   Li VC, Kanda T, Lin Z. The influence of fiber/matrix interface properties on complementary energy and composite damage tolerance. In: Proceedings of 3rd Conference on Fracture and Strength of Solid, December 1997; Hong Kong.

[9]   Kang GZ, Gao Q. Tensile properties of randomly oriented short δ-Al_2O_3 fiber reinforced aluminum alloy composites: II. Finite element analysis for stress transfer, elastic modulus and stress-strain curve. Composites Part A. 2002;33:657–667.

[10] Houshyar S, Shanks RA, Hodzic A. The effect of fiber concentration on mechanical and thermal properties of fiber-reinforced polypropylene composites. Journal of Applied Polymer Science. 2005;96:2260–2272. doi:10.1002/app.20874

[11] Hbaieb K, Wang, QX, Chia YHJ, Cotterell B. Modelling stiffness of polymer/clay nanocomposites. Polymer. 2007;48:901–909. doi:10.1016/j.polymer.2006.11.062

[12] Lee SH, Wang S, Pharr GM, Xu H. Evaluation of interphase properties in a cellulose fiber-reinforced polypropylene composite by nanoindentation and finite element analysis. Composites: Part A. 2007;38:1517–1524. doi:10.1016/j.compositesa.2007.01.007

[13] Houshyar S, Shanks RA. Hodzic A. Modelling of polypropylene fiber-matrix composites using finite element analysis. Express Polymer Letters. 2009;3(1):2–12. doi:10.3144/expresspolymett.2009.2

[14] Kim BR, Lee HK. An RVE-based micromechanical analysis of fiber-reinforced composites considering fiber size dependency. Composite Structures. 2009;90:418–427. doi:10.1016/j.compstruct.2009.04.025.

[15] Porfiri M, Gupta N. Effect of volume fraction and wall thickness on the elastic properties of hollow particle filled composites. Composites: Part B. 2009;40:166–173. doi:10.1016/j.compositesb.2008.09.002

[16] Pan Y, Pelegri AA. Influence of matrix plasticity and residual thermal stress on interfacial debonding of a single fiber composite. Journal of Mechanics of Materials and Structures. 2010;5(1):129–142.

[17] Pal B, Haseebuddin MR. Analytical estimation of elastic properties of polypropylene fiber matrix composite by finite element analysis. Advances in Materials Physics and Chemistry. 2012;2:23–30. doi:org/10.4236/ampc.2012.21004

[18] Sockalingam S, Nilakantan G. Fiber-matrix interface characterization through the microbond test. International Journal of Aeronautical and Space Sciences. 2012;13(3): 282–295. doi:10.5139/IJASS.2012.13.3.282

[19] Qing H. A new theoretical model of the quasistatic single-fiber pullout problem: analysis of stress field. Mechanics of Materials. 2013;60:66–79. doi:org/10.1016/j.mechmat.2013.01.006

[20] Sai VS, Satyanarayana MRS, Murthy VBK, Rao GS, Prasad AS. An experimental simulation to validate FEM to predict transverse Young's modulus of FRP composites. Hindawi Publishing. Corporation Advances in Materials Science and Engineering Article. ID 648527, 1–6, 2013. doi:org/10.1155/2013/648527

[21] Unterweger C, Brüggemann O, Fürst C. Effects of different fibers on the properties of short-fiber-reinforced polypropylene composites. Composites Science and Technology. 2014;103:49–55. doi:org/10.1016/j.compscitech.2014.08.014

[22] Alfonso I, Iglesias VR, Figueroa IA. Computational potentialities of the finite elements method for the modeling and simulation of composite materials: a review. Revista Materia. 2015;20(2):293–303. doi:10.1590/S1517-707620150002.0030

[23] Chang WX, Qing H, Gao CF. A new theoretical model of the quasistatic single-fiber pull-out problem: a rate-dependent interfacial bond strength. Mechanics of Materials. 2016;94:132–141. doi:org/10.1016/j.mechmat.2015.12.001

[24] Jones RM. Mechanics of composite materials. New York: (Taylor &Francis Group) CRC Press; 1998. 538 p.

[25] Paul B. Prediction of elastic constants of multiphase materials. Transactions of the Metallurgical Society of AIME. 1960;218:36–41.

[26] Cox HL. The elasticity and strength of paper and fibrous materials. Search Results British Journal of Applied Physics. 1952;3(72):72–79.

[27] Günay E, Ece Z, Esi MA. A comparative study of fiber-matrix interactions by using micromechanical models. Mechanics of Composite Materials. 2008;44(4):505–520. doi: 10.1007/s11029-008-9027-8

Estimation of Shallow Water Flow Based on Kalman Filter FEM

Takahiko Kurahashi, Taichi Yoshiara and
Yasuhide Kobayashi

Additional information is available at the end of the chapter

Abstract

In this chapter, we present numerical examples of an estimation of shallow water flow based on Kalman filter finite element method (Kalman filter FEM). Shallow water equations are adopted as the governing equations. The Galerkin method, using triangular elements, is employed to discretize the governing equation in space, and the selective lumping method is used to discretize time. We describe the influence on the numerical results of setting the observation points.

Keywords: Kalman filter FEM, shallow water equation, Galerkin method, selective lumping method

1. Introduction

Conventionally, shallow water flow analysis based on the FEM has been carried out to investigate the marine environment, specifically coastal drift sand, storm surges, tsunamis, and so on [1, 2]. However, the computed results are rarely close to the observed values if the appropriate governing equation is not employed, the appropriate discretization technique is not applied to the governing equation, or the boundary conditions are not defined appropriately. This has prompted a great deal of inverse analysis in recent years, aiming to obtain flow fields that more closely approach the observed values. Boundary control analysis is one of these inverse analytic techniques, in which an unknown boundary condition is numerically determined by iterative computation such that the computed water elevation homes in on the target value or the observed value [3, 4]. Deterministic methods such as the adjoint variable or sensitivity equation methods are commonly employed. On the other hand, the stochastic approach has also been adopted, in which estimation of the flow field is employed using a Kalman filter. Removal of the noise data from the observed values and the flow field estimation are also performed. Conventionally, flow fields are estimated using Kalman filter FEM, and this method is applied to the practical coastal model [5, 6]. However, the effect of boundary conditions on the estimated flow field has not been investigated. This prompted us to research and describe in detail in this chapter the formulation of Kalman filter FEM and numerical experiments for flow estimation when changing the positions of observation points [7].

2. Concept of state estimation

In the Kalman filter, system and observation equations are employed. Eqs. (1) and (2) are sample equations:

$$\phi^{n+1} = a\phi^n + q^n \tag{1}$$

$$z^{n+1} = \phi^{n+1} + r^{n+1} \tag{2}$$

where φ, z, a, q, and r indicate the true value of the state variable, the observation value, the constant coefficient, the system, and the observation noise, respectively. n denotes the number of time steps. **Figure 1** shows relationship between the observation and the estimation values.

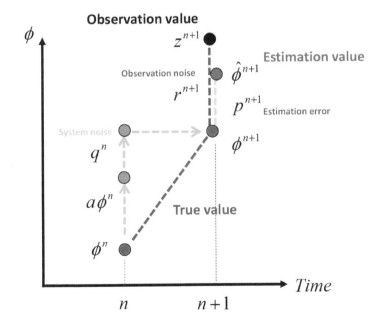

Figure 1. Diagram of the relationship between the observation and the estimation values.

Here, $\hat{\phi}$ and p indicate the estimation value for the state variable and estimation error. From **Figure 1**, it is found that the estimation value is expressed as a summation of the true value and the estimation error, and the observation value is expressed by the summation of the true value and the observation error. Based on this concept, our formulation of the Kalman filter is shown below.

3. Discretization of the governing equation

The shallow water equations, shown below, are employed as the governing equations.

$$\dot{u}_i + g\eta_{,i} = 0 \tag{3}$$

$$\dot{\eta} + hu_{i,i} = 0 \tag{4}$$

where u_i, η, g, and h indicate flow velocity component for the x and y directions, water elevation, gravitational acceleration, and water depth, respectively. The Galerkin method and the selective lumping method are applied to discretize the governing equation. The discretized governing equation is written as Eq. (5) and is represented by Eq. (6),

$$\begin{Bmatrix} \{u^{n+1}\} \\ \{v^{n+1}\} \\ \{\eta^{n+1}\} \end{Bmatrix} = \begin{bmatrix} [\overline{M}] & [0] & [0] \\ [0] & [\overline{M}] & [0] \\ [0] & [0] & [\overline{M}] \end{bmatrix}^{-1} \begin{bmatrix} [\tilde{M}] & [0] & -g\Delta t[S_x] \\ [0] & [\tilde{M}] & -g\Delta t[S_y] \\ -\bar{h}\Delta t[S_x] & -\bar{h}\Delta t[S_y] & [\tilde{M}] \end{bmatrix} \begin{Bmatrix} \{u^n\} \\ \{v^n\} \\ \{\eta^n\} \end{Bmatrix} \tag{5}$$

$$\{\hat{\phi}^{n+1}\} = [A]\{\hat{\phi}^n\} \tag{6}$$

where Δ, $\bar{h}$, $[S_i]$, $[M]$, and $[\overline{M}]$ denote the time increment, the mean water depth, the matrix for the pressure, the consistent mass matrix, and diagonal mass matrix, respectively. $[\tilde{M}]$ is represented by Eq. (7) by using the lumping parameter $e(0 \le e \le 1)$. $\{\hat{\phi}\}$ indicates the estimation value.

$$[\tilde{M}] = (1-e)[\overline{M}] + e[M] \tag{7}$$

The system equation in the Kalman filter is obtained by adding the vector represented by the multiplication of the driving matrix $[\Gamma]$ and the system noise vector $\{g\}$ and is shown as Eq.

(8). Here, the vector $\{\emptyset\}$ indicates the vector of true value. The observation equation shown in Eq. (9) is also introduced. The vectors $\{z\}$ and $\{r\}$ and the matrix $[H]$ denote the observation value and the observation noise vectors and the observation matrix.

$$\{\phi^{n+1}\} = [A]\{\phi^n\} + [\Gamma]\{q^n\} \tag{8}$$

$$\{z^{n+1}\} = [H]\{\phi^{n+1}\} + \{r^{n+1}\} \tag{9}$$

4. Derivation of computational equations in the Kalman filter FEM

The process of modification of the estimation vector $\{\hat{\phi}\}$ is referred to as "assimilation," and the estimation vector before and after assimilation is expressed by "(−)" and "(+)" marks, respectively. First of all, it is assumed that the estimated value after assimilation is expressed by the observation value and the estimated value before assimilation, and that the estimated value after assimilation, i.e., the optimal estimated vector, is expressed by Eq. (10).

$$\{\hat{\phi}_{(+)}^{n+1}\} = [K_1^{n+1}]\{z^{n+1}\} + [K_2^{n+1}]\{\hat{\phi}_{(-)}^{n+1}\} \tag{10}$$

where $\left[K_1^{n+1}\right]$ and $\left[K_2^{n+1}\right]$ indicate arbitrary matrices. In addition, the optimal estimated vector $\left\{\hat{\phi}_{(+)}^{n+1}\right\}$ is expressed by true value $\left\{\phi^{n+1}\right\}$ and estimation error $\left\{p_{(+)}^{n+1}\right\}$ as shown in Eq. (11).

$$\{\hat{\phi}_{(+)}^{n+1}\} = \{\phi^{n+1}\} + \{p_{(+)}^{n+1}\} \tag{11}$$

Consequently, Eq. (12) is obtained from Eqs. (9), (10), and (11).

$$\begin{aligned}
\{\phi^{n+1}\} + \{p_{(+)}^{n+1}\} = \\
[K_1^{n+1}]([H]\{\phi^{n+1}\} + \{r^{n+1}\}) \\
+ [K_2^{n+1}](\{\phi^{n+1}\} + \{p_{(-)}^{n+1}\})
\end{aligned} \tag{12}$$

Here, we consider the expected value for Eq. (12) in time. In addition, the expected value for vectors $\{r^{n+1}\}$, $\{p_{(+)}^{n+1}\}$ and $\{p_{(-)}^{n+1}\}$ in time is assumed to be zero, and Eq. (12) is represented as Eq. (13).

$$([K_2^{n+1}]+[K_1^{n+1}][H]-[I])\langle\{\phi^{n+1}\}\rangle = \{0\} \tag{13}$$

where $[I]$ denotes the unit matrix, and $\langle\{\phi^{n+1}\}\rangle$ indicates the expected value of $\{\phi^{n+1}\}$ in time. Because of $\langle\{\phi^{n+1}\}\rangle \neq \{0\}$, the following relation equation is obtained (see Eq. (14)).

$$[K_2^{n+1}]+[K_1^{n+1}][H]-[I] = [0] \tag{14}$$

Substituting Eq. (14) for Eq. (10), Eq. (15) is obtained.

$$\{\hat{\phi}_{(+)}^{n+1}\} = \{\hat{\phi}_{(-)}^{n+1}\}+[K_1^{n+1}](\{z^{n+1}\}-[H]\{\hat{\phi}_{(-)}^{n+1}\}) \tag{15}$$

where $\left[K_1^{n+1}\right]$ is referred to as the Kalman gain matrix.

Next, let us consider the Kalman gain matrix $\left[K_1^{n+1}\right]$ so as to minimize the trace norm of the error covariance matrix after assimilation. The estimation vector is represented by Eq. (16).

$$\{p_{(+)}^{n+1}\} = \{\hat{\phi}_{(+)}^{n+1}\}-\{\phi^{n+1}\} \tag{16}$$

Eq. (17) is obtained by substituting Eq. (15) with Eq. (16), and substituting Eq. (9) with the obtained equation.

$$\begin{aligned}\{p_{(+)}^{n+1}\} = \\ ([I]-[K_1^{n+1}][H])\{p_{(-)}^{n+1}\}+[K_1^{n+1}]\{r^{n+1}\}\end{aligned} \tag{17}$$

Here, the error covariance matrix after assimilation $\left[P_{(+)}^{n+1}\right]$, i.e., the predicted error covariance matrix, is expressed by the expected value of the error covariance matrix as shown in Eq. (18).

$$[P_{(+)}^{n+1}] = \langle\{p_{(+)}^{n+1}\}\{p_{(+)}^{n+1}\}^T\rangle \tag{18}$$

Also, in calculating Eq. (18), it is assumed that the expected value of the covariance matrix of the observation error and the estimation error before assimilation is a zero vector (see Eq. (19)).

$$\langle \{r^{n+1}\} \{p_{(-)}^{n+1}\}^T \rangle = [0] \tag{19}$$

Consequently, the predicted error covariance matrix can be expressed, such as in Eq. (20),

$$[P_{(+)}^{n+1}] =$$
$$([I] - [K_1^{n+1}][H])[P_{(-)}^{n+1}]([I] - [K_1^{n+1}][H])^T \tag{20}$$
$$+ [K_1^{n+1}][R^{n+1}][K_1^{n+1}]^T$$

where $[R^{n+1}]$ is the observation error covariance matrix, and is represented by $\langle \{r^{n+1}\}\{r^{n+1}\}^T \rangle$. Here, let us consider the Kalman gain matrix $[K_1^{n+1}]$ so as to minimize the trace norm of the predicted error covariance matrix such as $\dfrac{\partial}{\partial [K_1^{n+1}]} \mathrm{tr} \left[P_{(+)}^{n+1} \right] = 0$. Conse-quently, we can obtain the equation for calculating the Kalman gain matrix, as shown in Eq. (21).

$$[K_1^{n+1}] =$$
$$[P_{(-)}^{n+1}][H]^T ([H][P_{(-)}^{n+1}][H]^T + [R]^{n+1})^{-1} \tag{21}$$

In addition, Eq. (20) is represented by Eq. (22) taking Eq. (21) into account.

$$[P_{(+)}^{n+1}] = [P_{(-)}^{n+1}] - [K_1^{n+1}][H][P_{(-)}^{n+1}] \tag{22}$$

Next, let us consider the computation of the estimated error covariance matrix before assimi-lation $[P_{(-)}^{n+1}]$, i.e., the estimated error covariance matrix. First of all, Eq. (6) is represented as Eq. (23) based on the consideration expressed in Eq. (11).

$$\{\phi^{n+1}\} + \{p_{(-)}^{n+1}\} = [A](\{\phi^n\} + \{p_{(-)}^n\}) \tag{23}$$

Subtracting Eq. (8) from Eq. (23) gives us Eq. (24).

$$\{p_{(-)}^{n+1}\} = [A]\{p_{(+)}^n\} - [\Gamma]\{q^n\} \tag{24}$$

Here, the estimated error covariance matrix $[P_{(-)}^{n+1}]$ is also represented by the expected value of the error covariance matrix, as shown in Eq. (25).

$$[P_{(-)}^{n+1}] = \langle \{p_{(-)}^{n+1}\} \{p_{(-)}^{n+1}\}^T \rangle \tag{25}$$

Considering the relation equations $\left(\{p_{(+)}^n\}\{q^n\}^T \right) = [0]$ and $\left(\{q^n\}\{p_{(+)}^n\}^T \right) = [0]$ in the calculation in Eq. (25) allows Eq. (26) to be derived.

$$[P_{(-)}^{n+1}] = [A][P_{(+)}^{n+1}][A]^T + [\Gamma][Q^n][\Gamma]^T \tag{26}$$

where $[Q^n]$ is the system error covariance matrix and is represented by $\left(\{q^{n+1}\}\{q^{n+1}\}^T \right)$.

5. Computational algorithm based on the Kalman filter FEM

If the matrices $[A]$, $[Q]$, and $[R]$ are steady coefficient matrices, the computational algorithm can be divided into two parts: the computations of the Kalman gain matrix and the
estimated value in time. The computational algorithm for the Kalman filter FEM is shown
below.

5.1. Computation of Kalman gain matrix

1. Set input data: $[A]$, $\left[P_{(+)}^0 \right]$, $\left\{ \hat{\phi}_{(+)}^0 \right\}$, $[\Gamma]$, $[Q]$, $[R]$, ε, $(n = 0 \sim imax)$

2. Calculation of estimated error covariance matrix: $\left[P_{(-)} \right] = [A]\left[P_{(+)} \right][A]^T + [\Gamma][Q][\Gamma]^T$

3. Calculation of Kalman gain matrix: $[K_1] = \left[P_{(-)} \right][H]^T \left([H]\left[P_{(+)} \right][H]^T + [R] \right)^{-1}$

4. Calculation of predicted error covariance matrix: $\left[P_{(+)} \right] = \left[P_{(-)} \right] - [K_1][H]\left[P_{(-)} \right]$

5. Check of convergence: if $\sqrt{tr\left(\left(\left[P_{(+)}^{k+1} \right] - \left[P_{(+)}^k \right] \right)\left(\left[P_{(+)}^{k+1} \right] - \left[P_{(+)}^k \right] \right)^T \right)} \le \varepsilon$ then go to Step
   6, else go to Step 2.

5.2. Computation of estimated value in time

6. Calculation of estimated value: $\left\{ \hat{\phi}_{(-)}^{n+1} \right\} = [A]\left\{ \hat{\phi}_{(+)}^n \right\}$

7. Calculation of optimal estimated value: $\left\{ \hat{\phi}_{(+)}^{n+1} \right\} = \left\{ \hat{\phi}_{(-)}^{n+1} \right\} + [K_1]\left(\{z^{n+1}\} - [H]\left\{ \hat{\phi}_{(-)}^{n+1} \right\} \right)$

6. Numerical example 1

Figures 2 and **3**, respectively, show the computational model and the position of observation points in the computation using the Kalman filter FEM. The estimation of shallow water flow was carried out based on the Kalman filter FEM. **Table 1** shows the computational conditions. In this study, we simulated the observed data from the shallow water flow analysis based on the FEM. The boundary condition for the water elevation is given by $\eta(t) = \sin(t)$ on the left-hand side of the open channel, and the artificial observed data is obtained by summation of the numerical result and observation noise, i.e., the white noise. In the computation of the Kalman filter FEM shown in this section, the inflow boundary condition is ignored, and the artificial observation data flow velocities u_x, u_y, and water elevation η, i.e., the computational result by the FEM, are given at the observation points.

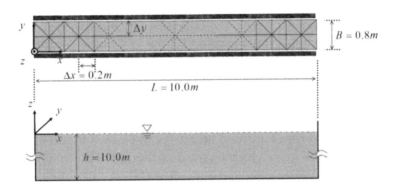

Figure 2. Computational model.

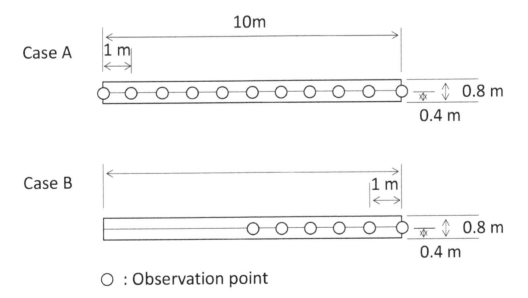

O : Observation point

Figure 3. Numerical examples.

Time increment Δt, s	0.001
Time steps	2000
Number of nodes	153
Number of elements	200
Gravitational acceleration g, m/s^2	9.8
Lumping parameter e	0.8
Initial of estimated error covariance $P^0_{(+)}$	1.0
Initial of estimated value $\hat{\varphi}^0_{(+)}$	0
Convergence determination constant ε	0.01

Table 1. Computational conditions.

The computational results are shown below. **Figures 4** and **5** show the convergence criterion expressed by the Frobenius norm. The equation for the Frobenius norm is shown in Step 5 of the flowchart in Section 4. It is seen that the convergence criterion monotonically decreases and converges. **Figures 6** and **7** show the time history of water elevation at $(x, y) = (5.0$ m, 0.4 m) in Case A and Case B, respectively. It is found that the observation noise can be removed in both cases. **Figures 8** and **9** show the distribution of water elevation on line $y = 0.4$ m in Case A and Case B, respectively. From **Figures 8** and **9**, it can be seen that if the observation point is not set at the upstream side in the channel, the distribution of the water elevation cannot be appropriately obtained. Conversely, from the result of Case A, it can be said that the distribution of water elevation can be correctly obtained if the position of the observation point is appropriately given in the computational model. **Figures 10** and **11** show the distribution of flow velocity u and v and water elevation η at $T = 2.0$ s. It can be seen that water elevation on the upstream side in Case B is not appropriately obtained in comparison with the result of Case A. Therefore, from this numerical example, it can be said that it is necessary to set the observation points uniformly in the computational domain.

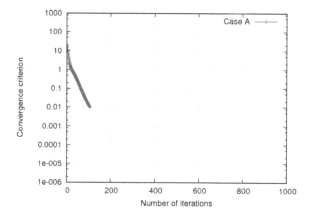

Figure 4. Convergence criterion in Case A.

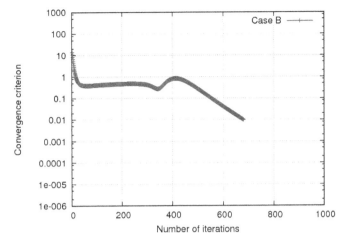

Figure 5. Convergence criterion in Case B.

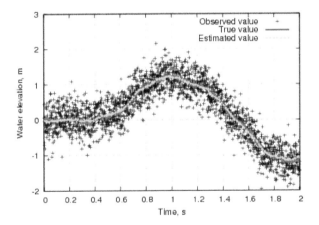

Figure 6. Time history of water elevation at (x, y) = (5.0 m, 0.4 m) in Case A.

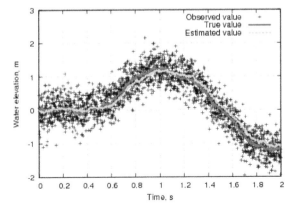

Figure 7. Time history of water elevation at (x, y) = (5.0 m, 0.4 m) in Case B.

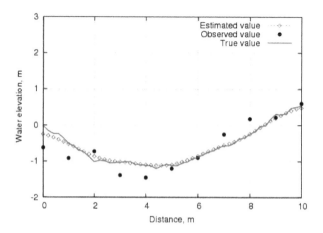

Figure 8. Distribution of water elevation on line $y = 0.4$ m in Case A.

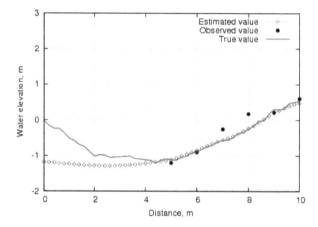

Figure 9. Distribution of water elevation on line $y = 0.4$ m in Case B.

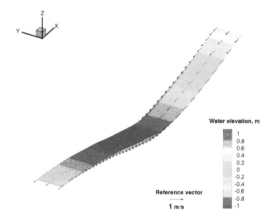

Figure 10. Distribution of flow velocity u and v and water elevation η at $T = 2.0$ s in Case A.

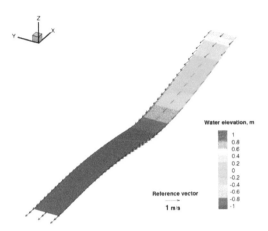

Figure 11. Distribution of flow velocity u and v and water elevation η at $T = 2.0$ s in Case B.

7. Numerical example 2

In this section, the numerical experiment is carried out with the inflow boundary conditions given in Case B, shown in the previous section. An image diagram of the numerical example is shown in **Figure 12**. The inflow boundary condition is given by $\eta(t) = \sin(t)$. The computational conditions in this section are the same as in **Table 1**. As the computational result, **Figure 13** shows the convergence criterion expressed by the Frobenius norm. It can be seen that the convergence criterion decreases and converges monotonically. **Figure 14** shows the time history of water elevation at $(x, y) = (5.0\text{ m}, 0.4\text{ m})$ in Case C. It is found that the observation noise can be removed. **Figure 15** shows the distribution of water elevation on line $y = 0.4$ m in Case C. From **Figure 15**, it is found that the distribution of the water elevation can be appropriately obtained in comparison with the result shown in **Figure 9**. In addition, **Figure 16** shows the distribution of flow velocity u and v and water elevation η at $T = 2.0$ s. It is seen that water elevation on the upstream side can be more accurately obtained than with the result for Case B. Therefore, from this numerical experiment, it is necessary to give the boundary conditions if the computation of the flow field estimation is carried out based on the Kalman filter FEM, and the observation point cannot be uniformly given.

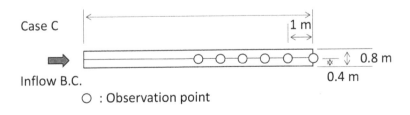

Figure 12. Numerical example.

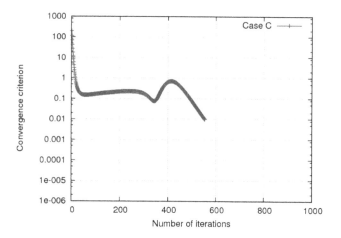

Figure 13. Convergence criterion in Case C.

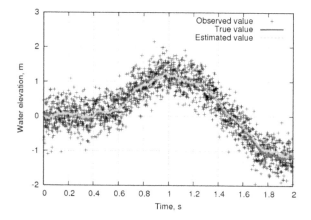

Figure 14. Time history of water elevation at $(x, y) = (5.0$ m, 0.4 m) in Case C.

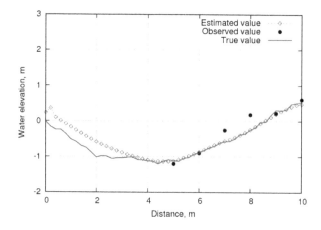

Figure 15. Distribution of water elevation on line $y = 0.4$ m in Case C.

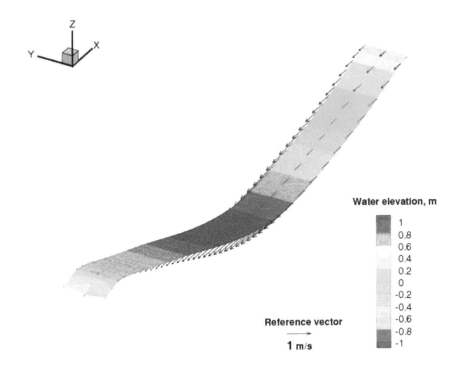

Figure 16. Distribution of flow velocity u and v and water elevation η at $T = 2.0$ s in Case C.

8. Comparison of estimation accuracy in Cases A, B, and C

Based on the estimation result at $(x, y) = (5.0$ m, 0.4 m$)$ shown in **Figures 6, 7**, and **14**, the numerical accuracy is investigated by comparison of data between the true and the estimated values in each case. The L_2 norm with respect to the difference between the true and the estimated values in each case is shown in **Table 2**.

Case	Number of observation points	Inflow boundary condition	L^2 norm
Case A	10	Not given	1.899
Case B	5 (only downstream side)	Not given	4.161
Case C	5 (only downstream side)	Given	2.463

Table 2. Comparison of L^2 norm.

A comparison of the results in Cases A and B shows that it is necessary to set the observation points uniformly in the computational domain to obtain a highly accurate estimation result. In addition, when comparing the results in Case B and Case C, it is found that the estimation accuracy increases if the inflow boundary condition is taken into account.

9. Conclusions

In this study, flow field estimation analysis in an open channel was carried out based on the Kalman filter FEM. The shallow water equations were employed as the governing equations, and the Galerkin and the selective lumping methods were used to discretize the governing equation in space and time, respectively. In the numerical experiments, the observed value is created by adding white noise to the simulation result in the open channel model. The following conclusions were obtained from this study.

- The observation noise can be removed from the observed value by using Kalman filter FEM.

- When the observation points are set only on the downstream side of an open channel, the estimated water elevation on the upstream side is almost constant.

- If the inflow boundary condition is given in the case where the observation points are positioned only on the downstream side of an open channel, the distribution of the water elevation can be appropriately obtained, including the upstream side in the open channel.

Nomenclature

u_i:	flow velocity component for x and y directions
η:	water elevation
g:	gravitational acceleration
h:	water depth
Δt:	time increment
$\bar{h}$:	mean water depth
$[S_i]$:	pressure matrix
$[M]$:	consistent mass matrix
$[\overline{M}]$:	diagonal mass matrix
e:	lumping parameter
$\{\hat{\phi}\}$:	estimation value vector
$[\Gamma]$:	driving matrix
$\{q\}$:	system noise vector
$\{\phi\}$:	true value vector
$\{z\}$:	observation value vector
$\{r\}$:	observation noise vector
$[A]$:	state transition matrix
$[H]$:	observation matrix

{p}:   estimation error vector

[K₁]:   Kalman gain matrix

[P]:   estimated error covariance matrix

[Q]:   system error covariance matrix

[R]:   observation error covariance matrix

Acknowledgements

This work was supported by Grants-in-Aid for Scientific Research (C) Grant Number 15K05786, and the contents of this work, i.e., formulation by FEM and the theory of the Kalman filter FEM, is based on seminars by Emeritus Professor Mutsuto Kawahara at Chuo University's Department of Civil Engineering. The computations were mainly carried out using the Fujitsu PRIMERGY CX400 computer facilities at Kyushu University's Research Institute for Information Technology. We wish to thank Emeritus Professor Mutsuto Kawahara and the staff at Kyushu University's Research Institute for Information Technology.

Author details

Takahiko Kurahashi*, Taichi Yoshiara and Yasuhide Kobayashi

*Address all correspondence to: kurahashi@mech.nagaokaut.ac.jp

Department of Mechanical Engineering, Nagaoka University of Technology, Nagaoka, Japan

References

[1] Kawahara, M., Kodama, T. and Kinoshita, M., Finite element method for tsunami wave propagation analysis considering the open boundary condition. Computers & Mathematics with Applications, Vol. 16 (1988), pp. 139–152.

[2] Tanaka, S., Bunya, S., Westerink, J.J., Dawson, C.N. and Luettich, R.A., Scalability of an unstructured grid continuous Galerkin-based hurricane storm surge model. Journal of Scientific Computing, Vol. 46, 3 (2011), pp. 329–358.

[3] Kawahara, M. and Shimada, Y., Gradient method of optimal control applied to the operation of a dam water gate. International Journal for Numerical Methods in Fluids, Vol. 19 (1994), pp. 463–477.

[4] Kurahashi, T. and Kawahara, M., Flood control of urban stormwater conduit systems using the finite element methods. International Journal for Numerical Methods in Fluids, Vol. 52 (2005), pp. 1029–1057.

[5] Yonekawa, K. and Kawahara, M., Application of Kalman filter finite element method and AIC. International Journal of Computational Fluid Dynamics, Vol. 17 (2003), pp. 307–317.

[6] Suga, R. and Kawahara, M., Estimation of tidal current using Kalman filter finite-element method. Computers and Mathematics with Applications, Vol. 52 (2006), pp. 1289–1298.

[7] Kurahashi, T., Yoshiara, T. and Kobayashi, Y., Verification of estimation accuracy of flow field in a shallow water region based on the Kalman filter finite element method. Transactions of the JSME (in Japanese), Vol. 82, 835 (2016), pp. 1–19.

8

The Discontinuous Galerkin Finite Element Method for Ordinary Differential Equations

Mahboub Baccouch

Additional information is available at the end of the chapter

Abstract

We present an analysis of the discontinuous Galerkin (DG) finite element method for nonlinear ordinary differential equations (ODEs). We prove that the DG solution is $(p + 1)$th order convergent in the L^2-norm, when the space of piecewise polynomials of degree p is used. A $(2p+1)$th order superconvergence rate of the DG approximation at the downwind point of each element is obtained under quasi-uniform meshes. Moreover, we prove that the DG solution is superconvergent with order $p+2$ to a particular projection of the exact solution. The superconvergence results are used to show that the leading term of the DG error is proportional to the $(p + 1)$-degree right Radau polynomial. These results allow us to develop a residual-based *a posteriori* error estimator which is computationally simple, efficient, and asymptotically exact. The proposed *a posteriori* error estimator is proved to converge to the actual error in the L^2-norm with order $p+2$. Computational results indicate that the theoretical orders of convergence are optimal. Finally, a local adaptive mesh refinement procedure that makes use of our local *a posteriori* error estimate is also presented. Several numerical examples are provided to illustrate the global superconvergence results and the convergence of the proposed estimator under mesh refinement.

Keywords: discontinuous Galerkin finite element method, ordinary differential equations, a priori error estimates, superconvergence, a posteriori error estimates, adaptive mesh refinement

1. Introduction

In this chapter, we introduce and analyze the discontinuous Galerkin (DG) method applied to the following first-order initial-value problem (IVP)

$$\frac{d\vec{u}}{dt} = \vec{f}(t,\vec{u}), \quad t \in [0,T], \quad \vec{u}(0) = \vec{u}_0, \tag{1}$$

where $\vec{u}:[0,T] \to \mathbb{R}^n$, $\vec{u}_0 \in \mathbb{R}^n$, and $\vec{f}:[0,T] \times \mathbb{R}^n \to \mathbb{R}^n$. We assume that the solution exists and is unique and we would like to approximate it using a discontinuous piecewise polynomial space. According to the ordinary differential equation (ODE) theory, the condition $\vec{f} \in C^1([0,T] \times \mathbb{R}^n)$ is sufficient to guarantee the existence and uniqueness of the solution to (1). We note that a general nth-order IVP of the form $y^{(n)} = g(t,y,y',...,y^{(n-1)})$ with initial conditions $y(0) = a_0$, $y'(0) = a_1,...,y^{(n-1)}(0) = a_{n-1}$ can be converted into a system of equations in the form (1), where $\vec{u} = [y,y',...,y^{(n-1)}]^t$, $\vec{f}(t,\vec{u}) = [u_2,u_3,...,u_n,g(t,u_1,...,u_n)]^t$, and $\vec{u}_0 = [a_0,a_1,...,a_{n-1}]^t$.

The high-order DG method considered here is a class of finite element methods (FEMs) using completely discontinuous piecewise polynomials for the numerical solution and the test functions. The DG method was first designed as an effective numerical method for solving hyperbolic conservation laws, which may have discontinuous solutions. Here, we will discuss the algorithm formulation, stability analysis, and error estimates for the DG method solving nonlinear ODEs. DG method combines the best proprieties of the classical continuous finite element and finite volume methods such as consistency, flexibility, stability, conservation of local physical quantities, robustness, and compactness. Recently, DG methods become highly attractive and popular, mainly because these methods are high-order accurate, nonlinear stable, highly parallelizable, easy to handle complicated geometries and boundary conditions, and capable to capture discontinuities without spurious oscillations. The original DG finite element method (FEM) was introduced in 1973 by Reed and Hill [1] for solving steady-state first-order linear hyperbolic problems. It provides an effective means of solving hyperbolic problems on unstructured meshes in a parallel computing environment. The discontinuous basis can capture shock waves and other discontinuities with accuracy [2, 3]. The DG method can easily handle adaptivity strategies since the h refinement (mesh refinement and coarsening) and the p refinement (method order variation) can be done without taking into account the continuity restrictions typical of conforming FEMs. Moreover, the degree of the approximating polynomial can be easily changed from one element to the other [3]. Adaptivity is of particular importance in nonlinear hyperbolic problems given the complexity of the structure of the discontinuities and geometries involved. Due to local structure of DG methods, physical quantities such as mass, momentum, and energy are conserved locally through DG schemes. This property is very important for flow and transport problems. Furthermore, the DG method is highly parallelizable [4, 5]. Because of these nice features, the DG method has been analyzed and extended to a wide range of applications. In particular, DG methods have been used to solve ODEs [6–9], hyperbolic [5, 6, 10–19] and diffusion and convection diffusion [20–23] partial differential equations (PDEs), to mention a few. For transient problems, Cockburn and Shu [17] introduced and developed the so-called Runge-Kutta discontinuous Galerkin (RKDG) methods. These numerical methods use DG discretizations in space and combine it with an explicit Runge-Kutta time-marching algorithm. The proceedings of Cockburn et al. [24] and

Shu [25] contain a more complete and current survey of the DG method and its applications. Despite the attractive advantages mentioned above, DG methods have some drawbacks. Unlike the continuous FEMs, DG methods produce dense and ill-conditioned matrices increasing with the order of polynomial degree[23].

Related theoretical results in the literature including superconvergence results and error estimates of the DG methods for ODEs are given in [7–9, 26–28]. In 1974, LaSaint and Raviart [9] presented the first error analysis of the DG method for the initial-value problem (1). They showed that the DG method is equivalent to an implicit Runge-Kutta method and proved a rate of convergence of $O(h^p)$ for general triangulations and of $O(h^{p+1})$ for Cartesian grids. Delfour et al. [7] investigated a class of Galerkin methods which lead to a family of one-step schemes generating approximations up to order $2p + 2$ for the solution of an ODE, when polynomials of degree p are used. In their proposed method, the numerical solution u_h at the discontinuity point t_n is defined as an average across the jump, i.e., $\alpha_n u_h(t_n^-) + (1 - \alpha_n)u_h(t_n^+)$. By choosing special values of α_n, one can obtain the original DG scheme of LeSaint and Raviart [9] and Euler's explicit, improved, and implicit schemes. Delfour and Dubeau [27] introduced a family of discontinuous piecewise polynomial approximation schemes. They presented a more general framework of one-step methods such as implicit Runge-Kutta and Crank-Nicholson schemes, multistep methods such as Adams-Bashforth and Adams-Moulton schemes, and hybrid methods. Later, Johnson [8] proved new optimal *a priori* error estimates for a class of implicit one-step methods for stiff ODEs obtained by using the discontinuous Galerkin method with piecewise polynomials of degree zero and one. Johnson and Pitkäranta [29] proved a rate of convergence of $O(h^{p+1/2})$ for general triangulations and Peterson [19] confirmed this rate to be optimal. Richter [30] obtained the optimal rate of convergence $O(h^{p+1})$ for some structured two-dimensional non-Cartesian grids. We also would like to mention the work of Estep [28], where the author outlined a rigorous theory of global error control for the approximation of the IVP (1). In [6], Adjerid et al. showed that the DG solution of one-dimensional hyperbolic problems exhibit an $O(h^{p+2})$ superconvergence rate at the roots of the right Radau polynomial of degree $p + 1$. Furthermore, they obtained a $(2p + 1)$th order superconvergence rate of the DG approximation at the downwind point of each element. They performed a local error analysis and showed that the local error on each element is proportional to a Radau polynomial. They further constructed implicit residual-based *a posteriori* error estimates but they did not prove their asymptotic exactness. In 2010, Deng and Xiong [31] investigated a DG method with interpolated coefficients for the IVP (1). They proved pointwise superconvergence results at Radau points. More recently, the author [12, 15, 26, 32–39] investigated the global convergence of the several residual-based *a posteriori* DG and local DG (LDG) error estimates for a variety of linear and nonlinear problems.

This chapter is organized as follows: In Section 2, we present the discrete DG method for the classical nonlinear initial-value problem. In Section 3, we present a detailed proof of the optimal *a priori* error estimate of the DG scheme. We state and prove our main superconvergence results in Section 4. In Section 5, we present the *a posteriori* error estimation procedure and prove that these error estimates converge to the true errors under mesh refinement. In Section 6, we propose an adaptive algorithm based on the local *a posteriori* error estimates. In Section 7, we present several numerical examples to validate our theoretical results. We conclude and discuss our results in Section 8.

2. The DG scheme for nonlinear IVPs

The error analysis of nonlinear scalar and vector initial-value problems (IVPs) having smooth solutions is similar. For this, we restrict our theoretical discussion to the following nonlinear initial-value problem (IVP)

$$u' = f(t,u), \quad t \in [0,T], \quad u(0) = u_0,$$ (2)

where $f(t,u) : [0,T] \times \mathbb{R} \to \mathbb{R}$ is a sufficiently smooth function with respect to the variables t and u. More precisely, we assume that $|f_u(t,u)| \leq M_1$ on the set $D = [0,T] \times \mathbb{R} \subset \mathbb{R}^2$, where M_1 is a positive constant. We note that the assumption $|f_u(t,u)| \leq M_1$ is sufficient to ensure that $f(t,u)$ satisfies a Lipschitz condition in u on the convex set D with Lipschitz constant M_1

$$| f(t,u) - f(t,v) | \leq M_1 | u - v |, \quad \text{for any (t,u) and (t,v)} \in D.$$ (3)

Next, we introduce the DG method for the model problem (2). Let $0 = t_0 < t_1 < \cdots < t_N = T$ be a partition of the interval $\Omega = [0,T]$. We denote the mesh by $I_j = [t_{j-1}, t_j]$, $j = 1, ..., N$. We denote the length of I_j by $h_j = t_j - t_{j-1}$. We also denote $h = \max_{1 \leq j \leq N} h_j$ and $h_{min} = \min_{1 \leq j \leq N} h_j$ as the length of the largest and smallest subinterval, respectively. Here, we consider regular meshes, that is, $\dfrac{h}{h_{min}} \leq \lambda$, where $\lambda \geq 1$ is a constant (independent of h) during mesh refinement. If $\lambda = 1$, then the mesh is uniformly distributed. In this case, the nodes and mesh size are defined by $t_j = jh$, $j = 0, 1, ..., N$, $h = T/N$.

Throughout this work, we define $v(t_j^-)$ and $v(t_j^+)$ to be the left limit and the right limit of the function v at the discontinuity point t_j, i.e., $v(t_j^-) = \lim_{s \to 0^-} v(t_j + s)$ and $v(t_j^+) = \lim_{s \to 0^+} v(t_j + s)$. To simplify the notation, we denote by $[v](t_j) = v(t_j^+) - v(t_j^-)$ the jump of v at the point t_j.

If we multiply (2) by an arbitrary test function v, integrate over the interval I_j, and integrate by parts, we get the DG weak formulation

$$\int_{I_j} v'u\,dt + \int_{I_j} f(t,u)v\,dt - u(t_j)v(t_j) + u(t_{j-1})v(t_{j-1}) = 0. \tag{4}$$

We denote by V_h^p the finite element space of polynomials of degree at most p in each interval I_j, i.e.,

$$V_h^p = \{v : v|_{I_j} \in P^p(I_j),\ j = 1,\ldots,N\},$$

where $P^p(I_j)$ denotes the set of all polynomials of degree no more than p on I_j. We would like to emphasize that polynomials in V_h^p are allowed to have discontinuities at the nodes t_j.

Replacing the exact solution $u(t)$ by a piecewise polynomial $u_h(t) \in V_h^p$ and choosing $v \in V_h^p$, we obtain the DG scheme: Find $u_h \in V_h^p$ such that $\forall\, v \in V_h^p$ and $j = 1, \ldots, N$,

$$\int_{I_j} v'u_h\,dt + \int_{I_j} f(t,u_h)v\,dt - \hat{u}_h(t_j)v(t_j^-) + \hat{u}_h(t_{j-1})v(t_{j-1}^+) = 0, \tag{5a}$$

where $\hat{u}_h(t_j)$ is the so-called numerical flux which is nothing but the discrete approximation u at the node $t = t_j$. We remark that u_h is not necessarily continuous at the nodes.

To complete the definition of the DG scheme, we still need to define $\hat{u}_h$ on the boundaries of I_j. Since for IVPs, information travel from the past into the future, it is reasonable to take $\hat{u}_h$ as the classical upwind flux

$$\hat{u}_h(t_0) = u_0, \quad \text{and} \quad \hat{u}_h(t_j) = u_h(t_j^-), \quad j = 1,\ldots,N. \tag{5b}$$

2.1. Implementation

The DG solution $u_h(t)$ can be efficiently obtained in the following order: first, we compute $u_h(t)$ in the first element I_1 using (5a) and (5b) with $j = 1$ since $u_h(t_0^-) = u_0$ is known. Then, we can find $u_h(t)$ in I_2 since $u_h(t)$ in I_1 is already available. We can repeat the same process to compute $u_h(t)$ in $I_3, \ldots, I_N$. More specifically, $u_h(t)$ can be obtained locally for each I_j using the following two steps: (i) express $u_h(t)$ as a linear combination of orthogonal basis $L_{i,j}(t)$, $i = 0, \ldots, p$, where $L_{i,j}$ is the ith degree Legendre polynomial on I_j, i.e., $u_h(t) = \sum_{i=0}^{p} c_{i,j} L_{i,j}(t)$, $t \in I_j$, where

$\{L_{i,j}(t)\}_{i=0}^{i=p}$ is a local basis of $P^p(I_j)$, and (ii) choose the test functions $v = L_{k,j}(t)$, $k = 0, ..., p$.
Thus, on each I_j, we get a $(p+1) \times (p+1)$ system of nonlinear algebraic equations, which can
be solved for the unknown coefficients $c_{0,j}, ..., c_{p,j}$ using, e.g., Newton's method for nonlinear
systems. Once we obtain the DG solution on all elements I_j, $j = 1, ..., N$, we get the DG solution
which is a piecewise discontinuous polynomial of degree $\leq p$. We refer to [7–9] for more details
about DG methods for ODEs as well as their properties and applications.

2.2. Linear stability for the DG method

Let us now establish a stability result for the DG method applied to the linear case, i.e.,
$f(t, u) = \lambda u$. Taking $v = u_h$ in the discrete weak formulation (5a), we get

$$\frac{u_h^2(t_j^-)}{2} + \frac{u_h^2(t_{j-1}^+)}{2} - u_h(t_{j-1}^-)u_h(t_{j-1}^+) = \lambda \int_{I_j} u_h^2 dt,$$

which is equivalent to

$$\frac{u_h^2(t_j^-)}{2} - \frac{u_h^2(t_{j-1}^-)}{2} + \frac{1}{2}\left(u_h(t_{j-1}^-) - u_h(t_{j-1}^+)\right)^2 = \lambda \int_{I_j} u_h^2 dt.$$

Summing over all elements, we get the equality

$$\frac{u_h^2(T^-)}{2} - \frac{u_0^2}{2} + \frac{1}{2}\sum_{j=1}^{N}\left(u_h(t_{j-1}^-) - u_h(t_{j-1}^+)\right)^2 = \lambda \int_{\Omega} u_h^2 dt.$$

Consequently, $\dfrac{u_h^2(T^-)}{2} - \dfrac{u_0^2}{2} \leq \lambda \int_{\Omega} u_h^2 dt$, which gives the stability result $u_h^2(T^-) \leq u_0^2$ provided
that $\lambda \leq 0$.

3. *A priori* error analysis

We begin by defining some norms that will be used throughout this work. We
define the L^2 inner product of two integrable functions, u and v, on the interval
$I_j = [t_{j-1}, t_j]$ as $(u, v)_{I_j} = \int_{I_j} u(t)v(t)dt$. Denote $\|u\|_{0,I_j} = (u, u)_{I_j}^{1/2}$ to be the standard
L^2 norm of u on I_j. Moreover, the standard L^∞ norm of u on I_j is defined by

$\|u\|_{\infty, I_j} = \sup_{t \in I_j} |u(t)|$. Let $H^s(I_j)$, where $s = 0, 1, ...,$ denote the standard Sobolev space

of square integrable functions on I_j with all derivatives $u^{(k)}$, $k = 0, 1, ..., s$ being square

integrable on I_j, i.e., $H^s(I_j) = \left\{ u : \int_{I_j} |u^{(k)}(t)|^2 dt < \infty, 0 \leq k \leq s \right\}$, and equipped with

the norm $\|u\|_{s, I_j} = \left(\sum_{k=0}^{s} \|u^{(k)}\|_{0, I_j}^2 \right)^{1/2}$. The $H^s(I_j)$ seminorm of a function u on

I_j is given by $|u|_{s, I_j} = \|u^{(s)}\|_{0, I_j}$. We also define the norms on the whole computational

domain Ω as follows:

$$\|u\|_{0, \Omega} = \left(\sum_{j=1}^{N} \|u\|_{0, I_j}^2 \right)^{1/2}, \quad \|u\|_{\infty, \Omega} = \max_{1 \leq j \leq N} \|u\|_{\infty, I_j}, \quad \|u\|_{s, \Omega} = \left(\sum_{j=1}^{N} \|u\|_{s, I_j}^2 \right)^{1/2}.$$

The seminorm on the whole computational domain Ω is defined as $|u|_{s, \Omega} = \left(\sum_{j=1}^{N} |u|_{s, I_j}^2 \right)^{1/2}$.

We note that if $u \in H^s(\Omega)$, $s = 1, 2, ...,$ then the norm $\|u\|_{s, \Omega}$ on the whole computational domain

is the standard Sobolev norm $\left(\sum_{k=0}^{s} \|u^{(k)}\|_{0, \Omega}^2 \right)^{1/2}$. For convenience, we use $\|u\|_{I_j}$ and $\|u\|$

to denote $\|u\|_{0, I_j}$ and $\|u\|_{0, \Omega}$, respectively.

For $p \geq 1$, we consider two special projection operators, $P_h^{\pm}$, which are defined as follows: For

a smooth function u, the restrictions of $P_h^+ u$ and $P_h^- u$ to I_j are polynomials in $P^p(I_j)$ satisfying

$$\int_{I_j} (P_h^- u - u) v \, dt = 0, \forall v \in P^{p-1}(I_j), \quad \text{and} \quad (P_h^- u - u)(t_j^-) = 0, \tag{6a}$$

$$\int_{I_j} (P_h^+ u - u) v \, dt = 0, \forall v \in P^{p-1}(I_j), \quad \text{and} \quad (P_h^+ u - u)(t_{j-1}^+) = 0. \tag{6b}$$

These two particular Gauss-Radau projections are very important in the proofs of optimal L^2

error estimates and superconvergence results. We note that the special projections $P_h^{\pm} u$ are

mainly utilized to eliminate the jump terms at the cell boundaries in the error estimate in order

to achieve the optimal order of accuracy [22].

For the projections mentioned above, it is easy to show that for any $u \in H^{p+1}(I_j)$ with $j = 1, ..., N$, there exists a constant C independent of the mesh size h such that (see, e.g., [40])

$$\left\| u - P_h^{\pm} u \right\|_{I_j} \leq C h_j^{p+1} |u|_{p+1, I_j}, \quad \left\| (u - P_h^{\pm} u)' \right\|_{I_j} \leq C h_j^p |u|_{p, I_j}. \tag{7}$$

Moreover, we recall the inverse properties of the finite element space V_h^p that will be used in our error analysis: For any $v_h \in V_h^p$, there exists a positive constant C independent of v_h and h, such that, $\forall \, j = 1, ..., N,$

$$\left\| v_h^{(k)} \right\|_{I_j} \leq C h_j^{-k} \| v_h \|_{I_j}, \quad k \geq 1, \quad \left| v_h(t_{j-1}^+) \right| + \left| v_h(t_j^-) \right| \leq C h_j^{-1/2} \| v_h \|_{I_j}. \tag{8}$$

From now on, the notation C, C_1, C_2, etc. will be used to denote generic positive constants independent of h, but may depend upon the exact solution of (1) and its derivatives. They also may have different values at different places.

Throughout this work, let us denote $e = u - u_h$ to be the error between the exact solution of (2) and the DG solution defined in (5a) and (5b), $\varepsilon = u - P_h^- u$ to be the projection error, and $\bar{e} = P_h^- u - u_h$ to be the error between the projection of the exact solution $P_h^- u$ and the DG solution u_h. We observe that the actual error can be written as $e = (u - P_h^- u) + (P_h^- u - u_h) = \varepsilon + \bar{e}$.

Now, we are ready to prove our optimal error estimates for e in the L^2 and H^1 norms.

Theorem 3.1. *Suppose that the exact solution of (2) is sufficiently smooth with bounded derivatives, i.e., $\|u\|_{p+1,\Omega}$ is bounded. We also assume that $\left| f_u(t, u) \right| \leq M_1$ on $D = [0,T] \times \mathbb{R}$. Let $p \geq 0$ and u_h be the DG solution of (5a) and (5b), then, for sufficiently small h, there exists a positive constant C independent of h such that,*

$$\|e\| \leq C \, h^{p+1}, \tag{9}$$

$$\sum_{j=1}^{N} \|e'\|_{I_j}^2 \leq C h^{2p}, \quad \|e\|_{1,\Omega} \leq C h^p. \tag{10}$$

Proof. We first need to derive some error equations which will be used repeatedly throughout this and the next sections. Subtracting (5a) from (4) with $v \in V_h^p$ and using the numerical flux (5b), we obtain the following error equation: $\forall \, v \in V_{h'}^p$

$$\int_{I_j} v'e\,dt + \int_{I_j} (f(t,u) - f(t,u_h))v\,dt + e(t_{j-1}^-)v(t_{j-1}^+) - e(t_j^-)v(t_j^-) = 0. \tag{11}$$

By integration by parts, we get

$$\int_{I_j} e'v\,dt - \int_{I_j} \left(f(t,u) - f(t,u_h)\right)v\,dt + [e](t_{j-1})v(t_{j-1}^+) = 0. \tag{12}$$

Applying Taylor's series with integral remainder in the variable u and using the relation $u - u_h = e$, we write

$$f(t,u) - f(t,u_h) = \theta(u - u_h) = \theta e, \quad \text{where } \theta = \int_0^1 f_u(t,u + s(u_h - u))\,ds = \int_0^1 f_u(t,u - se)\,ds. \tag{13}$$

Substituting (13) into (12), we arrive at

$$\int_{I_j} \left(e' - \theta e\right)v\,dt + [e](t_{j-1})v(t_{j-1}^+) = 0, \quad \forall \, v \in V_h^p. \tag{14}$$

To simplify the notation, we introduce the bilinear operator $\mathcal{A}_j(e;V)$ as

$$\mathcal{A}_j(e;V) = \int_{I_j} (e' - \theta e)V\,dt + [e](t_{j-1})V(t_{j-1}^+). \tag{15}$$

Thus, we can write (14) as

$$\mathcal{A}_j(e;v) = 0, \quad \forall \, v \in V_h^p. \tag{16}$$

A direct calculation from integration by parts yields

$$\mathcal{A}_j(e;V) = \int_{I_j} (-V' - \theta V)e\,dt + e(t_j^-)V(t_j^-) - e(t_{j-1}^-)V(t_{j-1}^+). \tag{17}$$

On the other hand, if we add and subtract $P_h^+ V$ to V then we can write (15) as

$$A_j(e;V) = A_j(e;V - P_h^+V) + A_j(e;P_h^+V). \tag{18}$$

Combining (18) and (16) with $v = P_h^+ V \in P^p(I_j)$ and applying the property of the projection P_h^+, i.e., $(V - P_h^+V)(t_{j-1}^+) = 0$, we obtain

$$A_j(e;V) = \int_{I_j} (e' - \theta e)(V - P_h^+V)dt + [e](t_{j-1})(V - P_h^+V)(t_{j-1}^+) = \int_{I_j} (e' - \theta e)(V - P_h^+V)dt. \tag{19}$$

If v is a polynomial of degree at most p then v' is a polynomial of degree at most $p - 1$. Therefore, by the property of the projection P_h^+, we immediately see

$$\int_{I_j} v'(V - P_h^+V)dt = 0, \quad \forall v \in P^p(I_j). \tag{20}$$

Substituting the relation $e = \varepsilon + \bar{e}$ into (19) and invoking (20) with $v = \bar{e}$, we get

$$A_j(e;V) = \int_{I_j} (\varepsilon' - \theta e)(V - P_h^+V)dt + \int_{I_j} \bar{e}'(V - P_h^+V)dt = \int_{I_j} (\varepsilon' - \theta e)(V - P_h^+V)dt. \tag{21}$$

Now, we are ready to prove the theorem. We construct the following auxiliary problem: find φ such that

$$-\varphi' - \theta\varphi = e, \quad t \in [0,T] \quad \text{subject to} \quad \varphi(T) = 0. \tag{22}$$

where $\theta = \theta(t) = \int_0^1 f_u(t, u(t) - se(t))ds$. Clearly, the exact solution to (22) is given by the explicit formula

$$\varphi(t) = \frac{1}{\Theta(t)} \int_t^T \Theta(y)e(y)dy, \quad \text{where} \quad \Theta(t) = \exp\left(-\int_t^T \theta(s)ds\right). \tag{23}$$

Next, we prove some regular estimates which will be needed in our error analysis. Using the assumption $|f_u(t,u)| \leq M_1$, we see that $\theta(t)$, $t \in [0,T]$ is bounded by M_1

$$|\theta(t)| \leq \int_0^1 |f_u(t, u(t) - se(t))| \, ds \leq \int_0^1 M_1 ds = M_1, \quad \forall \, t \in [0, T]. \tag{24a}$$

Using the definition of θ and the estimate (24a), we have

$$0 \leq \Theta(t) \leq \exp\left(\int_0^T |\theta(s)| \, ds\right) \leq \exp\left(\int_0^T M_1 ds\right) = \exp(M_1 T) = C_1. \tag{24b}$$

Similarly, we can easily estimate $\dfrac{1}{\Theta(t)}$ as follows

$$0 \leq \frac{1}{\Theta(t)} = \exp\left(\int_t^T \theta(s) ds\right) \leq \exp\left(\int_0^T |\theta(s)| \, ds\right) \leq \exp\left(\int_0^T M_1 ds\right) = \exp(M_1 T) = C_1. \tag{24c}$$

Applying the estimates (24b), (24c), and the Cauchy-Schwarz inequality, we get

$$|\varphi(t)| \leq \frac{1}{\Theta(t)} \int_t^T \Theta(y) \, |e(y)| \, dy \leq C_1 \int_t^T C_1 \, |e(y)| \, dy \leq C_1^2 \int_0^T |e(y)| \, dy \leq C_1^2 T^{1/2} \|e\|, \quad t \in [0, T].$$

Squaring both sides and intergrading over Ω yields

$$\|\varphi\|^2 \leq C_1^4 T^2 \|e\|^2 = C_2 \|e\|^2. \tag{25a}$$

We also need to obtain an estimate of $|\varphi|_{1,\Omega}$. Using (22) and (24a) gives

$$|\varphi'| = |\theta\varphi + e| \leq M_1 \, |\varphi| + |e|, \quad t \in [0, T].$$

Squaring both sides, applying the inequality $(a + b)^2 \leq 2a^2 + 2b^2$, integrating over the computational domain Ω, and using (25a), we get

$$|\varphi|_{1,\Omega}^2 = \int_0^T |\varphi'|^2 \, dt \leq 2(M_1^2 \|\varphi\|^2 + \|e\|^2) \leq 2(M_1^2 C_2 + 1) \|e\|^2 \leq C_3 \|e\|^2. \tag{25b}$$

Applying the projection result and the estimate (3.20b) yields

$$\|\varphi - P_h^+ \varphi\| \leq C_4 h |\varphi|_{1,\Omega} \leq C_5 h \|e\|. \tag{25c}$$

Now, we are ready to show (9). Using (17) with $V = \varphi$ and (22), we obtain

$$A_j(e;\varphi) = \int_{I_j} (-\varphi' - \theta\varphi)e\,dt - e(t_{j-1}^-)\varphi(t_{j-1}) + e(t_j^-)\varphi(t_j) = \int_{I_j} e^2\,dt - e(t_{j-1}^-)\varphi(t_{j-1}) + e(t_j^-)\varphi(t_j).$$

Summing over the elements and using the fact that $\varphi(T) = e(t_0^-) = 0$ yields

$$\sum_{j=1}^{N} A_j(e;\varphi) = \|e\|^2 - e(t_0^-)\varphi(t_0^-) + e(T^-)\varphi(T^-) = \|e\|^2. \tag{26}$$

On the other hand, if we choose $V = \varphi$ in (21) then we get

$$A_j(e;\varphi) = \int_{I_j} (\varepsilon' - \theta e)(\varphi - P_h^+\varphi)\,dt. \tag{27}$$

Summing over all elements and applying the Cauchy-Schwarz inequality, we get

$$\sum_{j=1}^{N} A_j(e;\varphi) \le (\|\varepsilon'\| + M_1\|e\|)\|\varphi - P_h^+\varphi\|.$$

Using the estimate (25c), we deduce that

$$\sum_{j=1}^{N} A_j(e;\varphi) \le (C_0 h^p |u|_{p+1,\Omega} + M_1\|e\|)C_1 h\|e\| \le C(h^{p+1} + h\|e\|)\|e\|. \tag{28}$$

Combining (26) and (28), we conclude that

$$\|e\| \le Ch^{p+1} + Ch\|e\|. \tag{29}$$

Thus, $(1 - Ch)\|e\| \le C\,h^{p+1}$, where C is a positive constant independent of h. Therefore, for sufficiently small h, e.g., $h \le \frac{1}{2C}$, we obtain $\frac{1}{2}\|e\| \le (1 - Ch)\|e\| \le C\,h^{p+1}$, which yields $\|e\| \le 2C\,h^{p+1}$ for h small. Thus, we completed the proof of (9).

To show (10), we use $e = \bar{e} + \varepsilon$, the classical inverse inequality (8), the estimate (9), and the projection result (7) to obtain

$$\left\| e' \right\| = \left\| \bar{e} + \varepsilon' \right\| \le \left\| \bar{e} \right\| + \left\| \varepsilon' \right\| \le C_1 h^{-1} \left\| \bar{e} \right\| + C_2 \, h^p \le C_1 h^{-1} \left(\left\| e \right\| + \left\| \varepsilon \right\| \right) + C_2 \, h^p \le C_3 h^p + C_2 \, h^p \le C h^p.$$

We note that $\left\| e \right\|_{1,\Omega}^2 = \left\| e \right\|^2 + \left\| e' \right\|^2$. Applying (9) and the estimate $\left\| e' \right\| \le C h^p$ yields $\left\| e \right\|_{1,\Omega}^2 \le C_1 h^{2p+2} + C_2 h^{2p} = o(h^{2p})$, which completes the proof of the theorem.

4. Superconvergence error analysis

In this section, we study the superconvergence properties of the DG method. We first show a $(2p+1)$th order superconvergence rate of the DG approximation at the downwind point of each element. Then, we apply this superconvergence result to show that the DG solution converges to the special projection of the exact solution $P_h^- u$ at $o(h^{p+2})$. This result allows us to prove that the leading term of the DG error is proportional to the $(p+1)$ degree right Radau polynomial.

First, we define some special polynomials. The pth degree Legendre polynomial can be defined by Rodrigues formula [41]

$$\tilde{L}_p(\xi) = \frac{1}{2^p \, p!} \frac{d^p}{d\xi^p} \left((\xi^2 - 1)^p \right), \quad -1 \le \xi \le 1.$$

It satisfies the following important properties: $\tilde{L}_p(1) = 1$, $\tilde{L}_p(-1) = (-1)^p$, and the orthogonality relation

$$\int_{-1}^{1} \tilde{L}_p(\xi) \tilde{L}_q(\xi) d\xi = \frac{2}{2p+1} \delta_{pq}, \quad \text{where } \delta_{pq} \text{ is the Kronecker symbol.} \tag{30}$$

One can easily write the $(p+1)$ degree Legendre polynomial on $[-1,1]$ as

$$\tilde{L}_{p+1}(\xi) = \frac{(2p+2)!}{2^{p+1}((p+1)!)^2} \xi^{p+1} + \tilde{q}_p(\xi), \quad \text{where } \tilde{q}_p \in P^p([-1,1]).$$

The $(p+1)$ degree right Radau polynomial on $[-1,1]$ is defined as $\tilde{R}_{p+1}(\xi) = \tilde{L}_{p+1}(\xi) - \tilde{L}_p(\xi)$. It has $p+1$ real distinct roots, $-1 < \xi_0 < \cdots < \xi_p = 1$.

Mapping I_j into the reference element $[-1,1]$ by the linear transformation $t = \dfrac{t_j + t_{j-1}}{2} + \dfrac{h_j}{2}\xi$, we obtain the shifted Legendre and Radau polynomials on I_j:

$$L_{p+1,j}(t) = \tilde{L}_{p+1}\left(\frac{2t - t_j - t_{j-1}}{h_j}\right), \quad R_{p+1,j}(t) = \tilde{R}_{p+1}\left(\frac{2t - t_j - t_{j-1}}{h_j}\right).$$

Next, we define the monic Radau polynomial, $\psi_{p+1,j}(t)$, on I_j as

$$\psi_{p+1,j}(t) = \frac{h_j^{p+1}[(p+1)!]^2}{(2p+2)!} R_{p+1,j}(t) = c_p h_j^{p+1} R_{p+1,j}(t), \quad \text{where } c_p = \frac{((p+1)!)^2}{(2p+2)!}. \tag{31}$$

Throughout this work the roots of $R_{p+1,j}(t)$ are denoted by $t_{j,i} = \dfrac{t_j + t_{j-1}}{2} + \dfrac{h_j}{2}\xi_i, \; i = 0, 1, ..., p$.

In the next lemma, we recall the following results which will be needed in our error analysis [32].

Lemma 4.1. *The polynomials $L_{p,j}$ and $\psi_{p+1,j}$ satisfy the following properties*

$$\left\|L_{p,j}\right\|_{I_j}^2 = \frac{h_j}{2p+1}, \quad \int_{I_j} \psi'_{p+1,j} \psi_{p+1,j}\, dt = -k_1 h_j^{2p+2}, \quad \left\|\psi_{p+1,j}\right\|_{I_j}^2 = (2p+2)k_2 h_j^{2p+3}, \tag{32}$$

where $k_1 = 2c_p^2$, $k_2 = \dfrac{k_1}{(2p+1)(2p+3)}$, and $c_p = \dfrac{((p+1)!)^2}{(2p+2)!}$.

Now, we are ready to prove the following superconvergence results.

Theorem 4.1. *Suppose that the assumptions of Theorem 1 are satisfied. Also, we assume that f_u is sufficiently smooth with respect to t and u (for example, $h(t) = f_u(t, u(t)) \in C^p([0,T])$ is enough.). Then there exists a positive constant C such that*

$$\left|e(t_k^-)\right| \leq Ch^{2p+1}, \quad k = 1, ..., N, \tag{33}$$

$$\left|\bar{e}(t_k^-)\right| \leq Ch^{2p+1}, \quad k = 1, ..., N, \tag{34}$$

$$\left\|\overline{e}'\right\| \le C\, h^{p+1},\tag{35}$$

$$\left\|\overline{e}\right\| \le C\, h^{p+2}.\tag{36}$$

Proof. To prove (33), we proceed by the duality argument. Consider the following auxiliary problem:

$$W' + \theta W = 0, \quad t \in [0, t_k] \quad \text{subject to} \quad W(t_k) = 1,\tag{37}$$

where $1 \le k \le N$ and $\theta = \theta(t) = \int_0^1 f_u(t, u(t) - se(t))ds$. The exact solution of this problem is

$$W(t) = \exp\left(\int_t^{t_k} \theta(s)ds\right), \quad t \in \Omega_k = [0, t_k].$$ Using the assumption $h(t) = f_u(t, u(t)) \in C^p([0, T])$

and the estimate (24a), we can easily show that there exists a constant C such that

$$\left\|W\right\|_{p+1, \Omega_k} \le C.\tag{38}$$

Using (17) and (37), we get

$$\mathcal{A}_j(e; W) = \int_{I_j}(-W' - \theta W)edt + -e(t_{j-1}^-)W(t_{j-1}) + e(t_j^-)W(t_j) = -e(t_{j-1}^-)W(t_{j-1}) + e(t_j^-)W(t_j).$$

Summing over the elements I_j, $j = 1, ..., k$, using $W(t_k) = 1$, and the fact that $e(t_0^-) = 0$, we obtain

$$\sum_{j=1}^{k}\mathcal{A}_j(e; W) = -e(t_0^-)W(t_0) + e(t_k^-)W(t_k) = e(t_k^-).\tag{39}$$

Now, taking $V = W$ in (21) yields

$$\mathcal{A}_j(e; W) = \int_{I_j}(\varepsilon' - \theta e)(W - P_h^+ W)dt.$$

Summing over all elements I_j, $j = 1, ..., k$ with $k = 1, ..., N$ and applying (39), we arrive at

$$e(t_k^-) = \sum_{j=1}^{k} \int_{I_j} (\varepsilon' - \theta e)(W - P_h^+ W)dt.$$

Using (24a) and applying the Cauchy-Schwarz inequality, we obtain

$$\left|e(t_k^-)\right| \le (\left\|\varepsilon'\right\|_{0,\Omega_k} + M_1 \left\|e\right\|_{0,\Omega_k}) \left\|W - P_h^+ W\right\|_{0,\Omega_k} \le (\left\|\varepsilon'\right\| + M_1 \left\|e\right\|) \left\|W - P_h^+ W\right\|_{0,\Omega_k}.$$

Invoking the estimates (7), (9), and (38), we conclude that

$$\left|e(t_k^-)\right| \le (C_0 h^p \left|u\right|_{p+1,\Omega} + M_1 C_1 h^{p+1}) C_2 h^{p+1} \left|W\right|_{p+1,\Omega_k} \le C(h^p + h^{p+1}) h^{p+1} = \mathcal{O}(h^{2p+1}), \tag{40}$$

for all $k = 1, ..., N$, which completes the proof of (33).

In order to prove (34), we use the relation $e = \bar{e} + \varepsilon$, the property of the projection P_h^-, i.e., $\varepsilon(t_k^-) = 0$, and the estimate (33) to get

$$\left|\bar{e}(t_k^-)\right| = \left|e(t_k^-) - \varepsilon(t_k^-)\right| = \left|e(t_k^-)\right| = \mathcal{O}(h^{2p+1}).$$

Next, we will derive optimal error estimate for $\left\|\bar{e}'\right\|$. By the property of P_h^-, we have

$$\int_{I_j} \varepsilon v' dt = 0, \quad \forall v \in P^p(I_j), \quad \text{and} \quad \varepsilon(t_j^-) = 0, \quad j = 1, \dots, N. \tag{41}$$

Using the relation $e = \varepsilon + \bar{e}$, applying (41) and (11) yields

$$\int_{I_j} v' \bar{e} dt + \int_{I_j} (f(t,u) - f(t,u_h)) v dt + \bar{e}(t_{j-1}^-) v(t_{j-1}^+) - \bar{e}(t_j^-) v(t_j^-) = 0.$$

By integration by parts on the first term, we obtain

$$\int_{I_j} (\bar{e}' - f(t,u) + f(t,u_h)) v dt + [\bar{e}](t_{j-1}) v(t_{j-1}^+) = 0. \tag{42}$$

Choosing $v(t) = \bar{e}'(t) - (-1)^p \bar{e}'(t^+_{j-1}) L_{p,j}(t) \in P^p(I_j)$ in (42), we have, by the property $\tilde{L}_p(-1) = (-1)^p$ and the orthogonality relation (30), $v(t^+_{j-1}) = 0$ and

$$
\begin{aligned}
\int_{I_j} (\bar{e}')^2 dt &= (-1)^p \bar{e}'(t^+_{j-1}) \int_{I_j} L_{p,j} \bar{e}' dt + \int_{I_j} (f(t,u) - f(t,u_h))(\bar{e}' - (-1)^p \bar{e}'(t^+_{j-1}) L_{p,j}) dt \\
&= \int_{I_j} (f(t,u) - f(t,u_h))(\bar{e}' - (-1)^p \bar{e}'(t^+_{j-1}) L_{p,j}) dt.
\end{aligned}
\tag{43}
$$

Using (3) and applying the Cauchy-Schwarz inequality gives

$$
\begin{aligned}
\|\bar{e}'\|^2_{I_j} &\leq \int_{I_j} |f(t,u) - f(t,u_h)| \left(|\bar{e}'| + |\bar{e}'(t^+_{j-1})| |L_{p,j}| \right) dt \leq M_1 \int_{I_j} |e| \left(|\bar{e}'| + |\bar{e}'(t^+_{j-1})| |L_{p,j}| \right) dt \\
&\leq M_1 \|e\|_{I_j} \left(\|\bar{e}'\|_{I_j} + |\bar{e}'(t^+_{j-1})| \|L_{p,j}\|_{I_j} \right).
\end{aligned}
\tag{44}
$$

Combining (44) with (8) and (32), we obtain

$$
\|\bar{e}'\|^2_{I_j} \leq M_1 \|e\|_{I_j} \left(\|\bar{e}'\|_{I_j} + \left(C_1 h_j^{-1/2} \|\bar{e}'\|_{I_j} \right) \frac{h_j^{1/2}}{(2p+1)^{1/2}} \right) \leq C \|e\|_{I_j} \|\bar{e}'\|_{I_j}.
$$

Consequently, $\|\bar{e}'\|_{I_j} \leq C \|e\|_{I_j}$. Taking the square of both sides, summing over all elements, and using (9), we conclude that

$$
\|\bar{e}'\|^2 \leq C \|e\|^2 \leq Ch^{2p+2}.
\tag{45}
$$

Finally, we will estimate $\|\bar{e}\|$. Using the fundamental theorem of calculus, we write

$$
|\bar{e}(t)| = |\bar{e}(t^-_j) + \int_{t_j}^t \bar{e}'(s) ds| \leq |\bar{e}(t^-_j)| + \int_{I_j} |\bar{e}'(s)| ds, \quad \forall t \in I_j.
$$

Taking the square of both sides, applying the inequality $(a+b)^2 \leq 2a^2 + 2b^2$, and applying the Cauchy-Schwartz inequality, we get

$$| \bar{e}(t) |^2 \le 2 | \bar{e}(t_j^-) |^2 + 2 \left(\int_{I_j} | \bar{e}'(s) | \, ds \right)^2 \le 2 | \bar{e}(t_j^-) |^2 + 2 h_j \int_{I_j} | \bar{e}'(s) |^2 \, ds = 2 | \bar{e}(t_j^-) |^2 + 2 h_j \| \bar{e}' \|_{I_j}^2 .$$

Integrating this inequality with respect to t and using the estimate (34), we get

$$\| \bar{e} \|_{I_j}^2 \le 2 h_j | \bar{e}(t_j^-) |^2 + 2 h_j^2 \| \bar{e}' \|_{I_j}^2 \le 2 C h_j^{4p+3} + 2 h_j^2 \| \bar{e}' \|_{I_j}^2 .$$

Summing over all elements and using the estimate (35) and the fact that $h = \max h_j$, we obtain

$$\| \bar{e} \|^2 \le C_1 h^{4p+2} + 2 h^2 \| \bar{e}' \|^2 \le C_1 h^{4p+2} + 2 C_2 h^{2p+4} = \mathcal{O}(h^{2p+4}), \tag{46}$$

where we used $4p + 2 \ge 2p + 4$ for $p \ge 1$. This completes the proof of the theorem.

The previous theorem indicates that the DG solution u_h is closer to $P_h^- u$ than to the exact solution u. Next, we apply the results of Theorem 2 to prove that the actual error e can be split into a significant part, which is proportional to the $(p + 1)$ degree right Radau polynomial, and a less significant part that converges at $o(h^{p+2})$ rate in the L^2 norm. Before we prove this result, we introduce two interpolation operators π and $\hat{\pi}$. The interpolation operator π is defined as follows: For smooth $u = u(t)$, $\pi u \big|_{I_j} \in P^p(I_j)$ and interpolates u at the roots of the $(p + 1)$ degree right Radau polynomial shifted to I_j, i.e., at $t_{j,i}$, $i = 0, 1, ..., p,$. The interpolation operator $\hat{\pi}$ satisfies $\hat{\pi} u \big|_{I_j} \in P^{p+1}(I_j)$ and $\hat{\pi} u \big|_{I_j}$ interpolates u at $t_{j,i}$, $i = 0, 1, ..., p$, and at an additional point $\bar{t}_j$ in I_j with $\bar{t}_j \ne t_{j,i}$, $i = 0, 1, ..., p$. The choice of the additional point is not important and can be chosen as $\bar{t}_j = t_{j-1}$.

Next, we recall the following results from [12] which will be needed in our analysis.

Lemma 4.2. *If $u \in H^{p+2}(I_j)$, then interpolation error can be split as*

$$u - \pi u = \phi_j + \gamma_j, \quad on \ I_j, \tag{47a}$$

where

$$\phi_j(t) = \alpha_j \psi_{p+1,j}(t), \quad \psi_{p+1,j}(t) = \prod_{i=0}^{p} (t - t_{j,i}), \quad \gamma_j = u - \hat{\pi} u, \tag{47b}$$

and α_j is the coefficient of t^{p+1} in the $(p+1)$ degree polynomial $\hat{\pi}u$. Furthermore,

$$\left\|\phi_j\right\|_{s,I_j} \le Ch_j^{p+1-s}\left\|u\right\|_{p+1,I_j}, \quad s = 0,\ldots,p, \tag{47c}$$

$$\left\|\gamma_j\right\|_{s,I_j} \le Ch_j^{p+2-s}\left\|u\right\|_{p+2,I_j}, \quad s = 0,\ldots,p+1. \tag{47d}$$

Finally,

$$\left\|\pi u - P_h^- u\right\|_{I_j} \le Ch_j^{p+2}\left\|u\right\|_{p+2,I_j}. \tag{48}$$

Proof. The proof of this lemma can be found in [12], more precisely in its Lemma 2.1.

The main global superconvergence result is stated in the following theorem.

Theorem 4.2. *Under the assumptions of Theorem 2, there exists a constant C independent of h such that*

$$\left\|u_h - \pi u\right\| \le Ch^{p+2}. \tag{49}$$

Moreover, the true error can be divided into a significant part and a less significant part as

$$e(t) = \alpha_j \psi_{p+1,j}(t) + \omega_j(t), \quad on\ I_j, \tag{50a}$$

where

$$\omega_j = \gamma_j + \pi u - u_h, \tag{50b}$$

and

$$\sum_{j=1}^{N}\left\|\omega_j\right\|_{I_j}^2 \le Ch^{2(p+2)}, \quad \sum_{j=1}^{N}\left\|\omega_{j'}\right\|_{I_j}^2 \le Ch^{2(p+1)}. \tag{50c}$$

Proof.   Adding   and   subtracting $P_h^- u$ to $u_h - \pi u$,   we   write

$u_h - \pi u = u_h - P_h^- u + P_h^- u - \pi u = -\bar{e} + P_h^- u - \pi u$. Taking the L^2 norm and using the triangle inequality, we get

$$\left\| u_h - \pi u \right\| \le \left\| \bar{e} \right\| + \left\| P_h^- u - \pi u \right\|.$$

Applying the estimates (36) and (48), we deduce (49). Next, adding and subtracting πu to e, we write $e = u - \pi u + \pi u - u_h$. Moreover, one can split the interpolation error $u - \pi u$ on I_j as in (47a) to get

$$e = \phi_j + \gamma_j + \pi u - u_h = \phi_j + \omega_j, \quad \text{where} \quad \omega_j = \gamma_j + \pi u - u_h. \tag{51}$$

Next, we use the Cauchy-Schwarz inequality and the inequality $|ab| \le \frac{1}{2}(a^2 + b^2)$ to write

$$\left\| \omega_j \right\|_{I_j}^2 = \left(\gamma_j + \pi u - u_h, \gamma_j + \pi u - u_h \right)_{I_j} = \left\| \gamma_j \right\|_{I_j}^2 + 2\left(\gamma_j, \pi u - u_h \right)_{I_j} + \left\| \pi u - u_h \right\|_{I_j}^2$$
$$\le 2\left(\left\| \gamma_j \right\|_{I_j}^2 + \left\| \pi u - u_h \right\|_{I_j}^2 \right).$$

Summing over all elements and applying (47d) with $s = 0$ and (49) yields the first estimate in (50c).

Using the Cauchy-Schwarz inequality and the inequality $|ab| \le \frac{1}{2}(a^2 + b^2)$, we write

$$\left\| \omega_{j'} \right\|_{I_j}^2 = \left(\gamma_{j'} + (\pi u - u_h)', \gamma_{j'} + (\pi u - u_h)' \right)_{I_j} \le 2\left(\left\| \gamma_{j'} \right\|_{I_j}^2 + \left\| (\pi u - u_h)' \right\|_{I_j}^2 \right). \tag{52}$$

Using the inverse inequality (8), i.e., $\left\| (\pi u - u_h)' \right\|_{I_j} \le C h^{-1} \left\| (\pi u - u_h) \right\|_{I_j}$, we obtain the estimate

$$\left\| \omega_{j'} \right\|_{I_j}^2 \le C\left(\left\| \gamma_{j'} \right\|_{I_j}^2 + h^{-2} \left\| \pi u - u_h \right\|_{I_j}^2 \right).$$

Summing over all elements and applying (49) and the estimate (47d) with $s = 1$, we establish the second estimate in (50c).

5. *A posteriori* error estimation

In this section, we use the superconvergence results from the previous section to construct a residual-based *a posteriori* error estimator which is computationally simple, efficient, and asymptotically exact. We will also prove its asymptotic exactness under mesh refinement. First, we present the weak finite element formulation to compute *a posteriori* error estimate for the nonlinear IVP (2).

In order to obtain a procedure for estimating the error e, we multiply (2) by arbitrary smooth function v and integrate over the element I_j to obtain

$$\int_{I_j} u'v\,dt = \int_{I_j} f(t,u)v\,dt. \tag{53}$$

Replacing u by $u_h + e$ and choosing $v = \psi_{p+1,j}(t)$, we obtain

$$\int_{I_j} e'\psi_{p+1,j}\,dt = \int_{I_j}\left(f(t,u_h+e)-u_h'\right)\psi_{p+1,j}\,dt. \tag{54}$$

Substituting (50a), i.e., $e(t) = \alpha_j\psi_{p+1,j}(t) + \omega_j(t)$, into the left-hand side of (54) yields

$$\alpha_j\int_{I_j} \psi_{p+1,j}'\psi_{p+1,j}\,dt = \int_{I_j}\left(f(t,u_h+e)-u_h'-\omega_j'\right)\psi_{p+1,j}\,dt. \tag{55}$$

Using (32) and solving for α_j, we obtain

$$\alpha_j = -\frac{1}{k_1 h_j^{2p+2}}\int_{I_j}\left(f(t,u_h+e)-u_h'-\omega_j'\right)\psi_{p+1,j}\,dt. \tag{56}$$

Our error estimate procedure consists of approximating the true error on each element I_j by the leading term as

$$e(t) \approx E(t) = a_j\psi_{p+1,j}(t), \quad t \in I_j, \tag{57a}$$

where the coefficient of the leading term of the error, a_j, is obtained from the coefficient α_j defined in (56) by neglecting the terms ω_j and e, i.e.,

$$a_j = -\frac{1}{k_1 h_j^{2p+2}} \int_{I_j} \left(f(t, u_h) - u_{h'} \right) \psi_{p+1,j} dt. \tag{57b}$$

We remark that our *a posteriori* error estimate is obtained by solving local problems with no boundary condition.

The global effectivity index, defined by $\sigma = \dfrac{\|E\|}{\|e\|}$, is an important criterion for evaluating the quality of an error estimator. The main results of this section are stated in the following theorem. In particular, we prove that the error estimate E, in the L^2 norm, converges to the actual error e. Moreover, we show that our *a posterior* error estimate is asymptotically exact by showing that the global effectivity index $\sigma \to 1$ as $h \to 0$.

Theorem 5.1. *Suppose that the assumptions of Theorem 2 are satisfied. If $E(t) = a_j \psi_{p+1,j}(t)$, $t \in I_j$, where a_j, $j = 1, ..., N$, are defined in (57b), then*

$$\left\| e - E \right\|^2 \leq C h^{2p+4}. \tag{58}$$

Thus, the post-processed approximation $u_h + E$ yields $\mathcal{O}(h^{p+2})$ superconvergent solution, i.e.,

$$\left\| u - (u_h + E) \right\|^2 = \sum_{j=1}^{N} \left\| u - (u_h + a_j \psi_{p+1,j}) \right\|_{I_j}^2 \leq C h^{2p+4}. \tag{59}$$

Furthermore, then there exists a positive constant C independent of h such that

$$\left| \left\| e \right\|^2 - \left\| E \right\|^2 \right| \leq C h^{2p+4}. \tag{60}$$

Finally, if there exists a constant $C = C(u) > 0$ independent of h such that

$$\left\| e \right\| \geq C h^{p+1}, \tag{61}$$

then the global effectivity index in the L^2 norm converges to unity at $\mathcal{O}(h)$ rate, i.e.,

$$\frac{\|E\|}{\|e\|} = 1 + \mathcal{O}(h). \tag{62}$$

Proof. First, we will prove (58) and (59). Since $e = \alpha_j \psi_{p+1,j} + \omega_j$ and $E = \alpha_j \psi_{p+1,j}$ on I_j, we have

$$\left\| e - E \right\|_{I_j}^2 = \left\| (\alpha_j - a_j)\psi_{p+1,j} + \omega_j \right\|_{I_j}^2 \leq 2(\alpha_j - a_j)^2 \left\| \psi_{p+1,j} \right\|_{I_j}^2 + 2\left\| \omega_j \right\|_{I_j}^2,$$

where we used the inequality $(a+b)^2 \leq 2a^2 + 2b^2$. Summing over all elements yields

$$\left\| e - E \right\|^2 = \sum_{j=1}^N \left\| e - E \right\|_{I_j}^2 \leq 2\sum_{j=1}^N (\alpha_j - a_j)^2 \left\| \psi_{p+1,j} \right\|_{I_j}^2 + 2\sum_{j=1}^N \left\| \omega_j \right\|_{I_j}^2. \tag{63}$$

Next, we will derive upper bounds for $\displaystyle\sum_{j=1}^N (\alpha_j - a_j)^2 \left\| \psi_{p+1,j} \right\|_{I_j}^2$. Subtracting (56) from (57b), we obtain

$$a_j - \alpha_j = \frac{1}{k_1 h_j^{2p+2}} \int_{I_j} \left(f(t,u_h + e) - f(t,u_h) - \omega_j' \right) \psi_{p+1,j} dt. \tag{64}$$

Thus,

$$\left| a_j - \alpha_j \right| \leq \frac{1}{k_1 h_j^{2p+2}} \int_{I_j} \left(\left| f(t,u_h + e) - f(t,u_h) \right| + \left| \omega_j' \right| \right) \left| \psi_{p+1,j} \right| dt. \tag{65}$$

Using the Lipschitz condition (3) and applying the Cauchy-Schwarz inequality yields

$$\left| a_j - \alpha_j \right| \leq \frac{1}{k_1 h_j^{2p+2}} \int_{I_j} \left(M_1 |e| + |\omega_j'| \right) \left| \psi_{p+1,j} \right| dt \leq \frac{\left\| \psi_{p+1,j} \right\|_{I_j}}{k_1 h_j^{2p+2}} \left(M_1 \|e\|_{I_j} + \|\omega_j'\|_{I_j} \right). \tag{66}$$

Applying the inequality $(a+b)^2 \leq 2(a^2 + b^2)$, we obtain

$$(a_j - \alpha_j)^2 \leq \frac{2\left\|\psi_{p+1,j}\right\|_{I_j}^2}{k_1^2 h_j^{4p+4}}\left(M_1^2\left\|e\right\|_{I_j}^2 + \left\|\omega_j'\right\|_{I_j}^2\right). \tag{67}$$

Multiplying by $\left\|\psi_{p+1,j}\right\|_{I_j}^2$ and using (32), i.e., $\left\|\psi_{p+1,j}\right\|_{I_j}^2 = (2p+2)k_2 h_j^{2p+3}$ yields

$$(a_j - \alpha_j)^2\left\|\psi_{p+1,j}\right\|_{I_j}^2 \leq \frac{2\left\|\psi_{p+1,j}\right\|_{I_j}^4}{k_1^2 h_j^{4p+4}}\left(M_1^2\left\|e\right\|_{I_j}^2 + \left\|\omega_j'\right\|_{I_j}^2\right) \leq k_3 h_j^2\left(\left\|e\right\|_{I_j}^2 + \left\|\omega_j'\right\|_{I_j}^2\right), \tag{68}$$

where $k_3 = \dfrac{2(2p+2)^2 k_2^2}{k_1^2}\max(M_1^2, 1)$ is a constant independent of the mesh size.

Summing over all elements and using $h = \max\limits_{1 \leq j \leq N} h_j$, we arrive at

$$\sum_{j=1}^{N}(a_j - \alpha_j)^2\left\|\psi_{p+1,j}\right\|_{I_j}^2 \leq k_3 h^2\left[\left\|e\right\|^2 + \sum_{j=1}^{N}\left\|\omega_j'\right\|_{I_j}^2\right].$$

Combining this estimate with (9) and (50c), we establish

$$\sum_{j=1}^{N}\left(a_j - \alpha_j\right)^2\left\|\psi_{p+1,j}\right\|_{I_j}^2 \leq Ch^{2p+4}. \tag{69}$$

Now, combining (63) and the estimates (50c) and (69) yields

$$\left\|e - E\right\|^2 \leq 2C_1 h^{2p+4} + 2C_2 h^{2p+4} = Ch^{2p+4},$$

which completes the proof of (58). Using the relation $e = u - u_h$ and the estimate (58), we obtain

$$\sum_{j=1}^{N}\left\|u - (u_h + a_j\psi_{p+1,j})\right\|_{I_j}^2 = \left\|u - (u_h + E)\right\|^2 = \left\|e - E\right\|^2 \leq Ch^{2p+4}.$$

Next, we will prove (60). Using the reverse triangle inequality, we have

$$\left| \|E\| - \|e\| \right| \leq \|E - e\|, \tag{70}$$

which, after applying the estimate (58), completes the proof of (60).

In order to show (62), we divide (70) by $\|e\|$ to obtain $|\sigma - 1| \leq \dfrac{\|E - e\|}{\|e\|}$. Applying the estimate (58) and the inverse estimate (61), we arrive at

$$|\sigma - 1| \leq Ch.$$

Therefore, $\sigma = \dfrac{\|E\|}{\|e\|} = 1 + o(h)$, which establishes (62).

Remark 5.1. The previous theorem indicates that the computable quantity $\|E\|$ converges to $\|e\|$ at $o(h^{p+2})$ rate. This accuracy enhancement is achieved by adding the error estimate E to the DG solution u_h.

Remark 5.2. The performance of an error estimator σ is typically measured by the global effectivity index which is defined as the ratio of the estimated error $\|E\|$ to the actual error $\|e\|$. We say that the error estimator is asymptotically exact if $\sigma \to 1$ as $h \to 0$. The estimate (62) indicates that the global effectivity index in the L^2 norm converge to unity at $o(h)$ rate. There-fore, the proposed estimator $\|E\|$ is asymptotically exact. We would like to emphasize that E is a computable quantity since it only depends on the DG solution u_h and f. It provides an asymptotically exact *a posteriori* estimator on the actual error $\|e\|$. Finally, we would like to point out that our procedure for estimating the error e is computationally simple. Furthermore, our DG error indicator is obtained by solving a local problem with no boundary condition on each element. This makes it useful in adaptive computations. We demonstrate this in Section 6.

Remark 5.3. Our proofs are valid for any regular meshes and using piecewise polynomials of degree $p \geq 1$. If $p = 0$ then (46) gives $\|\bar{e}\| = o(h)$ which is the same as $\|e\| = o(h)$. Thus, our superconvergence results are not valid when using $p = 0$. Also, our error estimate procedure does not apply.

Remark 5.4. The assumption (61), which is used to prove the convergence of σ to unity at $o(h)$, requires that terms of order $o(h^{p+1})$ are present in the error. If not, E might not be a good approximation of e. We note that the exponent of h in the estimate (9) is optimal in the sense that it cannot be improved. In fact, for the $h$version finite element method one may show that provided that the $(p + 1)$th order derivatives of the exact solution u do not vanish identically over the whole domain, then an inverse estimate of the form $\left\| e \right\| \geq C(u)h^{p+1}$ is valid for some positive constant $C(u)$ depending only on u [42–44].

Remark 5. Our results readily extend to nonlinear systems of ODEs of the form

$$\frac{d\vec{u}}{dt} = \vec{f}(t,\vec{u}), \quad t \in [0,T], \quad \vec{u}(0) = \vec{u}_0,$$

where $\vec{u} = [u_1, ..., u_n]^t : [0,T] \to \mathbb{R}^n$, $\vec{u}_0 \in \mathbb{R}^n$, and $\vec{f} = [f_1, ..., f_n]^t : [0,T] \times \mathbb{R}^n \to \mathbb{R}^n$. The DG method for this problem consists of finding $\vec{u}_h \in \vec{V}_h^p = \left\{ \vec{v} : \vec{v} \big|_{I_j} \in (P^p(I_j))^n, j = 1, ..., N \right\}$ such that: $\forall \, \vec{v} \in \vec{V}_h^p$ and $j = 1, ..., N$,

$$\int_{I_j} (\vec{v}')^t \vec{u}_h dt + \int_{I_j} (\vec{v})^t \vec{f}(t,\vec{u}_h) dt - (\vec{v})^t (t_j^-) \vec{u}(t_j^-) + (\vec{v})^t (t_{j-1}^+) \vec{u}(t_{j-1}^-) = 0.$$

6. Application: adaptive mesh refinement (AMR)

A posteriori error estimates play an essential role in assessing the reliability of numerical solutions and in developing efficient adaptive algorithms. Adaptive methods based on *a posteriori* error estimates have become established procedures for computing efficient and accurate approximations to the solution of differential equations. The standard adaptive FEMs through local refinement can be written in the following loop

$$\text{SOLVE} \quad \to \quad \text{ESTIMATE} \quad \to \quad \text{MARK} \quad \to \quad \text{REFINE}.$$

The local *a posteriori* errors estimator of Section 5 can be used to mark elements for refinement.

Next, we present a simple DG adaptive algorithm based on the local *a posteriori* error estimator proposed in the previous section. The adaptive algorithm that we propose has the following steps:

1. Select a tolerance *Tol* and a maximum bound on the number of interval (say $N_{max} = 1000$). Put $\left\| E \right\| = 1$.

2. Construct an initial coarse mesh with $N + 1$ nodes. For simplicity, we start with a uniform mesh having $N = 2$ elements.

3. While $N + 1 \leq N_{max}$ and $\left\| E \right\| \geq Tol$ do

(a) Solve the DG scheme to obtain the solution u_h as described in Section 2.

(b) For each element, use (57a) and (57b) to compute the local error estimators $\|E\|_{I_j}$, $j = 1, ..., N$ as described in Section 5 and the global error estimator

$$\|E\| = \left(\sum_{j=1}^{N} \|E\|_{I_j}^2\right)^{1/2}.$$

(c) For all elements I_j

i.   Choose a parameter $0 \le \lambda \le 1$. If the estimated global error $\|E\|_{I_j} < \lambda \max_{j = 1, ..., N} \|E\|_{I_j}$ then stop and accept the DG solution on the element I_j.

ii.   Otherwise, reject the DG solution on I_j and divide the element I_j into two uniform elements by adding the coordinate of the midpoint of I_j to the list of nodes.

4.   Endwhile.

Remark 6.1. *There are many possibilities for selecting the elements to be refined given the local error indicator* $\|E\|_{I_j}$. *In the above algorithm, we used the most popular fixed-rate strategy which consists of refining the element* I_j *if* $\|E\|_{I_j} > \lambda \max_{j = 1, ..., N} \|E\|_{I_j}$, *where* $0 \le \lambda \le 1$ *is a parameter provided by the user. Note that the choice* $\lambda = 0$ *gives uniform refinement, while* $\lambda = 1$ *gives no refinement. Also, there are other stopping criteria that may be used to stop the adaptive algorithm.*

7. Computational results

In this section, we present several numerical examples to (i) validate our superconvergence results and the global convergence of the residual-based *a posteriori* error estimates, and (ii) test the above local adaptive mesh refinement procedure that makes use of our local *a posteriori* error estimate.

Example 7.1. *The test problem we consider is the following nonlinear IVP*

$$u' = -u - u^2, \quad t \in [0,1], \quad u(0) = 1.$$

Clearly, the exact solution is $u(t) = \dfrac{1}{2e^t - 1}$. We use uniform meshes obtained by subdividing the computational domain $[0,1]$ into N intervals with $N = 5, 10, 20, 30, 40, 50$. This example is tested by using P^p polynomials with $p = 0 - 4$. **Figure 1** shows the L^2 errors $\|e\|$ and $\|\bar{e}\|$ with log-log scale as well as their orders of convergence. These results indicate that $\|e\| = O(h^{p+1})$ and $\|\bar{e}\| = O(h^{p+2})$. This example demonstrates that our theoretical convergence rates are optimal.

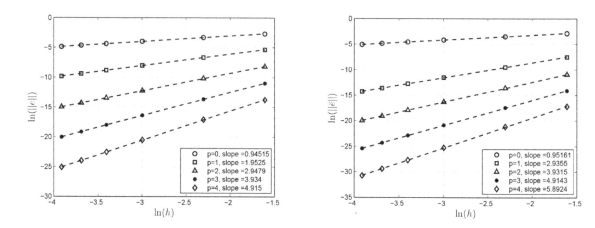

Figure 1. Log-log plots of $\|e\|$ (left) and $\|\bar{e}\|$ (right) versus mesh sizes h for Example 7.1 on uniform meshes having $N = 5, 10, 20, 30, 40, 50$ elements using P^p, $p = 0$ to 4.

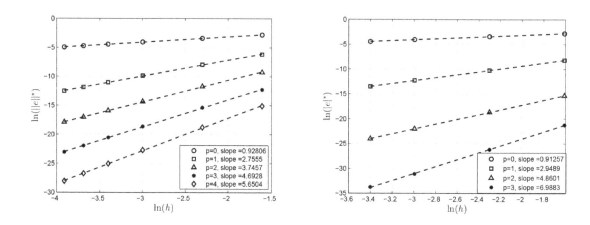

Figure 2. Log-log plots of $\|e\|^*$ (left) versus h for Example 7.1 using $N = 5, 10, 20, 30, 40, 50$ and P^p, $p = 0$ to 4. Log-log plots of $|e|^*$ (right) versus h using $N = 5, 10, 20, 30$ elements using P^p, $p = 0$ to 3.

Next, we compute the maximum error at the shifted roots of the $(p + 1)$ degree right Radau polynomial on each element I_j and then take the maximum over all elements. For simplicity, we use $\|e\|^*$ to denote $\max_{1 \le j \le N}\left(\max_{0 \le i \le p}\left|e(t_{j,i}^-)\right|\right)$, where $t_{j,i}$ are the roots of $R_{p+1,j}(t)$. Similarly, we compute the true error at the downwind point of each element and then we denote $|e|^*$ to be the maximum over all elements I_j, $j = 1, ..., N$, i.e.,

$|e|^* = \max_{1 \le j \le N} |e(t_j^-)|$. In **Figure 2**, we present the errors $\|e\|^*$, $|e|^*$ and their orders of convergence. We observe that $\|e\|^* = o(h^{p+2})$ and $|e|^* = o(h^{2p+1})$ as expected. Thus, the error at right Radau points converges at $o(h^{p+2})$. Similarly, the error at the downwind point of each element converge with an order $2p + 1$. This is in full agreement with the theory.

Next, we use (57a) and (57b) to compute the *a posteriori* error estimate for the DG solution. The global errors $\|e - E\|$ and their orders of convergence, using the spaces P^p with $p = 1 - 4$, are shown in **Figure 3**. We observe that $\|e - E\| = o(h^{p+2})$. This is in full agreement with the theory. This example demonstrates that the convergence rate proved in this work is sharp. Since $\|e - E\| = \|u - (u_h + E)\| = o(h^{p+2})$, we conclude that the computable quantities $u_h + E$ converges to the exact solution u at $o(h^{p+2})$ rate in the L^2 norm. We would like to emphasize that this accuracy enhancement is achieved by adding the error estimate E to the DG solution u_h only once at the end of the computation. This leads to a very efficient computation of the postprocessed approximation $u_h + E$.

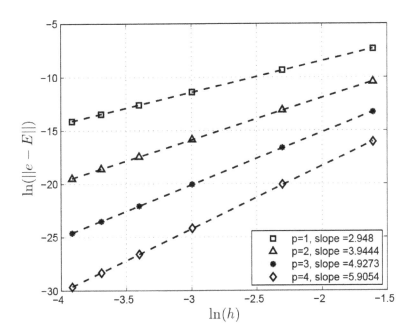

Figure 3. The errors $\|e - E\|$ and their orders of convergence for Example 1 on uniform meshes having $N = 5, 10, 20, 30, 40, 50$ elements using P^p, $p = 1$ to 4.

In **Table 1**, we present the actual L^2 errors and the global effectivity indices. These results demonstrate that the proposed *a posteriori* error estimates is asymptotically exact.

N	$p = 1$		$p = 2$		$p = 3$		$p = 4$	
	$\|e\|$	σ	$\|e\|$	σ	$\|e\|$	σ	$\|e\|$	σ
5	4.7637e-03	1.0362	2.7867e-04	1.0531	1.6847e-05	1.0637	1.0386e-06	1.0705
10	1.2750e-03	1.0179	3.7805e-05	1.0271	1.1742e-06	1.0326	3.7481e-08	1.0363
20	3.2849e-04	1.0089	4.8747e-06	1.0136	7.6227e-08	1.0164	1.2290e-09	1.0182
30	1.4736e-04	1.0059	1.4568e-06	1.0090	1.5201e-08	1.0109	1.6369e-10	1.0122
40	8.3262e-05	1.0044	6.1698e-07	1.0068	4.8296e-09	1.0082	3.9026e-11	1.0091
50	5.3429e-05	1.0035	3.1660e-07	1.0054	1.9827e-09	1.0066	1.2820e-11	1.0073

Table 1. The errors $\|e\|$ and the global effectivity indices for Example 7.1 on uniform meshes having $N = 5, 10, 20, 30,$ 40, 50 elements using $P^p, p = 1$ to 4.

In **Figure 4**, we show the errors $\delta e = |\|e\| - \|E\||$ and $\delta\sigma = |\sigma - 1|$. We see that $\delta e = o(h^{p+2})$ and $\delta\sigma = o(h)$ as the theory predicts.

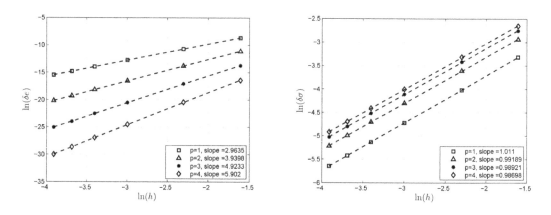

Figure 4. Convergence rates for δe (left) and $\delta\sigma$ (right) for Example 1 on uniform meshes having $N = 5, 10, 20, 30, 40,$ 50 elements using $P^p, p = 1$ to 4.

Example 7.2. In this example we test our error estimation procedure presented in Section 6 on adaptively refined meshes. We consider the following model problem

$$u' = \beta u, \quad t \in [0,5], \quad u(0) = 1,$$

where the exact solution is simply $u(t) = e^{\beta t}$. We apply our adaptive algorithm using $\beta = 1$ (unstable), $\beta = -1$ (stable), and $\beta = -20$ (stiff). The DG solutions and the sequence of meshes obtained by applying our adaptive algorithm with $Tol = 10^{-2}$ for $p = 1 - 4$ are shown in **Figures 5–7** for $\beta = 1, \beta = -1,$ and $\beta = -20,$ respectively. As can be expected, the adaptive algorithm refines in the vicinity of the endpoint $t = 5$ with coarser meshes for increasing polynomial degree p. Furthermore, we observe that, when λ is closer to 0, we get more uniform refinement near the portion with high approximation error. When λ is near 1, we get less uniform refinement near the portion with high approximation error. We also observed that, both for $\lambda = 0.2$ and $\lambda = 0.9$, the optimal convergence rates are achieved asymptotically and that the global effectivity indices converge to unity with increasing polynomial degree p. Furthermore, we tested our adaptive algorithm on other problems and observed similar conclusions. These results are not included to save space.

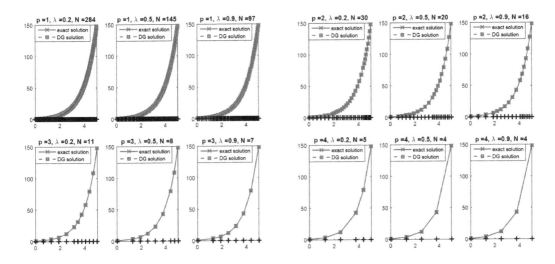

Figure 5. u, u_h, and final meshes for Example 7.2 with $\beta = -20$ using P^p, $p = 1$ to 4, and $Tol = 10^{-2}$.

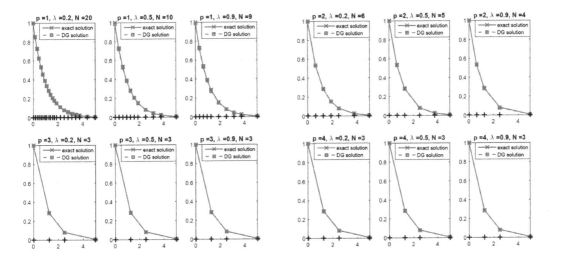

Figure 6. u, u_h, and final meshes for Example 7.2 with $\beta = -1$ using P^p, $p = 1$ to 4, and $Tol = 10^{-2}$.

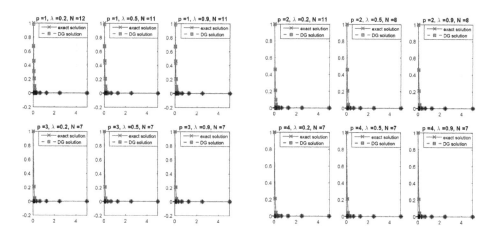

Figure 7. u, u_h, and final meshes for Example 7.2 with $\beta = -20$ using P^p, $p = 1$ to 4, and $Tol = 10^{-2}$.

8. Concluding remarks

In this chapter, we presented a detailed analysis of the original discontinuous Galerkin (DG) finite element method for the approximation of initial-value problems (IVPs) for nonlinear ordinary differential equations (ODEs). We proved several optimal error estimates and superconvergence results. In particular, we showed that the DG solution converges to the true solution with order $p + 1$, when the space of piecewise polynomials of degree p is used. We further proved the $(2p + 1)$th superconvergence rate at the downwind points. Moreover, we proved that the DG solution is $o(h^{p+2})$ superconvergent toward a particular projection of the exact solution. We used these results and showed that the leading term of the DG error is proportional to the $(p + 1)$ degree right Radau polynomial. This result allowed us to construct computationally simple, efficient, and asymptotically exact *a posteriori* error estimator. It is obtained by solving a local residual problem with no boundary condition on each element. Furthermore, we proved that the proposed *a posteriori* error estimator converges to the actual error in the L^2 norm. The order of convergence is proved to be $p + 2$. All proofs are valid for regular meshes and for P^p polynomials with $p \geq 1$. Finally, we presented a local adaptive procedure that makes use of our local *a posteriori* error estimate. Future work includes the study of superconvergence of DG method for nonlinear boundary-value problems.

Abbreviations

Symbols

AMR	Adaptive mesh refinement
DG	Discontinuous Galerkin
FEM, FEMs	Finite element method, finite element methods
IVP, IVPs	Initial-value problem, initial-value problems

ODE, ODEs	Ordinary differential equation, ordinary differential equations
PDE, PDEs	Partial differential equation, partial differential equations
RKDG	Runge-Kutta discontinuous Galerkin
$\mathbb{R}$	Set of real numbers
$\mathbb{R}^n$	Real n-dimensional vector space
$(a, b), [a, b]$	$\{x \in \mathbb{R}: a < x < b\}, \{x \in \mathbb{R}: a \leq x \leq b\}$
$C(X)$	Set of all functions continuous on X
$C^m(X)$	Set of all functions having m continuous derivatives on X
$C^\infty(X)$	Space of functions infinitely differentiable on X
$\overrightarrow{v}$	Typical vector in $\mathbb{R}^n$ of the form $\overrightarrow{v} = [v_1, v_2, ..., v_n]^t$
δ_{ij}	Kronecker symbol
v', v''	First and second derivatives of v with respect to t
$v^{(n)}$	nth derivative of v with respect to t
	"big oh" asymptotic bound
$\left| x_n - L \right| = O(h^m)$	The sequence $\{x_n\}$ converges to L with order m
M_1	Lipschitz constant
I_j	Interval $[t_{j-1}, t_j]$, $j = 1, ..., N$
h_j	Length of interval I_j, $h_i = t_j - t_{j-1}$
h	Maximum of h_j, $h = \displaystyle\max_{1 \leq j \leq N} h_j$
$v(t_j^-)$	Left limit of the function v at the point t_j
$v(t_j^+)$	Right limit of the function v at the point t_j
$[v](t_j)$	Jump of v at the point t_j
p	Degree of a polynomial (integer)
$P^p(I_j)$	Set of all polynomials of degree no more than p on I_j
V_h^p	Finite element space of polynomials of degree at most p in the interval I_j
$\forall$	For all
$(v, w)_{I_j}$	L^2 inner product of v and w on the interval I_j, $(v, w)_{I_j} = \displaystyle\int_{I_j} v(t)w(t)dt$
$\left\| v \right\|_{0, I_j}$ and $\left\| v \right\|_{I_j}$	Standard L^2-norm of v on I_j
$\left\| v \right\|_{0, \Omega}$ and $\left\| v \right\|$	L^2-norm of v on $\Omega = \cup_{j=1}^N I_j$
$\left\| v \right\|_{\infty, I_j}, \left\| v \right\|_\infty$	Standard L^∞-norm of v on I_j and Ω, respectively

$H^s(I_j)$

Sobolev space $H^s(I_j) = \left\{ v : \int_{I_j} |v^{(k)}(t)|^2 dt < \infty, \ 0 \leq k \leq s \right\}$

$\|v\|_{s, I_j}$

Norm of $H^s(I_j)$

$|v|_{s, I_j}$

$H^s(I_j)$-seminorm of v on I_j

$|v|_{s, \Omega}$ and $|v|_s$

$H^s(I_j)$-seminorm of v on Ω

$P_h^{\pm} v$

Gauss-Radau projections of v onto V_h^p

C, C_1, C_2, etc

Generic positive constants independent of h

$u(t)$

Exact solution at time t

$u_h(t)$

DG solution at time t

$\hat{u}_h(t_j)$

$\hat{u}_h(t_j) = u_h(t_j^-)$

e

True error, $e = u - u_h$

ε

Projection error, $\varepsilon = u - P_h^- u$

$\bar{e}$

Error $\bar{e} = u_h - P_h^- u$.

$\tilde{L}_i(\xi), \ i = 0, 1, ..., p$ ith degree Legendre polynomial on $[-1, 1]$

$\tilde{R}_i(\xi), \ i = 0, 1, ..., p$ ith degree right Radau polynomial on $[-1, 1]$

$L_{i, j}(t), \ i = 0, 1, ..., p$ ith degree Legendre polynomial on I_j

$R_{i, j}(t), \ i = 0, 1, ..., p$ ith degree right Radau polynomial on I_j

$\psi_{i, j}(t), \ i = 0, 1, ..., p$ ith degree monic Radau polynomial on I_j

$\xi_i, \ i = 0, 1, ..., p$ Roots of $\tilde{R}_{p+1}(\xi)$

$t_{j, i}, \ i = 0, 1, ..., p$ Roots of $R_{p+1, j}(t)$

πu Interpolant, interpolates $u(t)$ at $t_{j, i}, \ i = 0, 1, ..., p$,

$\hat{\pi} u$ Interpolant, interpolates $u(t)$ at $t_{j, i}, \ i = 0, 1, ..., p$, and at an additional point $\bar{t}_j$ in I_j

with $\bar{t}_j \neq t_{j, i}, \ i = 0, 1, ..., p$

γ_j $u - \hat{\pi} u$

$\phi_j(t)$ $\alpha_j \psi_{p+1, j}(t)$, where α_j is the coefficient of t^{p+1} in the $(p+1)$ degree polynomial $\hat{\pi} u$

ω_j $\gamma_j + \pi u - u_h$

$\sigma, \delta\sigma$ Global effectivity index, $\delta\sigma = |\sigma - 1|$

Tol, N_{max} Tolerance, maximum bound on the number of interval

$\|e\|_*$ Maximum error at Radau points

$|e|^*$ Maximum error at the downwind points

Author details

Mahboub Baccouch

Address all correspondence to: mbaccouch@unomaha.edu

Department of Mathematics, University of Nebraska at Omaha, Omaha, NE, USA

References

[1] W. H. Reed, T. R. Hill, Triangular mesh methods for the neutron transport equation, Tech. Rep. LA-UR-73-479, Los Alamos Scientific Laboratory, Los Alamos, 1973.

[2] R. Biswas, K. Devine, J. E. Flaherty, Parallel adaptive finite element methods for conservation laws, Applied Numerical Mathematics 14 (1994): 255–284.

[3] J.-F. Remacle, J. E. Flaherty, M. S. Shephard, An adaptive discontinuous Galerkin technique with an orthogonal basis applied to compressible flow problems, SIAM Review 45 (2002): 53–72.

[4] J. Flaherty, R. Loy, M. Shephard, J. Teresco, Software for the parallel adaptive solution of conservation laws by discontinuous Galerkin methods, in: B. Cockburn, G. Karnia-dakis, C.-W. Shu (eds.), Discontinuous Galerkin Methods, Vol. 11 of Lecture Notes in Computational Science and Engineering, Springer, Berlin Heidelberg, 2000, pp. 113–123.

[5] J. E. Flaherty, R. Loy, M. S. Shephard, B. K. Szymanski, J. D. Teresco, L. H. Ziantz, Adaptive local refinement with octree load-balancing for the parallel solution of three-dimensional conservation laws, Journal of Parallel and Distributed Computing 47 (1997): 139–152.

[6] S. Adjerid, K. D. Devine, J. E. Flaherty, L. Krivodonova, *A posteriori* error estimation for discontinuous Galerkin solutions of hyperbolic problems, Computer Methods in Applied Mechanics and Engineering 191 (2002): 1097–1112.

[7] M. Delfour, W. Hager, F. Trochu, Discontinuous Galerkin methods for ordinary differential equation, Mathematics of Computation 154 (1981): 455–473.

[8] C. Johnson, Error estimates and adaptive time-step control for a class of one-step methods for stiff ordinary differential equations, SIAM Journal on Numerical Analysis 25 (1988): 908–926.

[9] P. Lesaint, P. Raviart, On a finite element method for solving the neutron transport equations, in: C. de Boor (ed.), Mathematical Aspects of Finite Elements in Partial Differential Equations, Academic Press, New York, 1974.

[10] S. Adjerid, M. Baccouch, The discontinuous Galerkin method for two-dimensional hyperbolic problems. Part I: Superconvergence error analysis, Journal of Scientific Computing 33 (2007): 75–113.

[11] S. Adjerid, M. Baccouch, The discontinuous Galerkin method for two-dimensional hyperbolic problems. Part II: *A posteriori* error estimation, Journal of Scientific Computing 38 (2009): 15–49.

[12] S. Adjerid, M. Baccouch, Asymptotically exact *a posteriori* error estimates for a one-dimensional linear hyperbolic problem, Applied Numerical Mathematics 60 (2010): 903–914.

[13] S. Adjerid, M. Baccouch, Adaptivity and error estimation for discontinuous Galerkin methods, in: X. Feng, O. Karakashian, Y. Xing (eds.), Recent Developments in Discontinuous Galerkin Finite Element Methods for Partial Differential Equations, vol. 157 of The IMA Volumes in Mathematics and its Applications, Springer International Publishing, Switzerland, 2014, pp. 63–96.

[14] M. Baccouch, A local discontinuous Galerkin method for the second-order wave equation, Computer Methods in Applied Mechanics and Engineering 209–212 (2012): 129–143.

[15] M. Baccouch, *A posteriori* error estimates for a discontinuous Galerkin method applied to one-dimensional nonlinear scalar conservation laws, Applied Numerical Mathematics 84 (2014): 1–21.

[16] M. Baccouch, S. Adjerid, Discontinuous Galerkin error estimation for hyperbolic problems on unstructured triangular meshes, Computer Methods in Applied Mechanics and Engineering 200 (2010): 162–177.

[17] B. Cockburn, C. W. Shu, TVB Runge-Kutta local projection discontinuous Galerkin methods for scalar conservation laws II: General framework, Mathematics of Computation 52 (1989): 411–435.

[18] K. D. Devine, J. E. Flaherty, Parallel adaptive *hp*-refinement techniques for conservation laws, Computer Methods in Applied Mechanics and Engineering 20 (1996): 367–386.

[19] T. E. Peterson, A note on the convergence of the discontinuous Galerkin method for a scalar hyperbolic equation, SIAM Journal on Numerical Analysis 28 (1) (1991): 133–140.

[20] P. Castillo, A superconvergence result for discontinuous Galerkin methods applied to elliptic problems, Computer Methods in Applied Mechanics and Engineering 192 (2003): 4675–4685.

[21] F. Celiker, B. Cockburn, Superconvergence of the numerical traces for discontinuous Galerkin and hybridized methods for convection-diffusion problems in one space dimension, Mathematics of Computation 76 (2007): 67–96.

[22] Y. Cheng, C.-W. Shu, Superconvergence of discontinuous Galerkin and local discontinuous Galerkin schemes for linear hyperbolic and convection-diffusion

equations in one space dimension, SIAM Journal on Numerical Analysis 47 (2010): 4044–4072.

[23] B. Cockburn, C. W. Shu, The local discontinuous Galerkin method for time-dependent convection-diffusion systems, SIAM Journal on Numerical Analysis 35 (1998): 2440–2463.

[24] B. Cockburn, G. E. Karniadakis, C. W. Shu, Discontinuous Galerkin Methods Theory, Computation and Applications, Lecture Notes in Computational Science and Engineering, Vol. 11, Springer, Berlin, 2000.

[25] C.-W. Shu, Discontinuous Galerkin method for time-dependent problems: Survey and recent developments, in: X. Feng, O. Karakashian, Y. Xing (eds.), Recent Developments in Discontinuous Galerkin Finite Element Methods for Partial Differential Equations, Vol. 157 of The IMA Volumes in Mathematics and its Applications, Springer International Publishing Switzerland, 2014, pp. 25–62.

[26] M. Baccouch, Analysis of a posteriori error estimates of the discontinuous Galerkin method for nonlinear ordinary differential equations, Applied Numerical Mathematics 106 (2016): 129–153.

[27] M. Delfour, F. Dubeau, Discontinuous polynomial approximations in the theory of one-step, hybrid and multistep methods for nonlinear ordinary differential equations, Mathematics of Computation 47 (1986): 169–189.

[28] D. Estep, *A posteriori* error bounds and global error control for approximation of ordinary differential equations, SIAM Journal on Numerical Analysis 32 (1995): 1–48.

[29] C. Johnson, J. Pitkaranta, An analysis of the discontinuous Galerkin method for a scalar hyperbolic equation, Mathematics of Computation 47 (1986): 285–312.

[30] G. Richter, An optimal-order error estimate for discontinuous Galerkin method, Mathematics of Computation 50 (1988): 75–88.

[31] K. Deng, Z. Xiong, Superconvergence of a discontinuous finite element method for a nonlinear ordinary differential equation, Applied Mathematics and Computation 217 (2010): 3511–3515.

[32] M. Baccouch, Asymptotically exact *a posteriori* LDG error estimates for one-dimensional transient convection-diffusion problems, Applied Mathematics and Computation 226 (2014): 455–483.

[33] M. Baccouch, Global convergence of *a posteriori* error estimates for a discontinuous Galerkin method for one-dimensional linear hyperbolic problems, International Journal of Numerical Analysis and Modeling 11 (2014): 172–192.

[34] M. Baccouch, The local discontinuous Galerkin method for the fourth-order Euler-Bernoulli partial differential equation in one space dimension. Part II: *A posteriori* error estimation, Journal of Scientific Computing 60 (2014): 1–34.

[35] M. Baccouch, A superconvergent local discontinuous Galerkin method for the second-order wave equation on Cartesian grids, Computers and Mathematics with Applications 68 (2014): 1250–1278.

[36] M. Baccouch, Asymptotically exact *a posteriori* local discontinuous Galerkin error estimates for the one-dimensional second-order wave equation, Numerical Methods for Partial Differential Equations 31 (2015): 1461–1491.

[37] M. Baccouch, Asymptotically exact local discontinuous Galerkin error estimates for the linearized Korteweg-de Vries equation in one space dimension, International Journal of Numerical Analysis and Modeling 12 (2015): 162–195.

[38] M. Baccouch, Superconvergence and *a posteriori* error estimates of the DG method for scalar hyperbolic problems on Cartesian grids, Applied Mathematics and Computation 265 (2015): 144–162.

[39] M. Baccouch, B. Johnson, A high-order discontinuous Galerkin method for Itô stochastic ordinary differential equations, Journal of Computational and Applied Mathematics 308 (2016): 138–165.

[40] P. G. Ciarlet, The Finite Element Method for Elliptic Problems, North-Holland Pub. Co., Amsterdam/New York/Oxford, 1978.

[41] M. Abramowitz, I. A. Stegun, Handbook of Mathematical Functions, Dover, New York, 1965.

[42] M. Ainsworth, J. T. Oden, *A posteriori* Error Estimation in Finite Element Analysis, John Wiley, New York, 2000.

[43] L. Schumaker, Spline Functions: Basic Theory, Cambridge University Press, Cambridge/New York, 2007.

[44] K. Segeth, A posteriori error estimation with the finite element method of lines for a nonlinear parabolic equation in one space dimension, Numerische Mathematik 83 (3) (1999): 455–475.

9

Problems of Hierarchical Modelling and *hp*-Adaptive Finite Element Analysis in Elasticity, Dielectricity and Piezoelectricity

Grzegorz Zboiński

Additional information is available at the end of the chapter

Abstract

In this chapter, we consider theoretical and implementation difficulties in application of the hierarchical modelling and *hp*-adaptive finite element approach to elasticity, dielectricity and piezoelectricity. The main feature of the applied methodology is its generalizing character which is reflected by application of the same or analogous algorithms to three mentioned physical problems, including multi-physics problem of piezoelectricity, simple and complex physical description as well as simple and complex geometries. In contrast to the most common approaches dealing with a single physical phenomenon, described by a single physical model, within a single geometrical part, this chapter presents the ideas which brake and overcome such a simplicity. This presented chapter generalizes author's hitherto accomplishments, in hierarchical models and *hp*-approximations of linear elasticity, onto dielectricity and piezoelectricity. The same refers to error estimation and adaptivity control. In this context, the main similarities and differences of three physical problems are of interest in this work.

Keywords: physical complexity, elasticity, dielectricity, piezoelectricity, geometrical complexity, model complexity, hierarchical modelling, finite elements, hierarchical approximations, error estimation, *hp*-adaptivity

1. Introduction

In this chapter of the book we extend our hitherto propositions concerning 3D-based hierarchical models of liner elasticity onto 3D-based linear dielectric and piezoelectric media. In the case of hierarchical models of linear elasticity we apply 3D-elasticity model, hierarchical shell models, first-order shell model and the solid-to-shell or shell-to-shell transition models. In the case of dielectricity we utilize 3D-dielectricity model, and the 3D-based hierarchical dielectric models as well. The piezoelectric case needs combination of two mentioned mechanical and electric hierarchies, so as to generate the hierarchy of 3D-based piezoelectric models. Any combination of the mentioned elastic and dielectric models is possible. As far as the *hp*-discretization is concerned we extend the ideas of hierarchical approximations, constrained approximations and the transition approximations of the displacement field onto electric potential field of dielectricity or the coupled electro-mechanical field of piezoelectricity. The mentioned approximations allow *p*-adaptivity (three-dimensional or longitudinal), *q*-adaptivity (transverse one), *h*-adaptivity (three-dimensional or two-dimensional ones) and *M*-adaptivity (model adaptivity). The error assessment in three classes of problems is based on the equilibrated residual methods (ERM) applied to total and approximation error estimations. The modelling error is obtained as a difference of the previous two errors. The estimated error values are utilized for adaptivity control. The adaptive procedures for dielectricity and piezoelectricity are obtained through the generalization of the three- or four-step strategies applied so far to the elasticity case. The difficulties in generalization of the above-mentioned methods of hierarchical modelling, *hp*-approximations, error estimation and adaptivity control onto electrical and electro-mechanical problems are addressed in this chapter.

2. Considered problems

In the chapter we consider five problems. The first three correspond to stationary problems of mechanical, electric and electro-mechanical equilibrium of the elastic, dielectric and piezo-electric media, respectively. The last two problems deal with free vibration problems of linear elasticity and linear piezoelectricity.

2.1. Elastostatic problem

Let us start with the standard formulation of the linear elasticity [1]. The problem local equations include equilibrium, constitutive and geometric relations:

$$
\begin{aligned}
&\sigma_{ij,j} + f_i = 0, \\
&\sigma_{ij} = D_{ijkl}\varepsilon_{kl}, \\
&\varepsilon_{ij} = 1/2(u_{i,j} + u_{j,i}), \quad x \in V
\end{aligned}
\tag{1}
$$

where $D_{ijkl}, \sigma_{ij}, \varepsilon_{kl}, i,j,k,l = 1,2,3$ are the elasticity constants tensor, and the stress and strain tensors, respectively. The given vector of mass load is denoted as f_i, while u_i is the unknown vector of displacements. The above equations hold in volume V of the body.

The standard boundary conditions for stresses and displacements are:

$$\sigma_{ij}n_j = p_i, \qquad x \in S_P,$$
$$u_i = w_i, \qquad x \in S_W \tag{2}$$

where n_j denotes components of the normal to the body surface S, composed of its loaded S_P and supported S_W parts: $S = S_P \cup S_W$. The vectors p_i and w_i represent the given stresses and displacements on S_P and S_W, respectively.

The equivalent variational formulation results from minimization of the potential energy of the elastic body:

$$\int_V D_{ijkl} v_{i,j} u_{k,l} \, dV = \int_V v_i f_i \, dV + \int_{S_P} v_i p_i \, dS \tag{3}$$

where v_i represent admissible displacements conforming to the displacement boundary conditions.

The above variational functional can be utilized in the derivation of the global finite element equations of the form:

$$\mathbf{K}_M \mathbf{q}^{q,hp} = \mathbf{F}_V + \mathbf{F}_S \tag{4}$$

where $\mathbf{K}_M$, $\mathbf{F}_V$, $\mathbf{F}_S$, are the stiffness matrix within the mechanical equilibrium problem, and the vectors of the nodal forces due to volume and surface loadings. The term $\mathbf{q}^{q,hp}$ stands for the nodal displacement degrees of freedom (dofs). The applied hierarchical q,hp-approximation of displacements will be addressed in the next sections.

2.2. Electrostatic problem of dielectrics

The standard local formulation of linear dielectricity [2] consists of the Gauss law, here corresponding to the lack of volume charges, the constitutive relation and the electric field E_j definition:

$$d_{i,i} = 0,$$
$$d_i = \gamma_{ij} E_j,$$
$$E_j = -\phi_{,j}, \qquad x \in V \tag{5}$$

Above, γ_{ij}, $i,j = 1,2,3$ stands for the dielectric constants tensor, while d_i denotes the electric displacement vector. The scalar term ϕ represents the electric potential field, searched in the volume V of the dielectric.

The boundary conditions for the electric displacements and electric potential read:

$$d_i n_i = -c, \quad x \in S_Q,$$
$$\phi = \chi, \quad x \in S_F \tag{6}$$

where c and χ are the given scalar values of the surface charge and electric potential on the parts S_Q and S_F, respectively, of the surface S of the dielectric body ($S = S_Q \cup S_F$).

The corresponding variational formulation which reflects minimization of the potential electric energy can be described as follows:

$$\int_V \gamma_{ij} \psi_{,i} \phi_{,j} \, dV = \int_{S_Q} \psi c \, dS \tag{7}$$

with ψ being the admissible electric potential conforming to the second boundary condition of Eq. (6).

The finite element formulation can be expressed as follows:

$$\mathbf{K}_E \, \varphi^{\rho, h\pi} = \mathbf{F}_Q \tag{8}$$

where $\mathbf{K}_E$ is the characteristic matrix of dielectricity, $\mathbf{F}_Q$ denotes the characteristic nodal vector of electric charges and $\varphi^{\rho, h\pi}$ stands for the unknown nodal vector of electric potentials. The hierarchical $\rho, h\pi$-approximation of the potential will be explained later on in this chapter.

2.3. Stationary electro-mechanical problem

Formally, the local formulation of the piezoelectric problem of electro-mechanical equilibrium [3] can be treated as a combination of the linear elasticity and linear dielectricity Eqs. (1) and (5):

$$\sigma_{ij,j} + f_i = 0,$$
$$d_{i,i} = 0,$$
$$\sigma_{ij} = D_{ijkl}\varepsilon_{kl} - C_{kij}E_k,$$
$$d_i = C_{ikl}\varepsilon_{kl} + \gamma_{ij}E_j,$$
$$\varepsilon_{ij} = 1/2(u_{i,j} + u_{j,i}),$$
$$E_j = -\phi_{,j}, \quad x \in V \tag{9}$$

What couples both sets of equations are the modified constitutive relations, where the coupling piezoelectric constants tensor C_{kij} appears.

The boundary conditions of the coupled problem are:

$$
\begin{aligned}
\sigma_{ij} n_j &= p_i, & x \in S_P, \\
d_i n_i &= -c, & x \in S_Q, \\
u_i &= w_i, & x \in S_W, \\
\phi &= \chi, & x \in S_F
\end{aligned}
\tag{10}
$$

The variational functional of the electro-mechanical problem consists of the terms of functionals (3) and (7) completed with the terms describing the piezoelectric coupling through the tensor C_{ijk}, i.e.

$$
\int_V D_{ijkl} v_{i,j} u_{k,l} \, dV + \int_V C_{ijk} v_{i,j} \phi_{,k} \, dV + \int_V v_i f_i \, dV + \int_{S_P} v_i p_i \, dS
$$
$$
+ \int_V \gamma_{ik} \psi_{,i} \phi_{,k} \, dV + \int_V C_{ikl} \psi_{,i} u_{k,l} \, dV + \int_{S_Q} \psi c \, dS = 0
\tag{11}
$$

The above variational formulation leads to the following finite element equations

$$
\begin{aligned}
\mathbf{K}_M \, q^{q,hp} - \mathbf{K}_C \, \varphi^{p,h\pi} &= \mathbf{F}_V + \mathbf{F}_S \\
\mathbf{K}_C^T \, q^{q,hp} + \mathbf{K}_E \, \varphi^{p,h\pi} &= \mathbf{F}_Q
\end{aligned}
\tag{12}
$$

where $\mathbf{K}_C$ is the characteristic matrix of piezoelectric coupling.

The above finite element equations correspond to a very general case when both the direct and inverse piezoelectric phenomena are present. Substitution of the second Eq. (12) into the first one leads to the single combined equation from which the nodal displacements $q^{q,hp}$ can be calculated. The opposite substitution gives the combined equation from which the nodal electric potentials $\varphi^{p,h\pi}$ can be extracted. The first situation corresponds to the so-called actuation action of the piezoelectric, while the second one to the sensing action of the piezoelectric body. These two modes of action can be associated with the direct and inverse piezoelectric phenomena, respectively.

2.4. Mechanical problem of free vibration

The local formulation of the free vibration problem of linear elasticity is composed of the following equations

$$\sigma_{ij,j} = \varrho \ddot{u}_i,$$
$$\sigma_{ij} = D_{ijkl} \varepsilon_{kl},$$
$$\varepsilon_{ij} = 1/2(u_{i,j} + u_{j,i}), \quad x \in V \tag{13}$$

where ϱ is a density of the elastic body, while $\ddot{u}_i$ represents the acceleration vector. The displacements are of harmonic character, i.e. $u_i = a_i \sin \omega t$, with ω standing for the unknown natural frequencies of the body and a_i denoting the searched displacement amplitudes.

The boundary conditions are:

$$\sigma_{ij} n_j = 0, \quad x \in S_p,$$
$$u_i = 0, \quad x \in S_W \tag{14}$$

The variational formulation of the free vibration problem takes advantage of the Hamilton's principle and reads

$$\int_V D_{ijkl} v_{i,j} a_{k,l} \, dV - \omega^2 \int_V \varrho v_i a_i \, dV = 0 \tag{15}$$

The finite element formulation derived from the above variational functional represents a set of uniform algebraic equations. Such a set possesses a solution if the following characteristic equation is fulfilled:

$$\det(K_M - \omega^2 M) = 0 \tag{16}$$

From this equation N natural frequencies ω_n, $n = 1,2,...,N$ can be calculated, where N is the total number of degrees of freedom of the vibrating elastic body. Above, M represents the mass (or inertia) matrix.

For each natural frequency ω_n the nodal vector of displacement amplitudes $\mathbf{q}_n^{q,hp}$ can be determined with use of the below finite element equations:

$$(K_M - \omega_n^2 M) \, \mathbf{q}_n^{q,hp} = \mathbf{0},$$
$$(\mathbf{q}_n^{q,hp})^T \, M \, \mathbf{q}_n^{q,hp} = 1 \tag{17}$$

The second relation above is the normalization condition, completing $N - 1$ geometrically independent finite element equations of the first relation.

2.5. Coupled problem of free vibration

We start here with the local (strong) formulation of the undamped vibration problem of the piezoelectric medium

$$
\begin{aligned}
&\sigma_{ij,j} + f_i = \varrho \ddot{u}_i, \\
&d_{i,i} = 0, \\
&\sigma_{ij} = D_{ijkl}\varepsilon_{kl} - C_{kij}E_k, \\
&d_i = C_{ikl}\varepsilon_{kl} + \gamma_{ij}E_j, \\
&\varepsilon_{ij} = 1/2(u_{i,j} + u_{j,i}), \\
&E_j = -\phi_{,j}, \quad x \in V
\end{aligned}
\tag{18}
$$

completed with the following boundary conditions of the coupled electromechanical field

$$
\begin{aligned}
&\sigma_{ij}n_j = p_i, \quad x \in S_P, \\
&d_i n_i = -c, \quad x \in S_Q, \\
&u_i = w_i, \quad\ \ x \in S_W, \\
&\phi = \chi, \quad\ \ \ x \in S_F,
\end{aligned}
\tag{19}
$$

In the case of stationary mass $f_i = f_i(x)$ and surface $p_i = p_i(x)$ loadings and charges $c = c(x)$, and the stationary displacement $w_i = w_i(x)$ and electric potential $\chi = \chi(x)$ boundary conditions as well, the problem converts into two independent ones. The first of them is exactly the stationary task of the electro-mechanical equilibrium defined with the local formulation (9) and (10). The corresponding variational and finite element formulations are exactly described with Eqs. (11) and (12), respectively. The solution in displacements $u_i = u_i(x)$ to this stationary problem determines the equilibrium state around which the free vibrations of the piezoelectric are performed. This solution allows the determination of the initial stresses $\varsigma_{ij} = \varsigma_{ij}(u)$ which are taken into account in the second problem of free vibration.

The local formulation of the mentioned free vibration problem of the piezoelectric can now be determined in the following way:

$$\sigma_{ij,j} = \varrho\ddot{u}_i,$$
$$d_{i,i} = 0,$$
$$\sigma_{ij} = \varsigma_{ij} + D_{ijkl}\varepsilon_{kl} - C_{kij}E_k,$$
$$d_i = C_{ikl}\varepsilon_{kl} + \gamma_{ij}E_j,$$
$$\varepsilon_{ij} = 1/2(u_{i,j} + u_{j,i}),$$
$$E_j = -\phi_{,j}, \quad x \in V$$

$$(20)$$

where the displacement and the coupled potential fields are: $u_i = a_i \sin \omega t$ and $\varphi = \alpha \sin \omega t$, respectively, with a_i and α standing for the displacement and potential amplitudes.

The above set of differential equations has to be completed with the boundary conditions of the form

$$\sigma_{ij}n_j = 0, \quad x \in S_P,$$
$$d_i n_i = 0, \quad x \in S_Q,$$
$$u_i = w_i, \quad x \in S_W,$$
$$\phi = \chi, \quad x \in S_F$$

$$(21)$$

The equivalent variational formulation of the problem reads

$$\int_V \varsigma_{ij}v_{k,i}a_{k,j}\, dV - \int_V D_{ijkl}v_{i,j}a_{k,l}\, dV + \int_V C_{ijk}v_{i,j}\alpha_{,k}\, dV + \omega^2 \int_V \varrho v_i a_i\, dV$$
$$+ \int_V \gamma_{ik}\psi_{,i}\alpha_{,k}\, dV + \int_V C_{ikl}\psi_{,i}a_{k,l}\, dV = 0$$

$$(22)$$

while the corresponding finite element equation describing free vibration of the initially stressed piezoelectric medium is

$$(K_M + K_G - \omega^2 M)q^{q,hp} - K_C \varphi^{p,h\pi} = 0$$
$$K_C^T q^{q,hp} + K_E \varphi^{p,h\pi} = 0$$

$$(23)$$

where $q^{q,hp}$ and $\varphi^{p,h\pi}$ represent the nodal, displacement and electric potential, amplitude degrees of freedom, while K_G stands for the so-called geometric stiffness matrix due to the initial stresses.

As the above set of linear algebraic equations is homogeneous, the solution to it can be obtained if and only if the following characteristic equation:

$$\det(\boldsymbol{K}_M + \boldsymbol{K}_G + \boldsymbol{K}_C \boldsymbol{K}_E^{-1} \boldsymbol{K}_C^T - \omega^2 \boldsymbol{M}) = 0 \tag{24}$$

is fulfilled. This equation has been obtained after substitution of the second relation (23) into the first one. This allows to remove electric potential amplitudes $\boldsymbol{\varphi}^{p,h\pi}$ from the combined equation. From this equation $n = 1,2,...,N$ natural frequencies ω_n can be obtained, where N is the total number of degrees of freedom within the mechanical field.

The corresponding N normalized mode shapes can be obtained from

$$
\begin{aligned}
(\boldsymbol{K}_M + \boldsymbol{K}_G + \boldsymbol{K}_C \boldsymbol{K}_E^{-1} \boldsymbol{K}_C^T - \omega_n^2 \boldsymbol{M})\,\boldsymbol{q}_n^{q,hp} &= \boldsymbol{0}, \\
(\boldsymbol{q}_n^{q,hp})^T \boldsymbol{M}\, \boldsymbol{q}_n^{q,hp} &= 1
\end{aligned}
\tag{25}
$$

where the normalization condition, the same as in (17), has been applied.

3. Complexity of the modelling

There are three types of complexity considered in this chapter. The first one deals with physical complexity which consists in the presence of more than one physical phenomenon in the problem. The second complexity refers to geometry of the domain under consideration. The geometry is regarded as a complex one if more than one type of geometry is applied. One may deal with a three-dimensional geometry, thin-walled geometry and transition geometry, for example. The third type of complexity is model complexity. In this case, one employs more than one model for description of at least one physical phenomenon under consideration. Combination of these three types of complexity can be regarded as a unique feature of the presented research.

The examples of such complex modelling are electro-mechanical systems composed of geometrically complex elastic structures, joined with the geometrically complex piezoelectric actuators or sensors. In the general case of arbitrary geometry, such systems may require complex mechanical and electro-mechanical description.

3.1. Physical complexity

There are two physical sub-systems present in the considered electro-mechanical systems. The first sub-system concerns bodies subject to elastic deformation and representing structural or machine elements, while the second one concerns piezoelectric bodies acting as actuators or sensors, where the direct or inverse piezoelectric phenomena take place.

3.2. Geometrical complexity

In both, mechanical and piezoelectric, sub-domains we deal with the complex geometry of the structural and piezoelectric elements. In the case of the structural elements, they can be three-dimensional bodies, bounded with surfaces, thin- or thick-shell bodies [4] and solid-to-shell transition bodies. In the case of the piezoelectric members, they can be of three-dimensional, symmetric-thickness or transition character. The shell or symmetric-thickness elements are defined by means of the mid-surface and thickness concepts. In the case of both transition members, we deal with three-dimensional geometry, bounded with surfaces, apart from the boundary to be joined with the shell or symmetric-thickness elements. On this superficial boundary part the mid-surface and the symmetric thickness function have to be defined.

3.3. Model complexity

In the case of the mechanical sub-system complex geometry, the mechanical description may include: three-dimensional elasticity model, hierarchical shell models, the first-order shell model and the solid-to-shell or shell-to-shell transition models. The latter two models allow joining the first-order shell domains with the 3D elasticity and hierarchical shell ones, respectively. In the case of the piezoelectric sub-system, the dielectric model can either represent three-dimensional dielectricity or hierarchical symmetric-thickness dielectric models. The piezoelectric model can be any combination of the listed elastic and dielelectric models.

4. The applied methodology

There are five related aspects of the presented methodology of adaptive hierarchical modelling and adaptive *hp*-finite element analysis of elastic, dielectric and piezoelectric bodies. The first of them is the 3D-based approach proposed in [5]. The second issue, i.e. hierarchical mechanical models were initiated in [6], further developed in [7] and finalized in 3D-based version in [8], while the electric models were introduced in [9] for laminated piezoelectrics and in [10] for dielectrics. General rules of the next aspect of hierarchical approximations were given in [11]. Such approximations for hierarchical shells were developed in [7] and for complex structures in [8]. The latter work generalizes the former attempts given in [12–15]. Approximations for piezoelectric problems were elaborated in [9, 16]. The next issue of error estimation by the equilibrated residual method [17] for 3D elasticity was addressed in [18], for the hierarchical shells in [19], for the 3D-based first-order shells in [20, 21] and for the 3D-based complex structures in [22]. Application of the method in electric problems was proposed in [23]. Finally, adaptivity control with the three-step strategy for simple structures was presented in [24], while adaptivity for simple piezoelectrics was introduced in [25]. The first work was extended onto the 3D-based complex structures in [22].

4.1. 3D-based approach

The applied 3D-based approach [5, 8] lies in application of only three-dimensional degrees of freedom (dofs) regardless of the applied mechanical or electric models. This means that the conventional mid-surface dofs of the shell models, i.e. mid-surface displacements, rotations and other generalized displacement dofs of the mid-surface, are replaced with the equivalent through-thickness displacement dofs similar to the three-dimensional dofs of the 3D elasticity model. Also the mid-surface dofs of the two-dimensional dielectric theory are replaced with the through-thickness electric potential dofs of the three-dimensional dielectrics.

The equivalence of the displacement mid-surface dofs and the through-thickness dofs can be expressed through:

$$u'_j = \sum_{m=0}^{I} \xi_3^{\prime m} s_j^{\prime m} = \sum_{m=0}^{I} t_m(\xi_3') u_j^{\prime m} \tag{26}$$

where u'_j represents the local, tangent ($j = 1,2$) and normal ($j = 3$), displacement fields. The terms $\xi_3^{\prime m}$ and $t_m(\xi_3')$ stand for the mth power of the local, normal coordinate ξ_3' ($\xi_3' = 0$ on the mid-surface) and the mth polynomial through-thickness function of this coordinate, respectively. The mid-surface and through-thickness displacement dof functions are denoted as $s_j^{\prime m}$ and $u_j^{\prime m}$, respectively, with $m = 1,2,...,I$ and I being the order of the shell theory.

In the case of the electric potential field, the analogous equivalence can be seen in:

$$\phi = \sum_{m=0}^{J} \xi_3^{\prime m} \delta^m = \sum_{m=0}^{J} t_m(\xi_3') \phi^m \tag{27}$$

where ϕ denotes the scalar field of the potential, while δ^m and ϕ^m represent mth ($m = 1,2,...,J$) mid-surface and through-thickness potential dof functions, while J is the order of the two-dimensional dielectric theory.

4.2. Hierarchical models

In the case of the mechanical elastic models the hierarchy M of the 3D or 3D-based models M is [5, 8]:

$$M \in \mathrm{M}, \ \mathrm{M} = \{3D, MI, RM, 3D\,/\,RM, MI\,/\,RM\} \tag{28}$$

where $3D$ represents three-dimensional elasticity, MI denotes hierarchical higher-order shell models, RM is the first-order Reissner-Mindlin shell model, while $3D/RM$ and MI/RM denote the solid-to-shell or shell-to-shell transition models. It is worth mentioning that the second and last models form the following sub-hierarchies:

$$\begin{aligned} MI &= \{M2, M3, M4,...\}, \\ MI\,/\,RM &= \{M2\,/\,RM, M3\,/\,RM, M4\,/\,RM,...\} \end{aligned} \tag{29}$$

with I being the order of each particular theory.

The hierarchical character of the above models results from the mentioned order I of the applied 3D-based theories, i.e.

$$M = RM \Rightarrow I = 1, K \equiv I$$
$$M = M2 / RM, M3 / RM, M4 / RM, \ldots \Rightarrow I = 2,3,4, \ldots, K = 1$$
$$M = M2, M3, M4, \ldots \Rightarrow I = 2,3,4, \ldots, K \equiv I \tag{30}$$
$$M = 3D / RM \Rightarrow I \to \infty, K = 1$$
$$M = 3D \Rightarrow I \to \infty, K \equiv I$$

Note that for the pure models $(RM, MI, 3D)$ $K \equiv I$, while for the transition ones $(MI / RM, 3D / RM)$ $K \neq I$.

The hierarchy of 3D-based models possesses the following property:

$$\lim_{K=1,I} \left(\lim_{I \to \infty} \left\| u^{I/K(M)} \right\|_{U,V} \right) = \left\| u^{3D} \right\|_{U,V} \tag{31}$$

guaranteeing that the solutions $u^{I/K(M)}$ obtained with the subsequent models tend in the limit to the solution u^{3D} of the three-dimensional elasticity (the highest model of the hierarchy), when $I \to \infty$. In the above relation the norm of the strain energy U is applied in order to compare the solutions. The norm is defined as follows:

$$\left\| u^{I/K(M)} \right\|_{U,V} = \frac{1}{2} \int_V \sigma^T (u^{I/K(M)}) \, \varepsilon(u^{I/K(M)}) \, dV \tag{32}$$

where σ and ε are the stress and strain vectors, respectively.

In the case of the dielectric theories the hierarchy E of the 3D-based models E:

$$E \in E, \quad E = \{3D, EJ\} \tag{33}$$

is composed of the three-dimensional theory 3D and the set:

$$EJ = \{E1, E2, E3, \ldots\} \tag{34}$$

of the 3D-based hierarchical dielectric models EJ, where J is the order of the corresponding dielectric theory.

The hierarchy can be ordered with respect to the order J in the following way:

$$E = E1, E2, E3, \ldots \Rightarrow J = 1,2,3, \ldots, L \equiv J$$
$$E = 3D \Rightarrow J \to \infty, L \equiv J \tag{35}$$

and is characterized with the following property:

$$\lim_{L=1,J} \left(\lim_{J \to \infty} \left\| \phi^{J/L(E)} \right\|_{W,V} \right) = \left\| \phi^{3D} \right\|_{W,V} \tag{36}$$

which says that the solutions $\varphi^{J/L(E)}$ based on the subsequent models of the hierarchy give in the limit ($J \to \infty$) the solution φ^{3D} of the highest model of the hierarchy, i.e. the model of three-dimensional dielectricity. In the case of the applied pure models, EJ and $3D$, $L \equiv J$.

The norm applied for the model comparisons is based on the electrostatic energy W, i.e.

$$\left\| \phi^{J/L(E)} \right\|_{W,V} = \frac{1}{2} \int_V d^T(\phi^{J/L(E)}) \; E(\phi^{J/L(E)}) \; dV \tag{37}$$

with $\mathbf{d}$ and E being the electric displacement and electric field vectors, respectively.

4.3. Hierarchical approximations

The hierarchical approximations [6, 11] applied to the hierarchy of the 3D-based elastic models can be defined as follows [5, 8]:

$$M = RM, I \equiv K = 1 \Rightarrow u^{q(M),hp} = u^{hp}$$
$$M \in MI \,/\, RM, I \geq 2, K = 1 \Rightarrow u^{q(M),hp} = u^{hpq/hp}$$
$$M \in MI, I \equiv K \geq 2 \Rightarrow u^{q(M),hp} = u^{hpq} \tag{38}$$
$$M = 3D \,/\, RM, I \to \infty, K = 1 \Rightarrow u^{q(M),hp} = u^{hpp/hp}$$
$$M = 3D, I \equiv K \to \infty \Rightarrow u^{q(M),hp} = u^{hpp}$$

Above we applied the general notation, $q(M),hp$, valid for any hierarchical model, and the equivalent symbols of the approximations for each particular model (on the right side of the above relations), where h represents the generalized size of the element, p denotes the longitudinal order of approximation and $q \equiv q(M)$ is the transverse order of approximation, equivalent to the order of the theory, i.e. $q(M) \equiv I(M)$. The specific approximations are either two-dimensional (hp) or three-dimensional (hpq, hpp) or mixed (hpq/hp, hpp/hp).

The above approximations lead in the limit ($1/h \to \infty$, $p \to \infty$) to the exact solution of the appropriate mechanical model M of the order I/K, i.e.

$$\lim_{1/h,p\to\infty} \left\| \boldsymbol{u}^{q(M),hp} \right\|_{U,\cup\overset{e}{V}} = \left\| \boldsymbol{u}^{I/K(M)} \right\|_{U,V} \tag{39}$$

Combination of the models defined with (30) and the corresponding approximations of (38) leads to the hierarchical numerical models of the following property:

$$\lim_{K=1,I}\left[\lim_{I\to\infty}\left(\lim_{1/h,p\to\infty}\left\|\boldsymbol{u}^{q(M),hp}\right\|_{U,\cup\overset{e}{V}}\right)\right] = \lim_{K=1,I}\left(\lim_{I\to\infty}\left\|\boldsymbol{u}^{I/K(M)}\right\|_{U,V}\right) = \left\|\boldsymbol{u}^{3D}\right\|_{U,V} \tag{40}$$

As it can be seen above, the solutions to these models tend in the limit to the exact solution of the highest mechanical model (3D).

By analogy, the numerical approximations of the 3D-based dielectric models are:

$$\begin{aligned} E \in EJ, J \equiv L \geq 2 &\Rightarrow \phi^{\rho(E),h\pi} = \phi^{h\pi\rho} \\ E = 3D, J \equiv L \to \infty &\Rightarrow \phi^{\rho(E),h\pi} = \phi^{h\pi\pi} \end{aligned} \tag{41}$$

Above, for the sake of further considerations, the longitudinal approximation order p is denoted as π and the transverse one q as $\rho \equiv \rho(E)$, where $\rho(E) \equiv J(E)$. The principal property of the above electric potential approximations reads

$$\lim_{1/h,\pi\to\infty}\left\|\phi^{\rho(E),h\pi}\right\|_{W,\cup\overset{e}{V}} = \left\|\phi^{J/L(E)}\right\|_{W,V} \tag{42}$$

while for the hierarchical numerical dielectric models, being the combination of the electric models (35) and the above approximations (41), one has

$$\lim_{L=1,J}\left[\lim_{J\to\infty}\left(\lim_{1/h,\pi\to\infty}\left\|\phi^{\rho(E),h\pi}\right\|_{W,\cup\overset{e}{V}}\right)\right] = \lim_{L=1,J}\left(\lim_{J\to\infty}\left\|\phi^{J/L(E)}\right\|_{W,V}\right) = \left\|\phi^{3D}\right\|_{W,V} \tag{43}$$

where the limit solutions $\phi^{J/L(E)}$ and ϕ^{3D} are present.

4.4. Error estimation

It is well known [17–19, 22] that the equilibrated residual methods of error estimation require solution of the following approximated local (element) problems of mechanical equilibrium:

$$\overset{e}{B}(\boldsymbol{u}^{Q,HP},\boldsymbol{v}^{Q,HP}) - \overset{e}{L}(\boldsymbol{v}^{Q,HP}) - \int_{\overset{e}{S}\backslash(S_P\cup S_D)}(\boldsymbol{v}^{Q,HP})^T \left\langle \overset{e}{r}(\boldsymbol{u}^{q,hp}) \right\rangle \overset{e}{dS} = 0 \tag{44}$$

where $\overset{e}{B}$ and $\overset{e}{L}$ are the bilinear and linear forms representing virtual strain energy and the virtual work of the external forces. The last term stands for the virtual work of the inter-element stress fluxes $\langle \overset{e}{r}(u^{q,hp}) \rangle$. The element size in the local problems is denoted as H, the longitudinal approximation order is P, while the transverse one is $Q \equiv Q(M)$.

The above three terms can be defined as follows

$$\overset{e}{B}(u^{Q,HP}, v^{Q,HP}) = \int_{\overset{e}{V}} \epsilon^T(v^{Q,HP}) \, D\epsilon(u^{Q,HP}) \, d\overset{e}{V} = (\overset{e}{v}{}^{Q,HP})^T \overset{e}{k}_M \overset{e}{q}{}^{Q,HP},$$

$$\overset{e}{L}(v^{Q,HP}) = \int_{\overset{e}{V}} (v^{Q,HP})^T f \, d\overset{e}{V} + \int_{\overset{e}{S_P}} (v^{Q,HP})^T p \, d\overset{e}{S} = (\overset{e}{v}{}^{Q,HP})^T (\overset{e}{f}_M + \overset{e}{f}_S), \tag{45}$$

$$\int_{\overset{e}{S \backslash (S_P \cup S_W)}} (v^{Q,HP})^T \langle \overset{e}{r}(u^{q,hp}) \rangle \, d\overset{e}{S} = (\overset{e}{v}{}^{Q,HP})^T \overset{e}{f}_R$$

with D being the elasticity constants matrix. Thus, Eq. (44) can be written in the language of finite elements:

$$\overset{e}{k}_M \overset{e}{q}{}^{Q,HP} = \overset{e}{f}_V + \overset{e}{f}_S + \overset{e}{f}_R \tag{46}$$

where $\overset{e}{k}_M, \overset{e}{f}_V, \overset{e}{f}_S, \overset{e}{f}_R$ denote element stiffness matrix, and element forces vectors due to mass, surface and inter-element stress loadings, while $\overset{e}{q}{}^{Q,HP}$ and $\overset{e}{v}{}^{Q,HP}$ represent solution and admissible displacement dof vectors in the local problem. The solution vector is then utilized in the error estimation. The collection of the element solutions obtained this way leads to the global error estimate which constitutes the upper bound of the true error [18, 19, 22].

The above approach can be extended onto the mechanical problem of free vibration by replacing the linear form of (44) by the virtual work of the inertia forces [26]. These forces are: $\omega^2 \overset{e}{m} \overset{e}{q}{}^{q,hp}$, where $\overset{e}{m}$ is the element mass (or inertia) matrix, while the natural frequencies ω_n and the vector of the element displacement amplitudes $\overset{e}{q}{}^{q,hp}$ are taken from the global problem solution. These forces replace $\overset{e}{f}_V$ and $\overset{e}{f}_S$ in (45) and (46). Note that now the element solutions, analogous to this obtained from (46), do not guarantee the upper boundedness of the global error by its residual estimate.

In the case of electrostatic dielectricity, the local problems of the equilibrated residual method take the form [23]:

$$\overset{e}{b}(\phi^{P,H\Pi}, \psi^{P,H\Pi}) - \overset{e}{l}(\psi^{P,H\Pi}) - \int_{\overset{e}{S \backslash (S_Q \cup S_F)}} \psi^{P,H\Pi} \langle \overset{e}{h}(\phi^{p,h\pi}) \rangle \, d\overset{e}{S} = 0 \tag{47}$$

with the bilinear and linear forms, $\overset{e}{b}$ and $\overset{e}{l}$, representing virtual electrostatic energy and the virtual work of external charges. The right term above is equal to the virtual work of the equilibrated charge flux $\overset{e}{\langle h(\phi^{\rho,h\pi})\rangle}$. The indices H, Π, $P \equiv P(E)$ stand for the element size and the element longitudinal and transverse approximation orders.

Taking into considerations the below definitions:

$$\overset{e}{b}(\phi^{P,H\Pi}, \psi^{P,H\Pi}) = \int_{\overset{e}{V}} E^T(\psi^{P,H\Pi})\, \gamma E(\phi^{P,H\Pi})\, d\overset{e}{V} = (\overset{e}{\psi}{}^{P,H\Pi})^T \overset{e}{k_E}\, \overset{e}{\varphi}{}^{P,H\Pi},$$

$$\overset{e}{l}(\psi^{P,H\Pi}) = \int_{\overset{e}{S_Q}} \psi^{P,H\Pi}\, c\, d\overset{e}{S} = (\overset{e}{\psi}{}^{P,H\Pi})^T \overset{e}{f_Q}, \tag{48}$$

$$\int_{\overset{e}{S\setminus(S_Q\cup S_F)}} \psi^{P,H\Pi} \overset{e}{\langle h(\phi^{\rho,h\pi})\rangle}\, d\overset{e}{S} = (\overset{e}{\psi}{}^{P,H\Pi})^T \overset{e}{f_H}$$

where γ is the dielectricity constants matrix, one can transform (47) into the following local finite element equation

$$\overset{e}{k_E}\, \overset{e}{\varphi}{}^{P,H\Pi} = \overset{e}{f_Q} + \overset{e}{f_H} \tag{49}$$

Above $\overset{e}{k_E}, \overset{e}{f_Q}, \overset{e}{f_H}$ denote element dielectricity matrix, and element vectors due to surface and inter-element charges, while $\overset{e}{\varphi}{}^{P,H\Pi}$ and $\overset{e}{\psi}{}^{P,H\Pi}$ are the solution and admissible electric potential dof vectors of the local problem. This element solution is applied to the error estimation of the dielectric problems. The global error estimate obtained with use of the above element solutions upper-bounds the true global error.

4.5. Adaptive strategy

The adaptive strategy for the complex problems of elasticity is based on the Texas Three-Step Strategy [24]. The latter strategy consists in solution of the global problem thrice on the so-called initial, intermediate and final meshes. The intermediate mesh is obtained from the initial one based on the initial mesh estimated values of element errors and the hp convergence theory relating these errors to the discretization parameter h. Thanks to this the h-adaptation is performed. The final mesh is obtained from the intermediate one in the analogous way through p-refinement. This process takes advantage of the intermediate mesh estimated errors and the relation between these errors and the discretization parameter p. The original strategy can be enriched with the fourth step [5, 27], called the modification one, which is performed on the initial mesh and is applied when the unpleasant numerical phenomena due to the improper solution limit, numerical locking or boundary layers appear in the mechanical problem. The purpose of this additional step is to get rid of the numerical consequences of the mentioned phenomena before the error-controlled hp-adaptivity is started. The control of this step is based on the sensitivity analysis of the local (element) problems solutions to these three phenomena.

The above four-step strategy can be easily extended onto the complex dielectric problems. It has to account only for the boundary layer phenomenon within the modification step, as two other phenomena do not appear in the problems of dielectrics. Other steps do not change.

5. Problems within the methodology

In this section of the chapter we consider the main difficulties in generalization of the hierarchical models, hierarchical approximations, equilibration residual method of error estimation and three- or four-step adaptive strategies, presented in the previous sections for the problems of elasticity and dielectricity, onto coupled problems of piezoelectricity.

5.1. Hierarchical model and approximation issues

The first task here is to compose the elastic and dielectric models, defined with (28) and (33), respectively, into one consistent hierarchy of the piezoelectric media. Our proposition on how to perform this task follows from the main feature of both component hierarchies which are characterized with the independently changing orders I and J of the elastic and dielectric models, as shown in (30) and (35). Because of this we can propose the definition

$$P \in \mathrm{P}, \ \mathrm{P} = \left\{ (M,E): \ M \in \mathrm{M}, \ E \in \mathrm{E} \right\} \tag{50}$$

which determines the hierarchy P of piezoelectric models P as composed of all combinations (M,E) of the elastic M and dielectric E models. Even though the following property:

$$\lim_{K=1,I} \left\{ \lim_{I \to \infty} \left[\lim_{L=1,J} \left(\lim_{J \to \infty} \left\| (u^{I/K(M)}, \phi^{J/L(E)}) \right\|_{Z,V} \right) \right] \right\} = \left\| (u^{3D}, \phi^{3D}) \right\|_{Z,V} \tag{51}$$

is valid in the limit, the ordering of the coupled electro-mechanical solutions measured in the energy norm is not unique due to different signs of the strain (or elastostatic) U, electrostatic W and coupling C parts of the co-energy: $Z = W - U + C$, i.e.

$$\left\| (u^{I/K(M)}, \phi^{J/L(E)}) \right\|_{Z,V} = \frac{1}{2} \int_V | E^T \gamma E - \varepsilon^T D\varepsilon + 2\varepsilon^T CE | \, dV \tag{52}$$

where $\varepsilon = \varepsilon(u^{I/K(M)})$ and $E = E(\varphi^{J/L(E)})$, while C is the coupling (piezoelectric) constants matrix.

The most general case of the hp-approximation within the coupled field of displacements and electric potential may include totally independent h and p approximations within the mechanical and electric fields. However, such an approach requires the vice-versa projections of the displacements and potential solutions between the independent h-meshes of each field. The approach results in the additional projection error which should be included in the error estimation. Because of this we propose the simplified approach which consists in application of the common h mesh and the independent p and π approximations within the displacements and electric potential fields. This assumption leads to the following limit property of the coupled solution

$$\lim_{1/h,p\to\infty}\left(\lim_{1/h,\pi\to\infty}\left\|(\boldsymbol{u}^{q(M),hp},\phi^{\rho(E),h\pi})\right\|_{Z,\cup\overset{e}{V}}\right)=\left\|(\boldsymbol{u}^{I/K(M)},\phi^{J/L(E)})\right\|_{Z,V} \tag{53}$$

It should be noticed that the monotonic character of the co-energy of the consecutive approximate solutions is not guaranteed here due to the coupled character of the electro-mechanical field.

Practical realization of the above concepts of hierarchical modelling and approximations is implemented by means of the hpq- and $h\pi\rho$-adaptive piezoelectric finite elements, presented in **Figure 1**. As said before, h represents the assumed characteristic element size, common for both fields, while p and π denote independent longitudinal approximation orders within the displacements and electric potential fields. The transverse approximation orders q and ρ of the mechanical and electric fields, respectively, are equivalent to the independent hierarchical orders I and J of the elastic and dielectric models, i.e. $q \equiv I$, $\rho \equiv J$.

The normalized versions of the prismatic adaptive elements are presented above, where the 3D-based solid (or hierarchical shell), transition (an example of) and first-order shell mechanical elements are combined with the three-dimensional (or 3D-based symmetric-thickness) dielectric elements. In the figure the normalized coordinates are defined as $\xi_1,\xi_2,\xi_3 \in (0,1)$, while the vertex, mid-edge, mid-base, mid-side and middle nodes of mechanical character are denoted as either $\mathbf{a}_1, \mathbf{a}_2, ..., \mathbf{a}_{21}$ or $\mathbf{a}_1, \mathbf{a}_2, ..., \mathbf{a}_{18}$ or $\mathbf{a}_1, \mathbf{a}_2, ..., \mathbf{a}_{14}$, while the corresponding electric ones are marked with $\mathbf{b}_1, \mathbf{b}_2, ..., \mathbf{b}_{21}$.

5.2. Problems within error estimation

In order to generalize the equilibrated residual method for piezoelectricity the local elastic (44) and dielectric (47) problems have to be replaced with the coupled stationary problems describing the electro-mechanical equilibrium:

$$\overset{e}{\mathrm{B}}(\boldsymbol{u}^{Q,HP},\boldsymbol{v}^{Q,HP})-\overset{e}{\mathrm{C}}(\phi^{\mathrm{P},H\Pi},\boldsymbol{v}^{Q,HP})=\overset{e}{\mathrm{L}}(\boldsymbol{v}^{Q,HP})+\int_{\overset{e}{S}\backslash(S_P\cup S_D)}(\boldsymbol{v}^{Q,HP})^T\langle\overset{e}{\boldsymbol{r}}\rangle\,dS$$

$$\overset{e}{\mathrm{C}}(\boldsymbol{u}^{Q,HP},\psi^{\mathrm{P},H\Pi})+\overset{e}{\mathrm{b}}(\phi^{\mathrm{P},H\Pi},\psi^{\mathrm{P},H\Pi})=\overset{e}{\mathrm{l}}(\psi^{\mathrm{P},H\Pi})+\int_{\overset{e}{S}\backslash(S_Q\cup S_F)}\psi^{\mathrm{P},H\Pi}\langle\overset{e}{h}\rangle\,dS \tag{54}$$

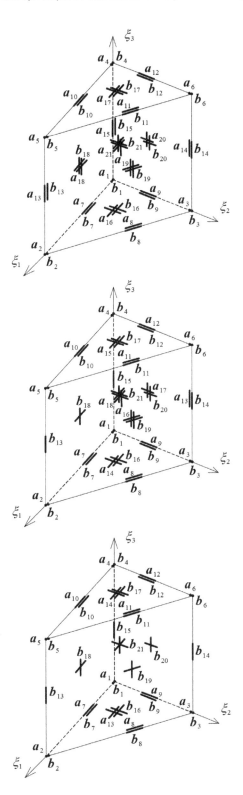

Figure 1. Piezoelectric solid/three-dimensional (top), transition/three-dimensional (middle), shell/three-dimensional (bottom) elements.

where $\langle \overset{e}{r} \rangle = \langle \overset{e}{r}(u^{q,hp}) \rangle$ and $\langle \overset{e}{h} \rangle = \langle \overset{e}{h}(\phi^{\rho,h\pi}) \rangle$, while the above coupling forms are determined as follows:

$$\overset{e}{C}(\phi^{P,H\Pi}, v^{Q,HP}) = \int_{V^e} \varepsilon^T(v^{Q,HP}) \, C \, E(\phi^{P,H\Pi}) \, d\overset{e}{V} = (\overset{e}{v}{}^{Q,HP})^T \overset{e}{k}_C \overset{e}{\phi}{}^{P,H\Pi}$$

$$\overset{e}{C}(u^{Q,HP}, \psi^{P,H\Pi}) = \int_{V^e} E^T(\psi^{P,H\Pi}) \, C^T \varepsilon(u^{Q,HP}) \, d\overset{e}{V} = (\overset{e}{\psi}{}^{P,H\Pi})^T \overset{e}{k}_C^T \overset{e}{q}{}^{Q,HP} \tag{55}$$

Definitions (45), (48) and (55) allow to rewrite (54) in the finite element language:

$$\overset{e}{k}_M \overset{e}{q}{}^{Q,HP} - \overset{e}{k}_C \overset{e}{\phi}{}^{P,H\Pi} = \overset{e}{f}_V + \overset{e}{f}_S + \overset{e}{f}_R$$

$$\overset{e}{k}_C^T \overset{e}{q}{}^{Q,HP} + \overset{e}{k}_E \overset{e}{\phi}{}^{P,H\Pi} = \overset{e}{f}_Q + \overset{e}{f}_H \tag{56}$$

The main disadvantage of the local solutions $\overset{e}{q}{}^{Q,HP}$ and $\overset{e}{\phi}{}^{P,H\Pi}$ obtained from the above set of equations is that they do not lead to the upper bound of the global approximation error of the global problem (12) due to the coupled character of piezoelectricity. Note that the upper bound property is present in the cases of pure elasticity and pure dielectricity. In these circumstances we propose the simplified approach which consists in decoupling of the local mechanical and electric fields:

$$\overset{e}{k}_M \overset{e}{q}{}^{Q,HP} = \overset{e}{k}_C \overset{e}{\phi}{}^{\rho,h\pi} + \overset{e}{f}_V + \overset{e}{f}_S + \overset{e}{f}_R$$

$$\overset{e}{k}_E \overset{e}{\phi}{}^{P,H\Pi} = -\overset{e}{k}_C^T \overset{e}{q}{}^{q,hp} + \overset{e}{f}_Q + \overset{e}{f}_H \tag{57}$$

The simplified solutions of the above two decoupled problems is suggested for serving the approximated error assessment of the coupled field.

In the case of the coupled free-vibration problem we propose to apply the same approach as for the purely elastic vibrations. This means that the inertia forces introduced in Subsection 4.4 have to replace the volume and surface forces in the first equations (56) and (57). The element constitutive stiffness matrix $\overset{e}{k}_M$ in both equations has to be changed for the following sum: $\overset{e}{k}_M + \overset{e}{k}_G$, where $\overset{e}{k}_G$ stands for the element geometric stiffness matrix due to the initial stresses which correspond to the electro-mechanical equilibrium. Because of this one may skip the electric charges $\overset{e}{f}_Q$ in the second equations (56) and (57).

5.3. Adaptivity control matters

The main problem with the piezoelectricity in the context of adaptivity control of the three- or four-step *hp*-adaptive procedure is that the convergence theorem for the finite element approximation of the coupled piezoelectric field is not at one's disposal. In these circumstances we propose to use the *hp*-convergence exponents of the elasticity and dielectricity problems for the mechanical and electric components of the coupled field.

With this assumption in mind we generalize the adaptive scheme applied successfully for the complex elastic structures [28]. It can also be adopted for the dielectricity problems. The generalization is presented in **Figure 2** in the form of a block diagram, where $i = 1,2,3,4$ represent the consecutive steps of the algorithm—the initial, modification, intermediate and final ones.

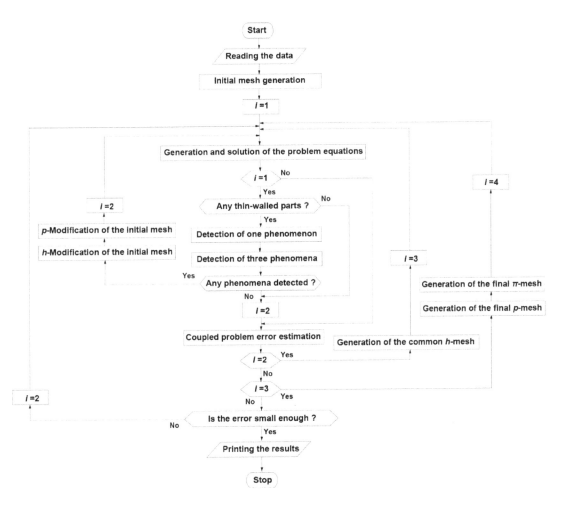

Figure 2. Four-step *hp*-adaptive scheme for complex piezoelectric or piezoelectric-elastic problems.

6. Conclusions

In the presented chapter we showed how to generalize hierarchical modelling, *hp*-adaptive hierarchical approximations, the equilibrated residual method of error estimation and the four-step adaptive procedure, originally applied to elasticity and possible also in dielectricity, for the coupled piezoelectric problems.

We suggest to combine the hierarchical models for complex elastic structures with the analogous models of dielectricity in order to obtain all coupled combinations of the component mechanical and electric models. In the case of the approximations, we suggest to apply the common h-mesh and independent p and π approximations for the displacement and electric potential fields.

In the error estimation, we propose to decouple the mechanical and electric fields in the local problems of the residual approach.

Our four-step hp-adaptive algorithm is based on the convergence theorems for the purely elastic and purely dielectric problems. These theorems are applied to the intermediate and final meshes generation.

Acknowledgements

The support of the Polish Scientific Research Committee (now the National Science Centre) under the research grant no. N N504 5153 040 is thankfully acknowledged.

Nomenclature

a_i – displacement amplitude vector components (i = 1,2,3),

$\mathbf{a}_j$ – a node with displacement degrees of freedom (dofs), j = 1,2,...,21,

$\overset{e}{b}$ – a bilinear form representing the element virtual electrostatic energy,

$\mathbf{b}_j$ – a node with electric potential dofs, j = 1,2,...,21,

$\overset{e}{B}$ – a bilinear form representing the element virtual strain energy,

c – the electric surface charge,

$\overset{e}{C}$ – a bilinear form representing the element coupling electro-mechanical energy,

C_{ikl} – components of the piezoelectricity tensor (i,k,l = 1,2,3),

$\mathbf{C}$ – the piezoelectric constants matrix,

d_i – components of the electric displacement vector (i = 1,2,3),

$\mathbf{d}$ – the electric displacement vector,

D_{ijkl} – elasticity tensor components, i,j,k,l = 1,2,3,

D – the elasticity constants matrix,

e – the number of an element,

E – a dielectric model,

E – the hierarchy of dielectric models,

E_j – electric field vector components ($j = 1,2,3$),

E – the electric field vector,

F_i – mass load vector components ($i = 1,2,3$),

f – the mass load vector,

$\overset{e}{\boldsymbol{f}}_H$ – the inter-element charge vector,

$\overset{e}{\boldsymbol{f}}_M$ – the element mass forces vector,

$\overset{e}{\boldsymbol{f}}_Q$ – the element charge vector,

$\overset{e}{\boldsymbol{f}}_R$ – the inter-element stress forces vector,

$\overset{e}{\boldsymbol{f}}_S$ – the element surface forces vector,

$\mathbf{F}_M$ – the global mass forces vector,

$\mathbf{F}_S$ – the global surface forces vector,

$\mathbf{F}_Q$ – the global charge vector,

h – measure of the element size,

$\overset{e}{\langle h \rangle}$ – the equilibrated inter-element charge,

H – a measure of the element size in the local problem,

I – the order of the hierarchical mechanical model,

J – the order of the hierarchical dielectric model,

$\overset{e}{\boldsymbol{k}}_C$ – the element piezoelectric (coupling) matrix,

$\overset{e}{\boldsymbol{k}}_E$ – the element dielectric matrix,

$\overset{e}{\boldsymbol{k}}_G$ – the element geometric stiffness matrix,

$\overset{e}{\boldsymbol{k}}_M$ – the element (constitutive) stiffness matrix,

$\mathbf{K}_C$ – the global piezoelectric (coupling) matrix,

$\mathbf{K}_E$ – the global dielectric matrix,

$\mathbf{K}_G$ – the global geometric stiffness matrix,

$\mathbf{K}_M$ – the global (constitutive) stiffness matrix,

$\overset{e}{\mathrm{l}}$ – a linear form equal to the element virtual work of the external charges,

$\overset{e}{\mathrm{L}}$ – a linear form representing the element virtual work of the external forces,

$\overset{e}{\boldsymbol{m}}$ – the element mass (inertia) matrix,

m – the number of a dof function,

M – mechanical model,

M – the hierarchy of mechanical models,

$\mathbf{M}$ – the global mass (inertia) matrix,

n – the number of a natural frequency,

n_j – vector components ($j = 1,2,3$) of the normal to the body surface,

N – the global number of dofs (degrees of freedom),

p – the element approximation order or the longitudinal order of approximation for displacements,

p_i – surface load vector components,

P – the longitudinal order of approximation for element displacements,

P – piezoelectric model,

P – the hierarchy of piezoelectric models,

$\mathbf{p}$ – the surface load vector,

q – the transverse order of approximation for displacements,

$\mathbf{q}^{q,\,hp}$ – the global displacement (or displacement amplitude) dofs vector,

$\overset{e}{\boldsymbol{q}}{}^{Q,HP}$ – the element displacement (or displacement amplitude) dofs vector,

Q – the local problem transverse order of approximation for displacements,

$\langle \overset{e}{\boldsymbol{r}} \rangle$ – a vector of the equilibrated inter-element stresses,

$s_j^{\prime m}$ – a mid-surface displacement dof function,

S – the surface of a body (or medium),

S_F – the body surface part with given electric potential,

S_P – the loaded part of the body surface,

S_Q – the electrically charged part of the body (or medium) surface,

S_W – the body surface part with given displacements,

t – time,

t_m – the mth polynomial through-thickness function,

$\mathbf{u}$ – the vector of global displacements,

u_i – the global displacement components, $i = 1,2,3$,

$\mathbf{u}^{Q,HP}$ – the displacement vector in the local (element) problem,

u'_j – local components ($j = 1,2,3$) of the displacement vector,

u'^m_j – a through-thickness displacement dof function,

$\ddot{u}_i$ – acceleration vector components, $i = 1,2,3$,

v_i – admissible displacement (or its amplitude) vector components ($i = 1,2,3$),

$\mathbf{v}^{Q,HP}$ – the admissible displacement vector in the local (element) problem,

$\overset{e}{v}{}^{Q,HP}$ – the admissible displacement dof vector of an element,

V – volume of a body (or medium),

w_i – given displacement vector components ($i = 1,2,3$) on the body surface,

$\mathbf{x}$ – global Cartesian coordinate vector,

γ_{ij} – components of the dielectricity tensor ($i,j = 1,2,3$),

γ – the dielectricity constants matrix,

δ^m – the mth mid-surface electric potential dof function,

ε_{ij} – strain tensor components ($i,j = 1,2,3$),

$\boldsymbol{\varepsilon}$ – the strain vector,

ξ_i – normalized coordinates of an element ($i = 1,2,3$),

ξ'_3 – the local normal coordinate,

π – the longitudinal approximation order of electric potential,

Π – the element longitudinal approximation order of electric potential,

ρ – the transverse approximation order of electric potential,

ϱ – mass density of the body,

P – the element transverse approximation order of electric potential,

ς_{ij} – initial stress tensor components $(i,j=1,2,3)$,

σ_{ij} – stress tensor components $(i,j=1,2,3)$,

$\boldsymbol{\sigma}$ – the stress vector,

$\boldsymbol{\varphi}^{\rho,h\pi}$ – the global electric potential (or potential amplitude) dofs vector,

$\overset{e}{\boldsymbol{\varphi}}{}^{P,H\Pi}$ – the local (element) electric potential dofs vector,

ϕ – the electric potential,

ϕ^m – the mth through-thickness electric potential dof function,

χ – the given electric potential on the body surface,

ψ – the admissible electric potential,

$\overset{e}{\boldsymbol{\psi}}{}^{P,H\Pi}$ – the admissible electric potential dofs vector of an element,

ω – a natural frequency,

ω_n – the nth natural frequency

Author details

Grzegorz Zboiński

Address all correspondence to: zboi@imp.gda.pl

1 Institute of Fluid Flow Machinery, Polish Academy of Sciences, Gdańsk, Poland

2 Faculty of Technical Sciences, University of Warmia and Mazury, Olsztyn, Poland

References

[1] Ciarlet PG. Mathematical Elasticity, Vol. 1: Three-Dimensional Elasticity. Amsterdam: North-Holland; 1988.

[2] Ramsey AS. Electricity and Magnetism: An Introduction to Mathematical Theory. Cambridge: Cambridge University Press; 2009.

[3] Preumont A. Mechatronics: Dynamics of Electromechanical and Piezoelectric Systems. Dordrecht: Springer; 2006.

[4] Ciarlet PG. Plates and Junctions in Elastic Multi-Structures. Berlin, Paris: Springer-Verlag, Masson; 1990.

[5] Zboiński G. Hierarchical modeling and finite element method for adaptive analysis of complex structures [D.Sc. thesis, in Polish]. 520/1479/2001. Gdańsk, Poland: Institute of Fluid Flow Machinery; 2001. 304 p.

[6] Szabó BA, Sahrmann GJ. Hierarchic plate and shell models based on p-extension. Int. J. Numer. Meth. Engng. 1988;26:1855–1881.

[7] Oden JT, Cho JR. Adaptive hpq finite element methods of hierarchical models for plate and shell-like structures. Comput. Methods Appl. Mech. Eng. 1996;136:317–345.

[8] Zboiński G. Adaptive hpq finite element methods for the analysis of 3D-based models of complex structures: Part 1. Hierarchical modeling and approximations. Comput. Methods Appl. Mech. Eng. 2010;199:2913–2940.

[9] Carrera E, Boscolo M, Robaldo A. Hierarchic multilayered plate elements for coupled multifield problems of piezoelectric adaptive structures: Formulation and numerical assessment. Arch. Comput. Methods Eng. 2007;14(4):384–430.

[10] Zboiński G. Hierarchical models for adaptive modelling and analysis of coupled electro-mechanical systems. In: Lodygowski T, Rakowski J, Litewka P, editors. Recent Advances in Computational Mechanics. London: CRC Press; 2014. pp. 339–334.

[11] Demkowicz L, Oden JT, Rachowicz W, Hardy O. Towards a universal hp adaptive finite element strategy. Part 1. A constrained approximation and data structure. Comput. Methods Appl. Mech. Eng. 1989;77:113–180.

[12] Zboiński G. Application of the three-dimensional triangular-prism hpq adaptive finite element to plate and shell analysis. Comput. Struct. 1997;65:497–514.

[13] Zboiński G, Jasiński M. 3D-based hp-adaptive first order shell finite element for modelling and analysis of complex structures: Part 1. The model and the approximation. Int. J. Numer. Meth. Eng. 2007;70:1513–1545.

[14] Zboiński G. 3D-based *hp*-adaptive first order shell finite element for modelling and analysis of complex structures: Part 2. Application to structural analysis. Int. J. Numer. Meth. Eng. 2007;70:1546–1580.

[15] Zboiński G, Ostachowicz W. An algorithm of a family of 3D-based solid-to-shell transition, *hpq/hp*-adaptive finite elements. J. Theoret. Appl. Mech. 2000;38:791–806.

[16] Lammering R, Mesecke-Rischmann S. Multi-field variational formulation and related finite elements for piezoelectric shells. Smart Mat. Struct. 2003;12:904–913.

[17] Ainsworth M, Oden JT. A Posteriori Error Estimation in Finite Element Analysis. New York: Wiley; 2000.

[18] Ainsworth M, Oden JT, Wu W. A posteriori error estimation for *hp*-approximation in elastostatics. Appl. Numer. Math. 1994;14:23–55.

[19] Cho JR, Oden JT. A priori error estimations of *hp*-finite element approximations for hierarchical models of plate and shell-like structures. Comput. Methods Appl. Mech. Eng. 1996;132:135–177.

[20] Zboiński G. A posteriori error estimation for *hp*-approximation of the 3D-based first order shell model: Part I. Theoretical aspects. Appl. Math. Informat. Mech. 2003;8(1):104–125.

[21] Zboiński G. A posteriori error estimation for *hp*-approximation of the 3D-based first order shell model: Part II. Implementation aspects. Appl. Math. Informat. Mech. 2003;8(2):59–83.

[22] Zboiński G. Adaptive *hpq* finite element methods for the analysis of 3D-based models of complex structures: Part 2. A posteriori error estimation. Comput. Methods Appl. Mech. Eng. 2013;267:531–565.

[23] Zboiński G. Application of the element residual methods to dielectric and piezoelectric problems. In: Kleiber M, et al., editors. Advances in Mechanics: Theoretical, Computational and Interdisciplinary Issues. London: CRC Press; 2016. pp. 605–609.

[24] Oden JT. Error estimation and control in computational fluid dynamics: The O. C. Zienkiewicz lecture. In: Proc. Math. of Finite Elements (MAFELAP VIII). Uxbridge: Brunel University; 1993. pp. 1–36.

[25] Vokas C, Kasper M. Adaptation in coupled problems. Int. J. Comput. Math. Electr. Electronic Eng. 2010;29(6):1626–1641.

[26] Jasiński M, Zboiński G. On some *hp*-adaptive finite element method for natural vibrations. Comput. Math. Appl. 2013;66:2376–2399.

[27] Zboiński G. Numerical tools for a posteriori detection and assessment of the improper solution limit, locking and boundary layers in analysis of thin-walled structures. In:

Diez P, Wiberg NE, editors. Adaptive Modeling and Simulation 2005. Barcelona: CIMNE; 2005. pp. 321–330.

[28] Zboiński G. Unresolved problems of adaptive hierarchical modelling and *hp*-adaptive analysis within computational solid mechanics. In: Kuczma M, Wilmański K, editors. Advanced Structural Materials: Vol. 1. Computer Methods in Mechanics. Berlin: Springer-Verlag; 2010. Ch. 7, pp. 111–145.

Permissions

All chapters in this book were first published in PFEM, by InTech Open; hereby published with permission under the Creative Commons Attribution License or equivalent. Every chapter published in this book has been scrutinized by our experts. Their significance has been extensively debated. The topics covered herein carry significant findings which will fuel the growth of the discipline. They may even be implemented as practical applications or may be referred to as a beginning point for another development.

The contributors of this book come from diverse backgrounds, making this book a truly international effort. This book will bring forth new frontiers with its revolutionizing research information and detailed analysis of the nascent developments around the world.

We would like to thank all the contributing authors for lending their expertise to make the book truly unique. They have played a crucial role in the development of this book. Without their invaluable contributions this book wouldn't have been possible. They have made vital efforts to compile up to date information on the varied aspects of this subject to make this book a valuable addition to the collection of many professionals and students.

This book was conceptualized with the vision of imparting up-to-date information and advanced data in this field. To ensure the same, a matchless editorial board was set up. Every individual on the board went through rigorous rounds of assessment to prove their worth. After which they invested a large part of their time researching and compiling the most relevant data for our readers.

The editorial board has been involved in producing this book since its inception. They have spent rigorous hours researching and exploring the diverse topics which have resulted in the successful publishing of this book. They have passed on their knowledge of decades through this book. To expedite this challenging task, the publisher supported the team at every step. A small team of assistant editors was also appointed to further simplify the editing procedure and attain best results for the readers.

Apart from the editorial board, the designing team has also invested a significant amount of their time in understanding the subject and creating the most relevant covers. They scrutinized every image to scout for the most suitable representation of the subject and create an appropriate cover for the book.

The publishing team has been an ardent support to the editorial, designing and production team. Their endless efforts to recruit the best for this project, has resulted in the accomplishment of this book. They are a veteran in the field of academics and their pool of knowledge is as vast as their experience in printing. Their expertise and guidance has proved useful at every step. Their uncompromising quality standards have made this book an exceptional effort. Their encouragement from time to time has been an inspiration for everyone.

The publisher and the editorial board hope that this book will prove to be a valuable piece of knowledge for researchers, students, practitioners and scholars across the globe.

List of Contributors

Yutaka Inaba, Hiroyuki Ike, Masatoshi Oba and Tomoyuki Saito
Department of Orthopaedic Surgery, Yokohama City University, Yokohama, Japan

Raymond C.W. Wong, John S.P. Loh and I. Islam
Discipline of Oral and Maxillofacial Surgery, National University Hospital, National University of Singapore, Singapore

Jayati Sarkar
Department of Chemical Engineering, Indian Institute of Technology Delhi, New Delhi, India

Hemalatha Annepu and Satish Kumar Mishra
Institute of Advanced Simulations-2, Forschungszentrum Gmbh, Jülich, Germany

Ara S. Avetisyan, Asatur Zh. Khurshudyan and Sergey K. Ohanyan
Department of Dynamics of Deformable Systems and Connected Fields, Institute of Mechanics, National Academy of Sciences of Armenia, Yerevan, Armenia

Takahiko Kurahashi, Taichi Yoshiara and Yasuhide Kobayashi
Department of Mechanical Engineering, Nagaoka University of Technology, Nagaoka, Japan

Ezgi Günay
Department of Mechanical Engineering, Gazi University, Maltepe, Ankara, Turkey

Ishan Ali Khan and Seyed M. Hashemi
Department of Aerospace Engineering, Ryerson University, Toronto, Canada

Mahboub Baccouch
Department of Mathematics, University of Nebraska at Omaha, Omaha, NE, USA

Grzegorz Zboiński
Institute of Fluid Flow Machinery, Polish Academy of Sciences, Gdańsk, Poland
Faculty of Technical Sciences, University of Warmia and Mazury, Olsztyn, Poland

Index

Printed in the USA
CPSIA information can be obtained
at www.ICGtesting.com
JSHW051352221024
72173JS00006B/1307